Rails Along the Fathew

The Story of the Talyllyn Railway

Ian Drummond

© Holne Publishing and Ian Drummond 2015
British Library Cataloguing in Publication Data
A record for this book is available from the British Library
ISBN 978-0-9563317-8-6
Published by: Holne Publishing, PO Box 343, LEEDS, LS19 9FW
Typesetting and Photo Restoration by: Holne Publishing Services, PO Box 343, LEEDS, LS19 9FW
Printed by: Charlesworth Press, Flanshaw Way, Flanshaw Lane, Wakefield, WF2 9LP

All rights reserved. No part of this book may be reproduced or transmitted in any form or by any means, electronic or mechanical including photocopying, recording or by any information storage and retrieval system, without permission from the publisher in writing.

Reasonable efforts have been made to discover the true copyright owners of the photographs reproduced in this volume, and no infringement of copyright is intended. If you have any evidence about the copyright owner of any photograph, or the photographer of any photograph listed as 'photographer unknown', please contact the publisher in the first instance. Uncredited photographs are by the author.

All documents are courtesy of the Talyllyn Railway Archive and the Narrow Gauge Museum Trust.

Photographs in this volume have been digitally adjusted to enhance clarity, and also remove blemishes, dust etc. However, no intentional alterations have been made to affect their historical significance.

For all maps and plans approximate scales are given where known, and unless indicated otherwise the top edge is north.

In the 1960s and 70s many place names in Wales were changed to their Welsh equivalents, for example Towyn became Tywyn, Aberdovey became Aberdyfi, Portmadoc became Porthmadog. For clarity the modern place names have been used throughout this book, except where they are included in titles of companies etc. or in quotations.

Some Welsh Place Names and Terms:

Afon - River	Bryneglwys - Church Hill	Ceunant - gorge	Coch or Goch - Red
Fach - Little	Hendy - Old House	Isaf - Lower	Nant - Stream
Plas - Place	Tanycoed - Until the trees	Tŷ Dŵr - Water House	Tŷ Mawr - Big House
Uchaf - Upper			

Holne Publishing
PO Box 343
LEEDS
LS19 9FW
enquiries@holnepublishing.co.uk
www.holnepublishing.co.uk

Cover Photos:

Front: *Dolgoch* stands at Abergynolwyn in April 1949. (Photo: The Elliot Collection)

Back: *Dolgoch* stands at Abergynolwyn on 6 June 2015 with a vintage train. (Photo: Barbara Fuller)

Contents

Introduction	5
History	
The McConnel Era	8
The Haydn Jones Era	28
The Preservation Era	39
The Route Described	
Tywyn Wharf	62
Tywyn Pendre	77
From Pendre to Rhydyronen	91
Rhydyronen	97
From Rhydyronen to Brynglas	103
Brynglas	106
From Brynglas to Dolgoch	113
Dolgoch	118
From Dolgoch to Abergynolwyn	124
Abergynolwyn	128
The Extension	137
Nant Gwernol	146
Passenger Operations	149
Goods Operations	161
Locomotives	167
Passenger Stock	186
Goods Stock	198
Signalling, Blocking and Permanent Way	204
People	208
The Narrow Gauge Railway Museum	220
The 150th Anniversary	222
Bibliography and Acknowledgements	223

Above: *Dolgoch* stands at Tywyn Wharf station with a mixed train in April 1949. The brake van was still out of service at the time and so only the four carriages are in use.
(Photo: The Elliot/Dan Quine Collection)

Wel hen dren bach yr Aber	This little train of ours
Chwibana heddyw'n dwt.	Today is spruce and spry
Dyrchafa mwg ir Awyr	And from its little chimney
O ben dy getyn pwt.	Smoke rises to the sky.
Bydd Towyn, Rhydyronen,	Now Towyn, Rhydyronen,
Dolgoch, an H, Aber ni	Dolgoch and Aber too
Yn rhedeg ith gyfarfod	Will meet you on your journeys
I roi Lwc Dda i ti.	To say "Good Luck" to you.

Above: A poem about the railway composed c. 1911 by 'Talfardd'. On the right is an English version.

Introduction

Above: In celebration of the 150th Anniversary locomotives No.1 *Talyllyn* and No.2 *Dolgoch* were repainted in what could have been their original delivery livery. Here *Talyllyn* is seen on a photographic charter on 17 March 2015. (Photo: David J. Mitchell)

In July 1975 I did my first volunteer turn on the Talyllyn Railway (TR) as a trainee at Dolgoch station. The Station Assistant was Sue Vincent (now Whitehouse) and the Stationmaster was Keith Stretch. What I remember of that day is Keith regaling us with all sorts of stories about the history of the railway. Little did I think then that 40 years later I would be writing a book of the railway's history for the 150th Anniversary.

The genesis of this book came shortly after the publication of my second book on the railways of the Isle of Wight in 2010. "Why not do something similar for the Talyllyn's 150th anniversary?" people said, "After all you've got five years to write it." How little did we know.

One thing that was said was that people wanted a history of the railway in one volume. Many previous books have concentrated on one era or another, but this book tries to cover them all. Part of the reason for the previous divisions has been a certain reluctance in general to regard the history of preserved lines as 'real' history. Some regard them as something 'artificial' and therefore their history should be discounted.

I would argue in the Talyllyn's case this is certainly not true. The Talyllyn has two unique claims:
1. It was the first narrow gauge railway, authorised by Parliament, designed for steam operation from the outset.
2. It is the World's First Preserved Railway.

There is another factor, which is that throughout its history it has been operated by one statutory company, the Talyllyn Railway Company.

The ownership of the company has changed through the years, and so the history of the line can be divided into three main eras. First of these is the time of the McConnel family, who led the development of the Bryneglwys quarry and the construction of the railway. Various branches of the family were to be involved in running the railway for over 45 years.

Then came the period when the company was owned by the local M.P., Sir Henry Haydn Jones. He kept the railway running, even subsidising it out of his own pocket, for nearly 40 years.

Finally, in the face of imminent closure, came the Talyllyn Railway Preservation Society, established by an enthusiastic group led by Tom Rolt and Bill Trinder. The Society effectively became the owners of the railway, and has continued to operate it for over 64 years, well over a third of its life.

In writing this book as well, I was determined to go back to contemporary material wherever it was available. This was to try and write as accurate a history as possible. Of course there are gaps in our knowledge, and so I have had to make (hopefully) educated guesses, but I have tried to flag up where there is hard evidence and where there has been some speculation.

In addition, as the work has progressed I became aware that others were working on books relating to the history of the railway. Martin Fuller has produced the first volume of his history of the locomotives, and Sara Eade has written a book about those who worked on the railway pre-preservation. Martin, Sara and myself have sought to liaise where possible to ensure that these books are complementary. Therefore, if you require additional information on these areas, their books are highly recommended.

Opportunity has also been taken to include as many photographs as is possible. Some of these form part of the Talyllyn Railway collection. We have tried to identify individual photographers as far as has been feasible, but I am conscious that some have still gone unidentified. If you therefore have information on any of the photographs which could help in their correct attribution, then please get in touch.

One pleasing thing has been that I have been able to include a number of photographs by Keith Stretch, who is sadly no longer with us. To him, and the many others, whom I have come to know down the years of working on this wonderful railway I owe a debt of thanks for years of friendship and fun. This book has turned into a labour of love, and I hope it will be judged worthy of the railway whose story it seeks to tell.

Ian Drummond
June 2015

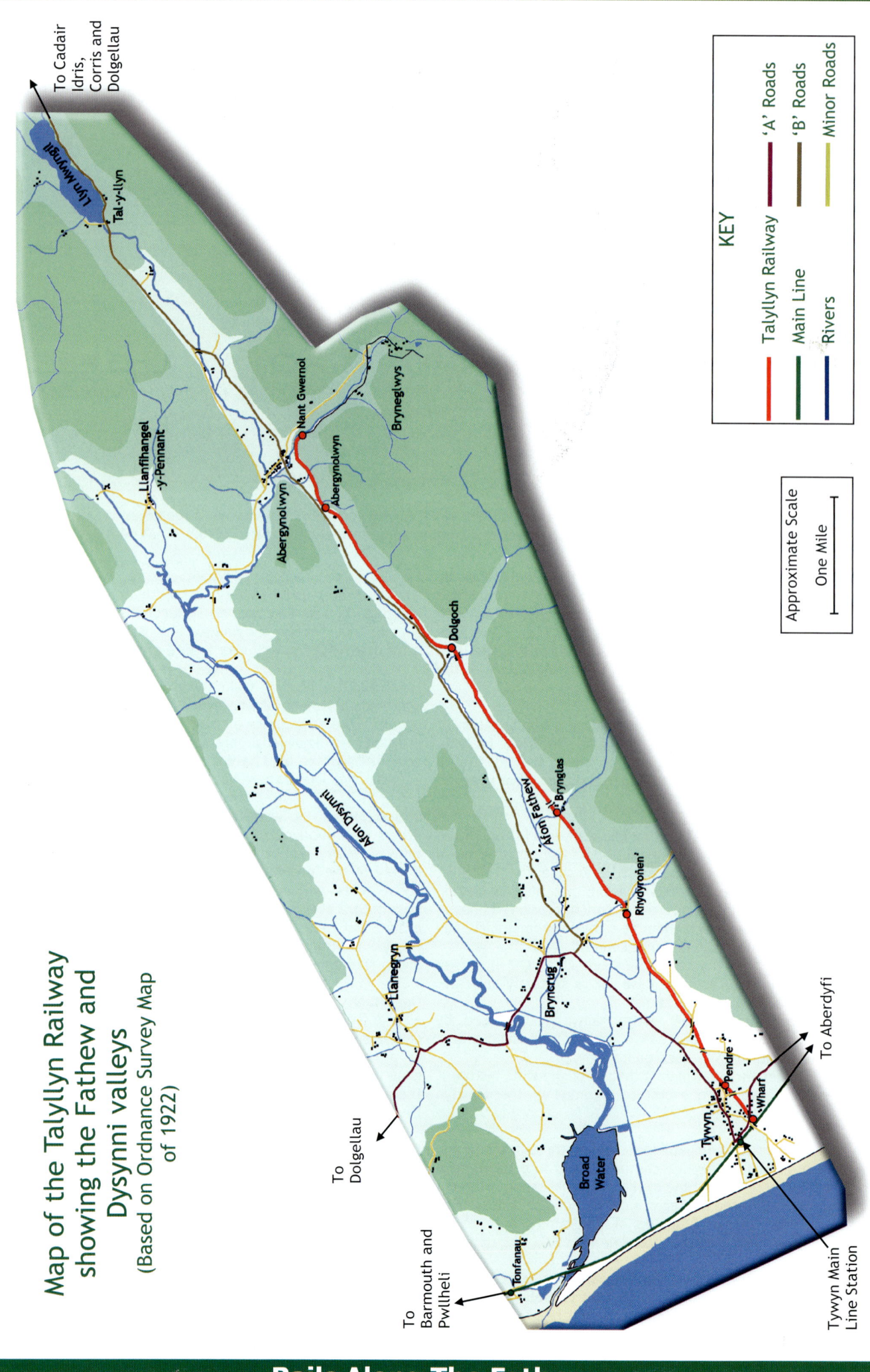

Rails Along The Fathew

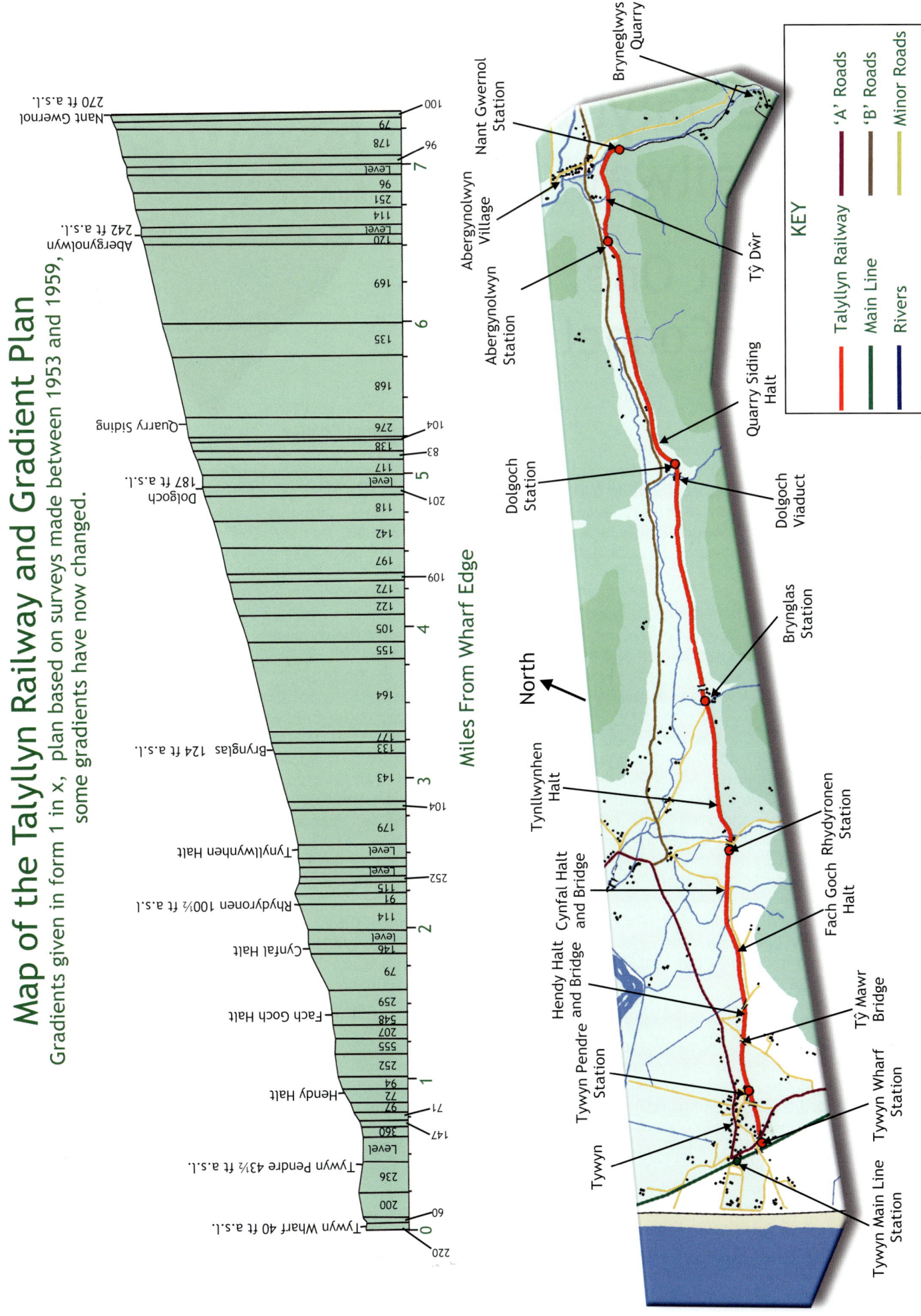

Rails Along The Fathew

History

The History of The Talyllyn Railway

Part One: The McConnel Era

Origins

Tywyn is situated on the west coast of Mid-Wales. To the south lies the town of Aberdyfi on the Dyfi estuary, while to the north lies the Dysynni estuary. Inland the Cambrian mountains of south Snowdonia rise to a peak at Cadair Idris. These formed natural barriers isolating this area from those around.

The first church settlement was founded at Tywyn in the early 6th century by St Cadfan, a missionary from Brittany. The later Norman church also houses St Cadfan's Stone, dating to the 8th or 9th century, which is inscribed with the earliest known example of the written Welsh language.

Much of the land in the area was owned by the Ynysymaengwyn estate, home for many years of the Corbet family. There was some ship-building on the Dysynni estuary, and some peat production, but the primary source of income was agriculture. By the early nineteenth century visitors were beginning to make their way to the area to take their holidays and enjoy the beauties of the area. These included Cadair Idris, Llyn Mwyngil, or Talyllyn Lake as it is commonly known, and the Bwlch Llyn Bach pass. The following comes from the book *England and Wales Delineated* by Thomas Dugdale published c.1850:

TOWYN, or TYWYN, is a small town situated on the mouth of the river from which it derives its appellation (sic). It is much frequented in the bathing season, the shore being delightful for either riding or bathing …. The inhabitants are chiefly employed in the herring fisheries; and a small coasting trade is carried on. A valuable slate quarry has lately been opened, and there are also several lead and copper mines in the vicinity. The church is a small neat structure … St Cadvan's well here is held in estimation for its medicinal properties; and the streams in the neighbourhood afford good sport to the angler. In many respects Towyn presents attraction to the visitor; the surrounding country is beautiful, and embellished with many seats of the gentry of the country."

A Decade of Change

The 1860s was a decade of enormous change for Tywyn. By 1869 the town gained a gas supply, new roads and a storm water drainage system. It also witnessed the construction, by John Corbet, of a series of dykes and ditches to drain the marshy land to the north of the town. In addition, by the middle of 1865 the town welcomed two new railways of very different characters and purpose.

Neither of these, however, was the first railway proposed for Tywyn. Previously plans had been presented to the Board of Trade (BoT) in December 1852 for the Corris, Machynlleth, Aberdovey and Towyn Railway. This standard gauge line would have followed the Dulas valley down from the slate quarries at Corris to the River Dyfi at Machynlleth. It would then have followed the north bank of the river to Aberdyfi before turning north to Tywyn. However, there was little further progress and the scheme was abandoned.

The first railway to be built was the standard gauge Aberystwith (sic) and Welsh Coast Railway (A&WCR), opened between Aberdyfi, Tywyn and Llwyngwril in October 1863. It would eventually give Tywyn connections to the north to Pwllheli and Dolgellau. At the latter location the line would later be connected through Bala to Ruabon and the north-west.

Meanwhile to the south a planned bridge across the Dyfi to connect with the line between Machynlleth and Aberystwyth never materialised. Therefore, a diversionary line between Aberdyfi and Machynlleth was eventually opened on 14 August 1867. This ran along the north side of the Dyfi, and would connect Tywyn to Birmingham and London. It became part of the Cambrian Railways system, and later the Great Western Railway.

Tywyn's second railway was originally a much more humble affair. It was to be a tramroad, built to serve the Bryneglwys slate quarry. This was situated above the village of Abergynolwyn some six miles inland. The line was also not to be standard gauge but narrow gauge, and

History

Left: The view towards Tywyn from the Cambrian Railways' station around 1869. As can be seen the town was very much smaller then and concentrated around the church and College Green. The church also has the tower at the west end, which would be altered in the rebuilding of 1880-1884. It would take several more years for the High Street to be built-up down to the station.

it was to be operated by steam locomotion from the outset.

The McConnels and Bryneglwys Quarry

Slate quarrying had begun in earnest at Bryneglwys in the mid 1840s when John Pughe took out a series of leases to quarry for slate in the area. When Pughe died in 1848 his widow carried on the quarry, although it appears to have stopped working by the early 1860s. In 1862 John Lloyd Jones took over the business, but it was not to remain in his hands for long.

At this point the McConnel family, whose background was in the Manchester cotton industry, became involved in the affairs of Bryneglwys. The McConnels were three brothers Thomas, James and William, the last being in charge of the family company.

It was a downturn in their business, caused by a shortage of raw cotton due to the American Civil War, that led William in particular to consider other possibilities. They became interested in Bryneglwys in 1863, eventually leading a consortium to form the Aberdovey Slate Company to take over the quarry in January 1864, with Thomas as Chairman.

The Tramroad

The first mention of a proposed tramroad comes in a newspaper report of 5 December 1863. It stated that the railway would run to the quarry from Tywyn, and that it would be steam powered. This would have replaced the pack horses then used. Certainly plans seem to have been well advanced, and £15,000 was set aside in the Aberdovey Slate Co.'s capital programme for the building of an 'exit tramway' to allow slate to be transported from the quarry.

By the end of January 1864 another newspaper report stated that the railway's engineer was already surveying the route. That engineer was James Swinton Spooner, the second son of James Spooner, who had assisted his father in surveying the route for the Festiniog Railway. This line was doubtless part of the inspiration that led to the building of the Talyllyn.

Originally opened in April 1836 between Porthmadog and the slate quarries at Blaenau Ffestiniog, the Festiniog had been built to a gauge of 1 ft 11½ in. Loaded slate trains were allowed to run down to Porthmadog by gravity with the empties being hauled back using horses. However, in 1863 it had introduced steam locomotives and had the intention of starting an official passenger service.

Returning to the Talyllyn story, on 16 April 1864 the *North Wales Chronicle* reported that agreement had been reached with the landowners for the sale of the land necessary for the building of the railway, which would soon start. It also stated that; 'We understand that the line will be extended to Talyllyn, and even further to meet the Corris tramroad', and that a passenger service would be run.

In the end the extension to Talyllyn and joining up with the Corris never came to pass, but a passenger service did

History

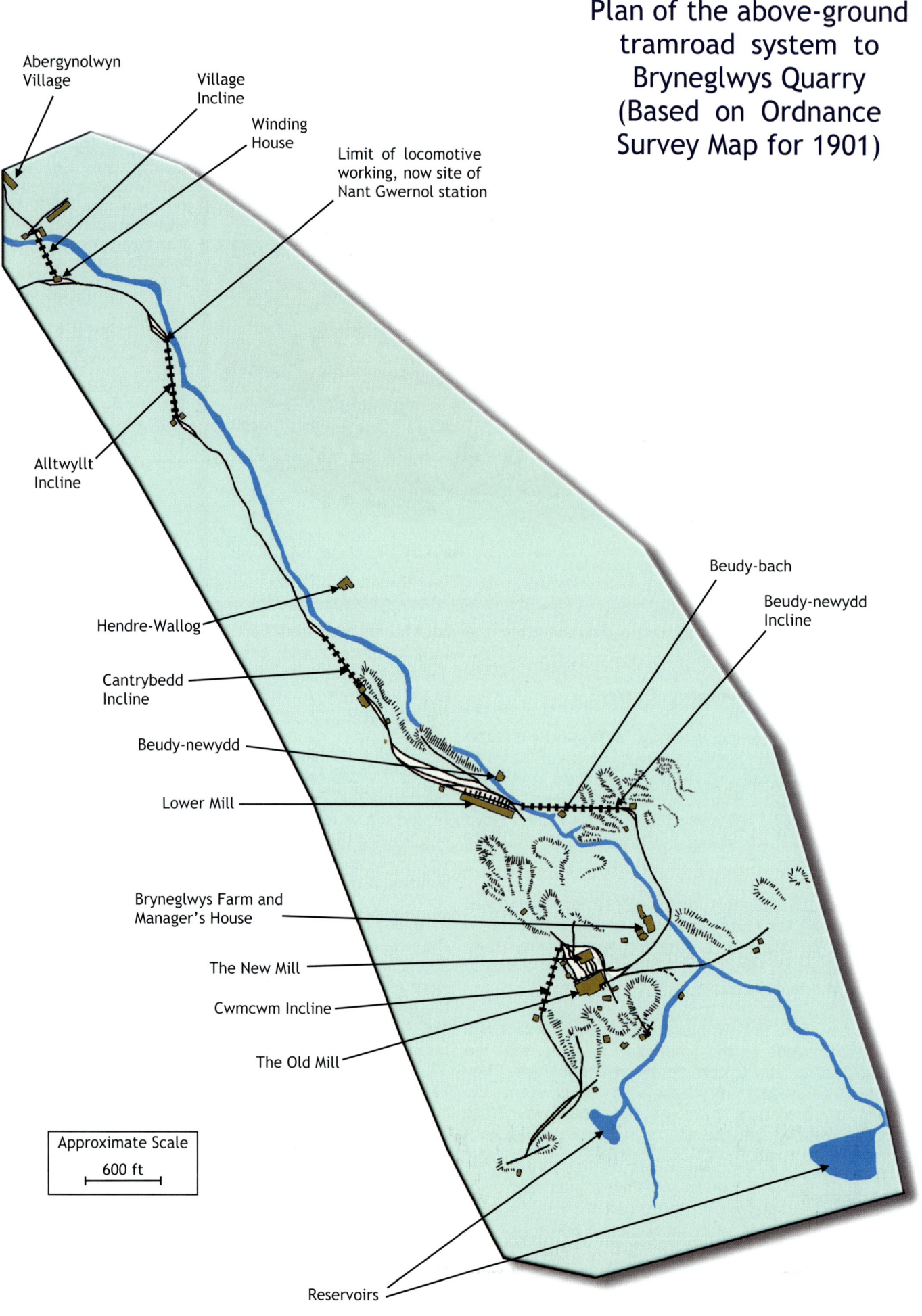

Plan of the above-ground tramroad system to Bryneglwys Quarry (Based on Ordnance Survey Map for 1901)

History

Above: The Lower Mill at Bryneglwys Quarry, with the tramway running through the middle of the picture. In the background is Beudy-newdd incline. Note the stocks of various sizes of slate and slab ready to be transported down the inclines and then to Tywyn.
(Photo: TR Collection)

start, although not for nearly three years. However, steps had already been taken for a steam locomotive to be built for the line.

Examination of the Fletcher, Jennings & Co. Ltd. order book indicates it was around this time that an order was placed by the Aberdovey Slate Company for an 0-4-0 saddle tank locomotive. This was to be built at their Lowca works in Whitehaven as works No.42 for a gauge of 2 ft 3 in. The locomotive *Talyllyn* was about to be born.

Meanwhile another report from the *North Wales Chronicle* on 9 July 1864 stated that the 'works of this line are proceeding with wonderful rapidity ... We hope to see the works completed about the end of the present year.' That was to prove slightly optimistic.

Construction

Construction was indeed moving ahead, but it was causing issues. At the monthly meeting of the Towyn Board of Health on 8 September 1864 a complaint was received from the tenant at Fach Goch Farm. This was that the parish road between Hendy and Rhydyronen had been rendered impassable by the 'tram road of the Aberdovey Slate Co.' At their October meeting the Board heard a report that the new bridges by Drefnewydd (the bridge at what would later be Wharf station) and at Hendy were progressing fast.

Obviously this indicates that construction was well under way. The cutting at Tywyn was the major earthwork to be dug, with the spoil being used to level the site of what would later become Wharf station. This had previously been a borrow pit to provide ballast during the construction of the A&WCR, and required a considerable amount of material to fill. It is likely too that material from the cutting was used for the embankments on the line east of Pendre station.

At the Tywyn end it is reasonable to assume that there were at least two gangs involved in constructing the tramroad. One gang was probably working up from the site of Wharf digging out the cutting. The other may well have started from what is now Pendre station working westwards through the cutting, and tipping the spoil to form the embankments east of Pendre. There were doubtless others working from where there was access to the line e.g. Tŷ Mawr/Hendy and Brynglas.

This leads to the possibility that Pendre was the principal construction base at Tywyn, where the first sod might have been turned, although there is no record of a ceremony. It could also partly explain why the locomotive and carriage sheds were eventually built there.

On most railways of the period there was usually an engineer responsible for the survey, drawings and engineering specifications of the construction, as well as

History

Left: The quarrymen of Bryneglwys taken in 1897.
(Photo: C.H. Young/TR Collection)

Right: The top of the Cantrybedd incline on 16 April 1946 shortly before the quarry ceased working.
(Photographer Unknown/Dan Quine Collection)

Left: The Lower Mill seen from the top of the Beudy-newydd incline in June 1970. (Photo: J.H.L. Adams)

Right: The Broad Vein water-wheel at Bryneglwys. This supplied power for drainage and also the use of rock drills. It was supplied by Williams and White of Aberystwyth, and was 18 ft in diameter.
(Photo: R. Holcombe)

Rails Along The Fathew

History

Left: View of the New Mill on the left and the Old Mill on the right on 29 July 1953 with the Manager's House and Bryneglwys Farm in the background. (Photo: J.H.L. Adams)

Right: The Lower Mill in June 1970. (Photo: J.H.L. Adams)

Left and Below: Two photographs showing the remains of some of the equipment left underground when the quarry was closed. (Photos: Ian Cooper)

Rails Along The Fathew

History

Above: An engraving from October 1869 looking west across Abergynolwyn. Note the stylised train on the mineral extension in the left background, and also the representation of the winding house.

the overall oversight. The actual construction though was usually in the hands of a Contractor.

We are not sure who was the Contractor for the tramway, or if there even was one, but there are a number of options. Some suggest it was Thomas Savin, Contractor to the A&WCR, but there is no firm evidence to support this. Another option comes from a report in November 1864 about a William E. Williams, an apprentice of Spooner, who was described as an 'inspector on the railway between Towyn and Talyllyn'.

Therefore, another theory is that the line was constructed by gangs directly employed by the slate company, or by Spooner, who operated under Spooner's supervision through men like William E. Williams. Alternatively they could have made use of some of the sub-contractors working on the A&WCR. Certainly a later newspaper report, commenting on the speed and quality of the construction work, only specifically mentions Spooner. There can be no doubt though, that someone with significant experience was involved.

However, what was happening at the quarry end? Here direct evidence is sketchy but there is some information available. There are, for example, plans of the new houses that were constructed by McConnel at Abergynolwyn, which are dated July 1864. These would have required construction materials.

It is possible, therefore, that the inclines and tram routes down from the quarry were also being constructed early in 1864. These could have included the incline down to the village at Abergynolwyn, shown in the engraving above, which was to be a feature for many years.

Meanwhile Dolgoch was where the largest civil engineering structure on the route had to be built, namely the viaduct across the ravine. Again little is known about the construction of this, but it is reputed to have cost £3,000. It would have been a large undertaking, and probably started in isolation from the rest of the line.

The Talyllyn Railway Act 1865

By November 1864 construction of the tramway was well advanced, but then the slate company decided to apply for an Act of Parliament for its railway. The question of why the company did this is an interesting one. Certainly it wasn't to allow them to begin construction of the line as it was well under way at this time. There are though a number of possibilities.

The first is that there were some landowners holding out against the company. According to the papers submitted to Parliament there were two parcels of land, one near what is now Rhydyronen station and the second around Abergynolwyn station, not occupied by the company. Against this theory, though, is the fact the landowners

History

lodged no objection to the Bill.

A second reason was that the tramway was constructed through the use of wayleaves. It could be the company wished to use the statutory compulsory purchase powers if any of the landowners refused to sell their property when these expired. Certainly there is some later evidence from a court case that the powers were used for this purpose.

Yet another possibility was to force the A&WCR to allow the Talyllyn access to their goods yard at Tywyn. The original Bill allowed for the construction of two railways, the first, known as Railway No.1, is what we now know as the Talyllyn Railway. A second line, known as Railway No.2, was to be a link from what is now Wharf station into the goods yard at the Welsh Coast station (see plan below). It was planned that a substantial portion of this would be mixed gauge. The A&WCR, however, was clearly not happy with the proposal and objected to the Bill.

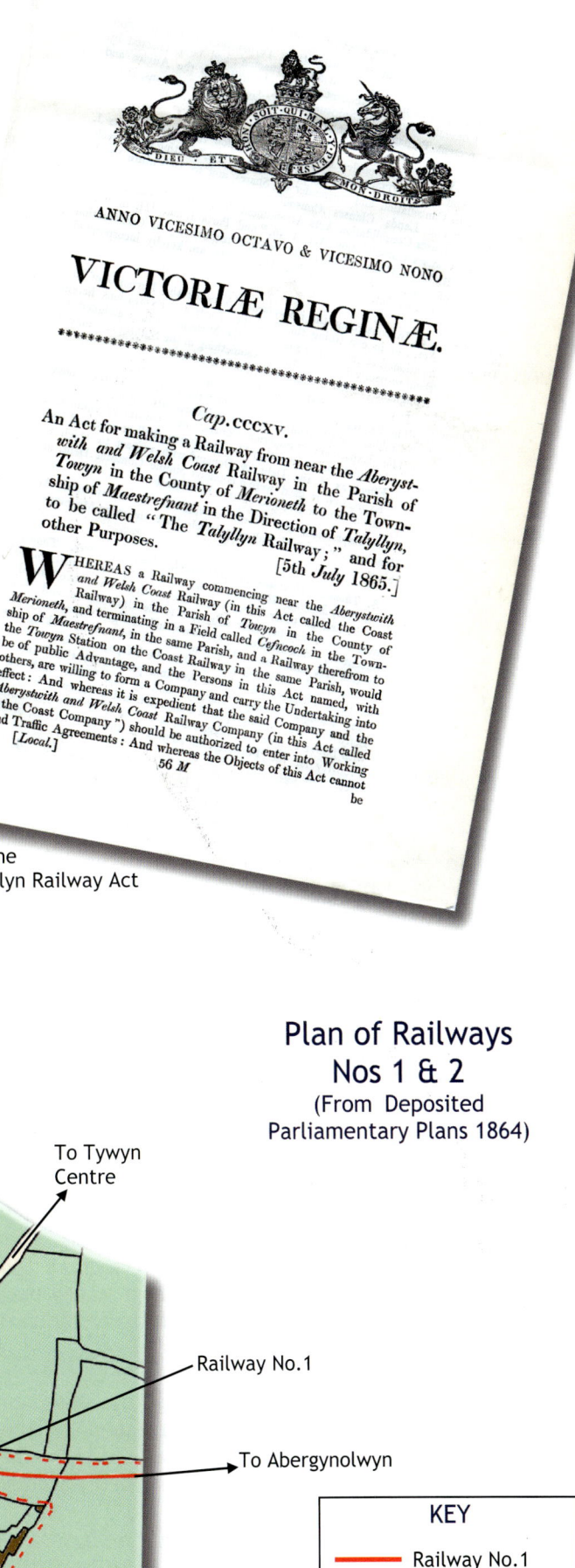

Above: Copy of the Original 1865 Talyllyn Railway Act

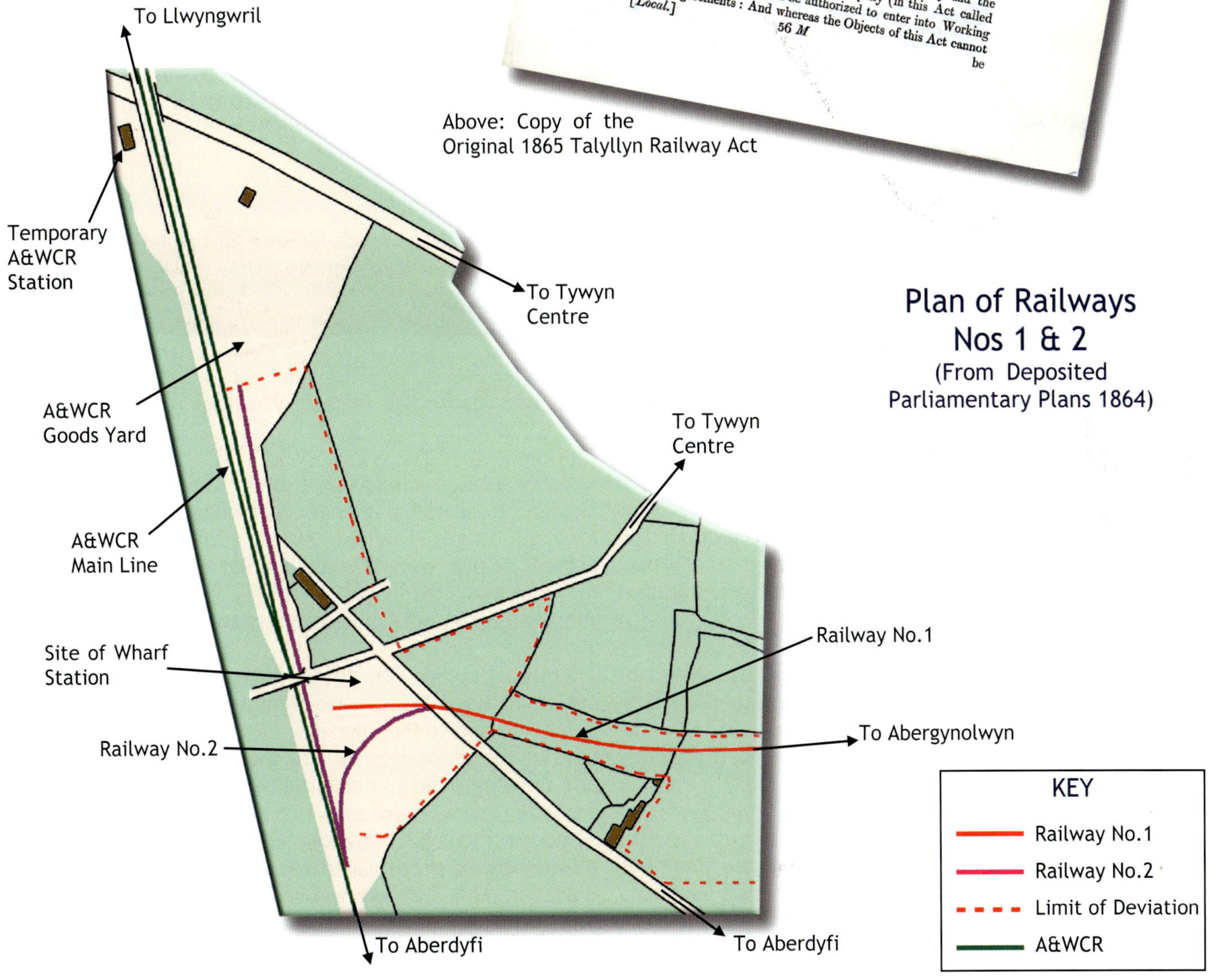

Plan of Railways Nos 1 & 2
(From Deposited Parliamentary Plans 1864)

KEY
- Railway No.1
- Railway No.2
- Limit of Deviation
- A&WCR

Rails Along The Fathew

History

This led to the Bill being modified with the mixed gauge being withdrawn. Clauses were also inserted that there would be no compulsory purchase of any land belonging to the Coast Railway. In addition, any railway laid into their goods yard was to be subject to their engineer's approval, but the A&WCR had to make provision for a 'double line of rails'. This was agreed in May 1865 when the A&WCR withdrew its objection.

There were possibly other reasons for obtaining the Act. The first is that it would formally separate the railway and the quarry into two distinct companies, the Talyllyn Railway Company (TRCo.) would own and operate the line between Tywyn and Abergynolwyn station. The Aberdovey Slate Company owned the track from there to the quarry, known as the mineral line or extension, as well as the quarry itself.

In practice this was a technicality with the two companies effectively being operated as one entity with separate divisions, the slate company holding the TRCo's shares. The directors of TRCo. were also all shareholders in the slate company.

There was also another provision in the Act that could have some bearing on the matter, and that was that the TRCo. would be permitted to raise £15,000 of share capital and an additional £5,000 in borrowing. As stated the Aberdovey Slate Company had a provision of £15,000 for the building of a tramroad, but almost immediately after the Talyllyn Railway Act was passed the slate company held a rights issue to raise its capital by £37,500. Was this part of a larger financial plan to justify the raising of further capital for the quarry?

an exception. Therefore, could it be that the Act was required because the Talyllyn wanted to run a passenger service on a narrow gauge line, and so it was felt that Parliamentary authority was necessary to set a precedent? The Talyllyn Railway Act certainly acknowledges the 1846 Act in that it states that the gauge of the line should be no less than 2 ft 3 in and no wider than standard gauge.

In truth the Act was probably obtained for a combination of reasons. Certainly it came at no little cost, so the McConnels must have felt the effort was worthwhile. It received its Royal Assent on 5 July 1865.

Why Talyllyn?

One other matter relating to the Act is that of the name. Up until this point the line was referred to variously in newspaper reports as the Bryneglwys, or Bryn-yr-Eglwys tramroad or the Towyn and Bryneglwys Railroad or variations thereof. Now the Act set the name of the railway as the Talyllyn.

Some have suggested that the name was an indication of a future desire to extend the line, but other than the reference in the newspaper report of 1864 there is no further mention of this possibility. Others have suggested that the name came because the line ran to the Parish of Talyllyn, but the line only skirted the border of the parish for a couple of field lengths around milepost 5¾. But the name was also used to describe the region and not just the parish, and certainly the Act states that the line is to be built in the direction of Talyllyn.

Above: What is believed to be one of the sleepers from the original construction track found in Wharf cutting in the late 1970s.

It seems though that the main reason the slate company obtained the Act was to run the passenger service. This relates to how the Talyllyn was able to overcome the Railway Regulation (Gauge) Act 1846, which stated that no railway was to be authorised other than standard gauge.

There survives a copy of the advice that the Board of Trade gave to Parliamentary Committee examining the Talyllyn Bill. This states that the 1846 Act did allow for exceptions in local situations such as had already happened with the Corris Railway.

Here an Act had been passed in 1864 allowing steam locomotives to be used on the narrow gauge line, but specifically excluding the provision of passenger services. The Talyllyn being nearly completed obviously counted as

Another reason could have been that the name was chosen to entice passenger patronage. Certainly Llyn Mwyngil, to give Talyllyn Lake its proper name, and the associated pass were already popular tourist destinations. In addition, the Coast Railway was now bringing substantial numbers of passengers to Tywyn.

Therefore, could it be that the McConnels had hopes of enticing these visitors onto their train with the vision of being whisked to the lakeside? Certainly from the earliest days of the passenger service the scenic features of the line were extolled to potential passengers.

Of course the reality was that they would find their train journey ended over three miles short of their destination. However, the Talyllyn would not be the only railway possessing a name that did not wholly reflect the

History

destination it served. In truth it was probably a combination of reasons that led to the name being chosen.

The Gauge

A subject that has not yet been explored fully is the that of the choice of gauge. Given the railway's connection with the Spooner family, why not adopt the 1 ft 11½ in of the Festiniog Railway? The fact that they did not implies some pre-existing reason for the choice of 2 ft 3 in. One suggestion has been the example of the Corris Railway which had opened in 1858 with the same gauge, but its origins appear to go back further.

Recent research indicates that the 2 ft 3 in gauge was widely used in the North Wales slate industry around the 1820s, including the Lord quarry at Ffestiniog, where a sleeper from a 2 ft 3 in gauge tramroad was recently discovered.

It seems that the gauge was probably brought to Corris by Joseph Tyson in the early 19th Century. In addition, before John Pughe took out his lease on Bryneglwys, some work was done there by 'two Ffestiniog men' in the early 1840s. Could either of these two routes be how 2 ft 3 in became the gauge for the quarry and the Talyllyn?

The Railway Completed and the Locomotive Arrives

In November 1864 it was reported in the *North Wales Chronicle* that the earthworks on the line were nearly completed. The cutting, between what would later be Tywyn Wharf and Pendre stations, was 'through' and the bridges were in operation. Furthermore it stated that a locomotive would be on the line in the New Year.

One of the mysteries of the Talyllyn story is what happened to *Talyllyn* after it was completed at Lowca Works, for the order book states that it was delivered on 24 September 1864. Instead, according to the newspaper reports, it was over six months before it arrived in Tywyn.

A possible reason is that it would have had no adequate rails to run on as only light construction track was in use. It seems that while the earthworks might be well under way, the correct rails were probably not ordered until late 1864, only arriving in the early days of 1865. This could have been due to a short-term 'cashflow' issue caused by the application for the Act of Parliament. In addition, before then the rails could not have been physically moved from the site of Wharf station, as the cutting was still incomplete.

There is also the issue of how *Talyllyn* travelled to Tywyn, as there was no direct rail connection, except between Aberdyfi and Tywyn. Evidence suggests that, although the first of the contractor's locomotives for the construction of the A&WCR was delivered to Aberdyfi by horse and cart from Machynlleth, at least one more was floated across the Dyfi estuary on a barge. Later a locomotive was transferred between Aberdyfi and Barmouth by sea. It is likely that *Talyllyn* would either have been floated across the estuary to Aberdyfi, from the railhead on the south shore, and then moved to Tywyn by rail, or would have come all the way from Whitehaven by sea to Aberdyfi.

With the winter storm season now upon them it is possible the McConnels might have been unwilling to risk their valuable locomotive to the elements. This means that the rails would have been laid by the navvies with only horse power for assistance. They certainly earned their wages!

There were other issues with the construction work as well. The *North Wales Chronicle* of 25 February 1865 reported that the railway was 'nearly completed … with the exception of the bridges, which are delayed by the frost'. Unfortunately which bridges this refers to is not clear.

In December 1864 the Board of Health had more concerns, particularly about the parish road between Tŷ Mawr Lane and Rhydyronen. This was said to be 'entirely obstructed in several places'. In fact the deposited plans show that the parish road was to be diverted. Instead a new road was to be built running on the north side of the line between Tŷ Mawr Lane and the bridge at Hendy Farm. Here it would cross to the south side of the line for the remainder of the distance to Rhydyronen. The Clerk of the Board of Health was instructed to write to the company asking for a guarantee that the road would be dealt with before they gave their consent to the Talyllyn Railway Bill.

It would not be until mid-April 1865 that *Talyllyn* arrived. The *North Wales Chronicle* stated that:

In a few days … we will see the iron horse with breath of flame and smoke rushing up this beautiful valley, and startling with its screams the echoes of these quiet ravines, and astonishing the natives of this otherwise secluded and quiet spot.

Goods Traffic Begins

But the sight of the iron horse rushing up the valley was not seen immediately, because the locomotive had been damaged in transit. It would not be long, though, before it was repaired, by William Boustead, a fitter sent down from Lowca works. He and the railway clearly got on, because a few weeks later he was to move with his family to work on the railway and would remain there until 1884.

On 13 May 1865 the *North Wales Chronicle* reported *Talyllyn* was now in working order and was bringing 'large quantities' of slate down from the quarry. Before this there was a incident which befell 'a woman named Roberts' reported by the *Chronicle* the week before. She had an accident where she slipped and fell on the railway at Tywyn in the act of dismounting from some trucks she had been riding on.

This was the railway's first recorded accident, but fortunately she was only bruised. However, this incident was curious because the report records that there was no locomotive attached to the train. Therefore, had *Talyllyn* been attached and then uncoupled? Alternatively was she

History

Site of Wharf Station | School Bridge | Site of Pendre Station | Tŷ Mawr Crossing | Hendy Farm

Above: A plan of the land occupied by the railway between Tywyn and Hendy Farm. Unfortunately there is no date on the original, but Tŷ Mawr is still indicated as a road crossing, although the land for the bridge seems to have been acquired. This possibly indicates a dating of mid to late 1865 after the A&WCR had become part of the Cambrian Railway. (TR Collection)

using the wagon to ride down the line on, or was some form of gravity working or shunting being used before *Talyllyn* was ready for service? It is quite possible that the locals were being given rides on the horse-drawn construction trains and free-wheeling down in wagons.

Once more the Board of Health was concerned about the newly opened railway, to the extent that they decided to hold a site meeting on 22 May 1865. The particular cause of this was the crossing gates that had been put up across Tŷ Mawr Lane and at Rhydyronen. Previously the Board had written to McConnel stating that gatekeepers and cottages should be provided at any crossing in the Board's area, and they were concerned that their instructions had not been complied with.

In the end 'having proceeded up the line' they decided that the crossings were 'sufficient for the traffic'. Unfortunately the minutes do not record how the members went up the line, but as *Talyllyn* was in use by then the probability was that it was by wagon hauled by the engine. In fact one has the suspicion that the 'site visit' was probably an excuse to have a ride on the railway.

After the Act

Strangely enough, after the passing of the Act there was not a rush to obtain the necessary equipment to pass a Board of Trade Inspection and introduce passenger trains. This is particularly peculiar as passing the Inspection would mean the company could recover its £1,200 Parliamentary deposit, which it had had to lodge to obtain the Act. In addition, passenger services could have produced extra revenue. Possibly the TRCo. knew there was still a lot of work to do to come up to standard.

Instead for several months the railway seems to have settled into a steady pattern of trains bringing slate down from the quarry. Possibly this was a product of a cash-flow crisis produced by the costs of obtaining the Act and also finishing the line. In addition, there was a general financial depression, which could have contributed to the situation. Therefore it could be that the TRCo.'s finances had to improve in order to pay for the extra items of motive power and rolling stock required.

The only recorded event during this period was an act of sabotage that could have had potentially serious consequences. On 26 August 1865 a stonemason, James Humphreys, attempted to derail a train near Brynerwest Farm. At the subsequent trial in March 1866 the story came out that Humphreys had been engaged in building houses at Abergynolwyn. He had placed an obstruction on the line, because he had been refused permission to ride on the train to Tywyn.

From the trial reports we learn the name of one of the first platelayers on the line, William Roberts, who saw Humphreys on the line. Another witness was Richard Richards, who described himself as a stoker on the railway. We also learn that although Humphreys was not allowed to travel, fifty men were riding on what was supposed to be a ballast train. This indicates that work was still in progress on the line. It was fortunate Richards saw the obstruction in time. Humphreys was found guilty and sentenced to five years penal servitude.

The Start of Passenger Operations

The first move towards an official passenger service seems to have come late in 1865 when an order was apparently placed with the carriage manufacturer Brown, Marshall and Co. of Birmingham for a four-wheel carriage. This was delivered in January 1866, and is now No.3 in the Talyllyn Railway carriage fleet. The present numbering system dates from the early days of the preservation era.

History

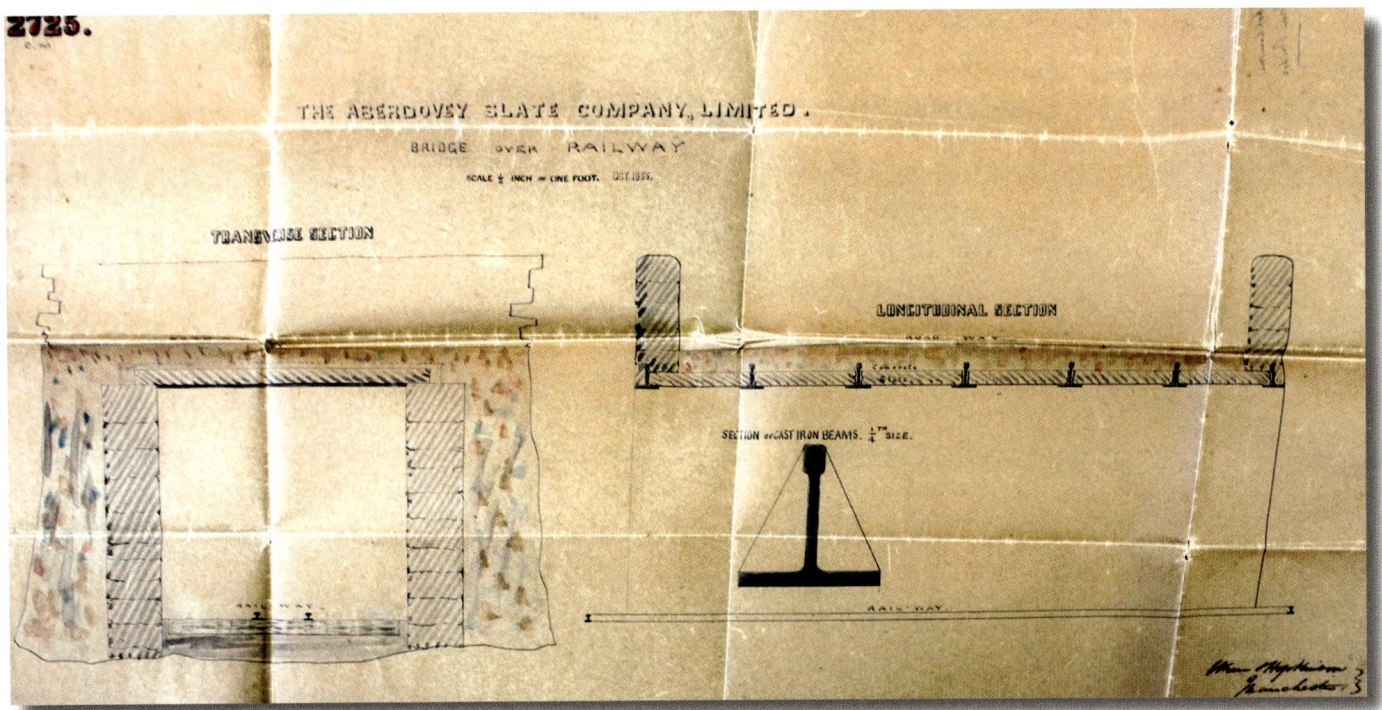

Above: A copy of the original plans for the bridges at Tŷ Mawr and Rhydyronen, dated October 1865. Interestingly the title indicates that it was drawn for the Aberdovey Slate Company even though the Talyllyn Railway Company had been established the previous July, possibly emphasising that the railway was regarded as a sub-section of the slate company. (TR Collection)

Thomas McConnel then wrote to the Board of Trade in February 1866 requesting an initial inspection of the line. This was to determine what work needed doing in order to permit the start of passenger operations before a full inspection. The Board refused, instead pointing McConnel to the Festiniog Railway for assistance, as if he might be unaware of its existence. Even a letter from the local Member of Parliament failed to sway them.

Possibly it was the problems the Festiniog had in getting permission that caused McConnel to write in the first place. When Captain Tyler had carried out his inspection there in October 1864 he required several items to be attended to. Among these was that the bridges only had 9 in of clearance to the side of the carriages.

Therefore, he recommended that all the carriage windows should be barred and the doors locked, the latter practice is still carried out on the railway today. Tyler also proposed the Festiniog fit trailing wheels to their locomotives to prevent vertical oscillation, a recommendation he was later to make on the Talyllyn.

McConnel had also decided to replace the crossings at Tŷ Mawr Lane and Rhydyronen by bridges, with drawings being prepared in October 1865. This was probably due to the need to provide crossing keepers to comply with legislation. By the time Captain Tyler came for his inspection in September 1866 the new bridges were in place, constructed of slab brought down from the quarry.

On 5 February 1866 McConnel and James Murray, one of the first directors, obtained a ruling from the Court of Chancery that permitted the release of the company's Parliamentary deposit and other fees amounting to some £1,375. This would have released the funds necessary for a number of items that seem to have been authorised around this time.

Chief of these was the order placed with Fletcher, Jennings for a second locomotive. This would also be an 0-4-0T but this time of a wholly different design, complete with Fletcher's Patent valve gear. This permitted a longer wheelbase, and was doubtless recommended to McConnel by Boustead as a way of overcoming the vertical oscillation of the short wheelbase *Talyllyn*.

Dolgoch was probably delivered in the summer of 1866, possibly along with the second vehicle for the passenger service. This was a brake van built by Brown, Marshall to the same general dimensions as the first carriage (although there is a suggestion it was delivered before the first carriage, see page 186).

The *North Wales Chronicle* for 31 March 1866 reported that the new station at Pendre was under construction, while at what they termed the south station (now Wharf) the buildings and yards were being extended. It was stated that an immense traffic in slate was being carried by the railway, but that it was hoped to start the passenger service in May. This again proved optimistic, but at least one passenger train was run that summer, on Tuesday 28 August 1866.

This was laid on for a party from the Cambrian Archaeological Society, one of whose members was Mr David Howell, the TRCo's Solicitor. He had also been the Secretary to the Newtown and Machynlleth Railway. The train was probably formed of the carriage and brake van, along with a set of slate trucks. An extract from a report of the outing stated:

History

Right: An original fencing post, from the type of post and rail fencing that can be seen in the postcard to the right.

The Talyllyn Railway, as your readers know is one of those two foot lines constructed for the purpose of carrying slates, but also used to convey passengers. As the passenger traffic from the Talyllyn Railway is not expected to be very extensive, the coach accommodation was only just sufficient for the ladies and most of the party were stowed away in slate trucks.

With this initial excursion completed, all seemed ready for the visit of Captain Tyler on 25 September 1866, but it did not go well.

His main concerns were:

- Locked chock blocks needed to be added to sidings and duplicate connecting rods to the switches.
- The fencing and hedging needed improvement.
- One bridge 3½ miles from Tywyn needed repair.
- Two bridge arches 1¼ and ¾ miles from Talyllyn (sic) needed to be rebuilt. (These are probably the cattle creeps located at Ceunant Coch and just east of Quarry Siding loop).
- The bridge openings did not leave adequate clearance for the carriages.
- One locomotive *Talyllyn* suffered from undue vertical oscillation and needed to be fitted with a set of trailing wheels.
- The second locomotive *Dolgoch* had too much horizontal motion and needed its crank pins shortening.

McConnel proposed that the doors on one side of the carriage be locked and the windows barred. This was a variation of the solution applied on the Festiniog and indicates that McConnel was aware of the problem. The Inspector agreed to this but noted the risk of passengers being trapped if the carriage tipped over, but considered that the slow speeds on the line made this unlikely. In addition, the track was to be slewed under the bridges to improve the clearances, but there is no evidence that this was ever done.

Later, McConnel was to write to the Board of Trade effectively pleading with them that the costs of rectifying any faults should not be too onerous. In particular he was concerned about the modifications to the locomotives, pointing out that he did not intend to run trains at a greater speed than 10 mph. He also stated that one further carriage was on order, and nearly completed.

Captain Tyler returned on 8 November 1866 and found much improvement. The bridges, or 'cattle arches', had been rebuilt and other modifications he had requested had been completed. He recommended some gates being put up near Pendre station were placed further from the line. Presumably these were the crossing gates at the east end of the station. He also suggested that extra carriages should be ordered before the following spring. Interestingly he did not suggest bogie coaches as he had done on his visit to the Festiniog.

McConnel had agreed to the necessary modifications to the locomotives. The Inspector therefore gave permission for the railway to be opened, on the proviso that it ran only with 'one engine in steam' and at a speed 'not exceeding 10 mph'.

One might have thought that after all this effort passenger operations would have commenced immediately, but the *Chronicle* on 17 November 1866 stated that it would not be opened for passenger traffic until January. In the event on 22 December the same paper reported that passenger trains had recently started running on the line. This possibly indicates when the second carriage arrived.

History

Above: The earliest known photograph of the Talyllyn Railway dating from c.1870 shows *Talyllyn* with a weatherboard and trailing wheels, but without a cab, on Dolgoch viaduct. The brake van still has an open verandah. It is possible that William Boustead is the figure sat on *Talyllyn*'s footplate.   (Photo supplied by Llyfrgell Genedlaethol Cymru/National Library of Wales)

The Early Years

Two trains a day were run starting from Abergynolwyn as this was where the locomotive and crew were then based, a locomotive shed having been built at Tŷ Dŵr. The first known timetable poster was issued for 19 February 1867. By this time services were originating at Tywyn Pendre. In addition, the first intermediate station had also opened at Rhydyronen.

This indicates that the locomotive shed at Tywyn Pendre was now in use. William Boustead, the locomotive fitter, and his family, had originally moved from Whitehaven to Abergynolwyn. Now a cottage was provided for them at Pendre, which was part of the shed and workshop, and adjacent to the crossing. It would seem possible that Annie Boustead also acted as crossing keeper.

After all this the railway settled into its daily routine. Passengers and goods were conveyed up and down the valley, while slates came down from the quarry. However, there were exceptional days as well, such as Good Friday and the Easter Monday fair. On these occasions it was reported that the company's carriages 'were well filled'.

A new timetable poster was issued with train times from 1 August 1867 showing that the station at Dolgoch was now open. An extra two carriages had evidently also been obtained, as they were included in the returns to the Board of Trade in September 1867. Another development came in April 1869 when the railway secured the contract for carrying the mails between Tywyn and Abergynolwyn, although mails were not carried until August 1870. This would have been a welcome source of additional revenue.

Of course the main fortunes of the railway were inextricably linked to the fortunes of the quarry as its main source of traffic. In 1867 the Aberdovey Slate Company changed its name to the Abergynolwyn Slate Company, a fairer reflection of the geographical location of its operation. By 1870 production of slate from the quarry had reached 6,000 tons *per annum*.

During the succeeding years of the following decade production of slate ebbed and flowed reaching a peak of 7,951 tons in 1877. This was nowhere near the original aspirations of the owners, and was to lead to a series of financial issues for the quarry at the end of the decade.

The quarry was also a dangerous place, with nine workers killed there during the 1870s. One person that did enjoy a lucky escape was the 16 year old mentioned in the *Cambrian News* of 24 September 1870.

This records that when he was riding down on a train of two wagons on the Alltwyllt incline (The incline that ended on the site of what is now Nant Gwernol station), the brake on the incline drum failed and the wagons ran away down the incline. On reaching the bottom the wagons plunged into the ravine and were smashed on the banks of the Nant Gwernol. The young man was catapulted across the river, and seems to have only sustained relatively minor injuries on landing. James Boyd in his book records that there was a man at the quarry known as 'Flying Dick' because of his lucky escape from such an incident.

Brynglas station is first mentioned in *Bradshaw's Guide* in July 1872, although it could have opened before this time. Then in October 1873 came the news of the death of Thomas McConnel after a long illness. He was replaced as Chairman of both the TRCo. and the Abergynolwyn Slate Company by William McConnel.

On 3 April 1876 the railway began to operate the first of the early Monday morning trains for the quarrymen. These were for the benefit of those living beyond Abergynolwyn, who lodged in the 'barracks' at the quarry during the week. The railway had been running extra trains on a Saturday afternoon for a while, which allowed the workmen to ride back down.

The Winds of Change

There was heavy snow on 8 January 1879 blocking the line around Fach Goch. Other storm clouds were gathering as well, only these were financial ones over the fortunes of the slate company.

Originally the capital of the Aberdovey Slate Company was £75,000. This was increased to £112,500 in August 1865 and, after the change of name to the Abergynolwyn Slate Company, to £129,000 in October 1869. The upshot of this was that the quarry was heavily over-capitalised and would never make sufficient profit. A general depression in the economy also affected business. The *Cambrian News* reported on 18 April 1879, that the quarry workers had been put on a four day week, as they had been quarrying slate for stock for several months.

Eventually on 9 October 1879 the assets of the quarry were put up for auction at Chester. These included all its properties in Abergynolwyn, said to be eighty-eight cottages and two farms, the quarries and equipment as well as the remaining leases. In addition the auction lot contained the 750 £20 shares in the TRCo. These were at the time potentially attractive as the railway was in the midst of its most profitable period pre-preservation, with a surplus of £501 for the twelve months to 30 September 1877 and £414 for a similar period in 1878.

Despite this only one bid of £10,000, by a 'gentleman from Manchester', was made and so it all went unsold. There were further problems from a severe storm on 7 August 1880. This damaged several bridges on the railway, and the water had 'risen so high as to put out the fire on the locomotive engines'. More seriously it caused the reservoir above the quarry to burst sending a cascade of water down through the quarry workings, reaching Abergynolwyn itself and sweeping away the bridges en-route. Fortunately there was no loss of life, but the loss to the slate company was estimated at £5,000 to £6,000.

Therefore, it is no surprise that the slate company's assets were again offered for sale at an auction in Manchester on 16 March 1881. This time they were sold for £18,000 to none other than William McConnel.

McConnel now owned the assets of the slate company, and the shares in the TRCo., but he did not own the slate company's shares. These were still in the hands of the previous shareholders. However, with the assets of the slate company sold its shares were effectively worthless. As a result the shareholders agreed to wind up the Abergynolwyn Slate Company and place it in liquidation on 7 March 1882.

William now established a new company to take over the quarries and the railway, The Abergynolwyn Slate Quarries Co. He also increasingly handed over the running of the quarry and railway to his son, William Houldsworth McConnel. Freed from some of the financial issues they invested in the quarry again with production reaching its all-time peak of 7,996 tons in 1883. This was to be the high point of the quarry's fortunes.

In 1885 McConnel enquired whether the Corris Railway was prepared to sell one of their locomotives. The reason being that major repairs were probably required to either *Talyllyn* or *Dolgoch*, or even both.

A Major Accident

On Friday 3 February 1882 the *Cambrian News* carried the following story:

THE TALYLLYN RAILWAY.—A NARROW ESCAPE OF LIFE.— As the working men's train, which starts Towyn every Monday morning at six a.m., conveying quarrymen residing at Aberdovey, Towyn, and Bryncrug, had reached a little beyond Dolgoch station the engine went off the rails and was precipitated to the bye-road leading to Tygwyn and Erw (now the crossing at Quarry Siding), dragging with it two carriages, one of which overturned with the engine. Fortunately, however, the occupants of the engine and carriage escaped without injury. Had the carriage given another turn no doubt a sad catastrophe would have ensued, it being full of occupants. It appears that during the storm of last Sunday the streams flowing from the Dolgoch hills had brought down a quantity of soil and gravel which was deposited on the line, and had not been removed before the coming of the train, to which fact no doubt the accident must be attributed. A number of quarrymen from Bryneglwys were summoned down to clear the line and to re-adjust the engine and carriages, and the line was opened for usual traffic before one p.m. on the same day.

The date of the incident would have been Monday 30 January 1882 at about 6.30 am, and therefore in the dark. Examining the description of the accident it seems that if one of the carriages overturned then it would probably have been onto its north side with the opening doors. If there were any workers inside they would have been trapped, which would have been a very frightening experience for anyone involved.

History

Right: Advertisement for the second auction of the assets of the Abergynolwyn Slate Company, which included the full 750 shares in the Talyllyn Railway Company. It is worth noting the name John Roberts as the contact point for enquiries about the railway.

The line seems to have been speedily restored after help had arrived, which would have taken several hours to summon, along with presumably the second locomotive from Tywyn. In addition, although the accident was reported to the Board of Trade, it appears it was not deemed serious enough to send out an Inspector. All of this suggests that possibly the event was not as dramatic as the account made out.

Unfortunately the report does not say which locomotive was involved, although it has been speculated that it could explain the denting on *Dolgoch's* pre-preservation cab. In recent years damage has been discovered on carriage No.4 consistent with it being involved with such an accident.

There was a later incident on 16 August 1884 when the evening down train came to a halt, as, *the water had suddenly found its way out of the* (presumably locomotive) *tank*. The passengers were then loaded into slate wagons and rode by gravity to Tywyn. This seems to have been most likely due to a burst boiler tube, rather than an actual leak in the water tank.

Relationships with the Cambrian Railways

Originally relationships with the A&WCR and its successor the Cambrian had been cordial, although there was a blip when the Talyllyn Act was going through Parliament. Unfortunately, things seem to have gradually deteriorated over time. In August 1872 the Cambrian directors decided to double the rate for slate haulage between Tywyn and Aberdyfi to 6d per ton. It seems to have been doubled again not long afterwards.

Then in May 1883 the Cambrian increased it again to 1s 6d per ton. This the slate company refused to pay. In June 1885 the Cambrian offered a compromise rate of 1s 4d per ton, but the TRCo. decided to appeal to the Railway Commissioners. As a way of settling the dispute, the Cambrian Traffic Manager had even proposed adapting old standard gauge wagons to carry Talyllyn wagons to Aberdyfi, much as was originally planned. However, it is reported that the Talyllyn did not possess enough wagons for a rake to be away from the line. At a hearing on 2 February 1886 the Commissioners upheld the TRCo. position, but this did not finally settle the matter, as the Cambrian wanted to recoup the unpaid fees, and so the issue rumbled on.

Things were not helped when on 10 July 1886 a rake of Talyllyn wagons broke free from a train heading up the cutting towards Pendre. They ran over the wharf edge overturning a Cambrian wagon standing on the siding, and proceeded to block, albeit briefly, the main line. The Cambrian Traffic Manager reported that he had asked the TRCo. 'to state what means they propose to adopt to prevent the recurrence of an accident of this kind'. It would however be nearly seventy years before a buffer stop appeared on the wharf edge.

Finally in December 1886 the rate dispute led the Cambrian to impose a severe sanction: W.H. McConnel's cheap rate season ticket was withdrawn. Eventually a settlement was reached in January 1887, and the season ticket was issued.

Resisting Regulation

A substantial portion of the McConnels' time in the late 1880s and early 1890s was spent dealing with what they considered to be one of the more onerous new legislative requirements that had come in, namely the fitting of continuous brakes. There were several letters between W.H. McConnel and the Board of Trade, much of which has been published elsewhere. This started with a circular

Rails Along The Fathew

History

from the Board in October 1889, and finally ended in July 1891 when the Board gave an exemption to the railway from the fitting of continuous brakes.

This was on the proviso that trains should not operate above 12 mph. As Thomas McConnel had promised that trains would not operate above 10 mph during Tyler's 1866 inspection, this could be said to actually be a speed increase! This exemption was to remain in force for a hundred years.

The Rise of Tourism

During the 1870s there was a move to increase tourism to the area and provide extra facilities. In 1876 plans were announced for the building of a pier, which was to have been 1,200 ft long. Construction began, but was stalled, and a substantial portion of it was washed away in a storm. Eventually the remains were dismantled.

A more successful enterprise was the construction of houses on the sea front, and a terrace of houses was built near Neptune Hall in 1878. That same year the Ynysymaengwyn estate was purchased by John Corbett from Droitwich. He had made his money in salt extraction, and was no relation to the previous owners of the estate. Corbett invested in the town, helping with the construction of the seafront promenade, the Market Hall, the Assembly Room (now the cinema) and also rebuilt what became the Corbett Arms Hotel. All this helped in the development of Tywyn's tourist trade, which was becoming increasingly significant and in turn was of benefit to the railway.

It is rumoured that in the 1890s, when the promenade was being constructed, a tramway was laid from what was then known as King's station. This apparently ran up onto the road (which was then much lower), over the Cambrian line on Neptune Road bridge and down to the Promenade. It enabled wagon loads of slate slab to be taken directly to the construction site.

The railway also began to feature in various articles on the attractions of the area obviously aimed at the tourist market. For example the following comes from the *Towyn-on-Sea & Merioneth County Times* for 31 August 1899:

THE NARROW-GUAGE (sic) RAILWAY.
This little railway runs from Towyn to Abergynolwyn and the varied scenery through which it passes is most impressive. There are four stations – Rhydyronen, Brynglas, Dolgoch, and Abergynolwyn. At each of these villages there is much to be seen and admired. The waterfalls are not far from Dolgoch Station, and the trains run conveniently so that visitors can, if they wish it, go by one train and return by the next. Dolgoch is also the station to alight for the Bird Rock ... The railway station at Towyn is in a turning out of Maengwyn Street, on the right. The carriages are, of course, very small and convenient, and the fares are moderate.

The 1890s

During the 1880s the operating surplus enjoyed between 1875 and 1884, turned to a string of losses. This was, with a few exceptions, to remain the pattern prior to preservation. Part of the losses was due to locomotive repairs. *Dolgoch* received a new boiler at the Brush Engineering's Falcon works in Loughborough in the early summer of 1891. The work seems to have cost in the order of £200.

Between 1898 and 1900 there was again heavy additional locomotive expenditure, of the order of £500 in total, suggesting significant work was done on both locomotives. Possibly *Talyllyn* was the first, and then *Dolgoch*. This would fit with *Dolgoch* being repainted in June 1900. All of which would have placed a strain on the company's finances.

Passenger traffic increased to a peak of 30,918 journeys in 1898. There is then a divergence with a general decrease in Third Class travel, presumably caused by the gradual decline in the quarry, but Second Class travel increased, probably due to increasing numbers of tourists. The latter though was not sufficient to balance a decline in overall numbers.

After legislative changes in 1888 the charges for goods were put up again in 1893, which did not go down well with the local population. Between Saturday 7 and Sunday 8 January that year there was also a major snow storm, sufficient that trains did not run on Saturday and Monday.

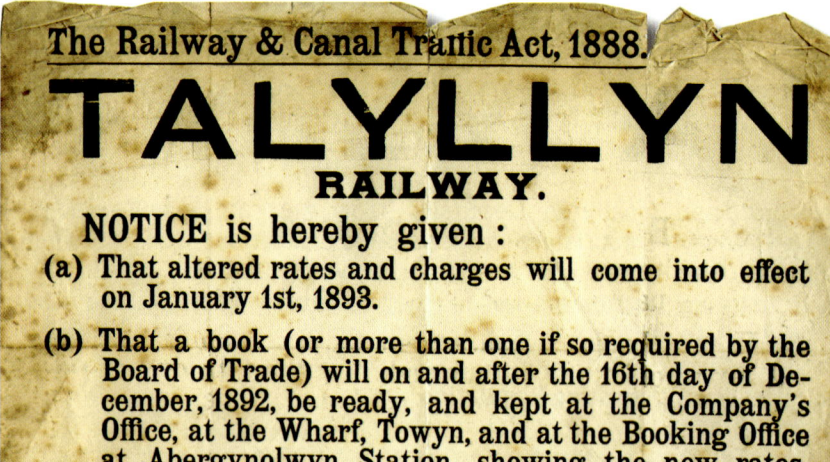

Left: Notice of what was to prove a less than popular goods rates increase from 1 January 1893.

History

By the end of the decade however, the railway was also getting some unfavourable comments in the press about the state of the carriages and the level of service offered. The *Towyn-on-Sea and Merioneth County Times* commented on 3 August 1899: *Could not the Talyllyn Railway Company see their way to do away with the existing carriages and provide carriages something similar to the Corris Railway Company?*

Similarly, in March the following year the paper commented: *Not only are the carriages on the narrow gauge of a primitive description, but the rate of speed is painfully slow …. A suggestion is made that the line of railway should be continued to Talyllyn Lake. If this could be carried out, the passenger traffic of the Company would be increased by some thousands.*

By May 1900 things had improved; the same paper reported: *The carriages on this railway have been beautifully painted and decorated by Mr W Rowlands. More frequent trains are also run, whilst trees have been planted at the stations. These are small improvements but they indicate progress.*

Into the Twentieth Century

In 1900 the 'slate wharf station' was first mentioned in the advertised passenger timetables, albeit as a footnote. This stated that trains would depart from there five minutes before the advertised departure time (from Tywyn Pendre). There was no mention of trains returning to the wharf, as officially all down trains still terminated at Pendre. This would remain the case until the early 1920s.

One major piece of international news was also celebrated on the railway. On 5 June 1900, during the Second Boer War, British troops captured Pretoria. News of this spread rapidly around Tywyn and great celebrations ensued, as some of the troops involved had local connections. At the same time in the workshop at Pendre *Dolgoch* was receiving a new coat of paint, probably by Mr Rowlands who had just painted the carriages. It was therefore decided to rename *Dolgoch*, *Pretoria*, to commemorate the event, a name it would carry for a number of years.

Above: A recently discovered photograph of *Talyllyn* in the Brain Collection at the National Railway Museum. Other photographs in the collection date from around 1897 -1900. *Talyllyn* is seen here at Abergynolwyn with some shiny paintwork, suggesting it was soon after the overhaul when its second saddletank was fitted.
(Photo: Copyright National Railway Museum (NRM)/Science and Society Picture Library (SSPL))

History

Above: *Dolgoch* was renamed *Pretoria* to commemorate the relief of that city during the Boer War in June 1900. It is seen here at Abergynolwyn in 1903 in its new guise. There are also two firemen in this photo, Bob Thomas is on the footplate, while the young man with the hoop is David Ellis Davies who served as fireman between 1920 and 1927. (Photo: Michael Whitehouse Collection)

The new century also brought a new General Manager and Company Secretary when Robert Burton Yates arrived on the railway. He was to instigate a number of significant changes to the line.

In 1902 two major events occurred. Firstly in May of that year Robert Jones Roberts, a pharmacist from Tywyn, leased the Dolgoch ravine to the local council. For several years he had been laying out the ravine with paths and trees as a public recreation area, but now he effectively made a gift of the land to the local community. This was to be a major attraction for the tourist trade in the years ahead.

On Friday 10 October came the news of the death of William McConnel at the age of 95. He was said to have been well-liked and respected in the area, and there was a genuine sense of loss at his passing. With his death, and the impending end of the leases on the quarry, the McConnel era was drawing to a close. Not long after this the railway company also lost its chief accountant, and sometime manager, with the death of Hugh Thomas in January 1903.

During these early years of the new century there was a series of accidents. The first occurred on the mineral extension near Tŷ Dŵr in March 1902 when a rake of loaded slate wagons derailed with a fair amount of damage resulting. Then in April 1904 a locomotive propelling a wagon at Pendre also derailed with considerable damage. Finally there was a near accident in October 1910, during the final weeks of the McConnel era, when a train narrowly avoided hitting a tree that had been felled by a storm.

One amusing incident that occurred on the railway came from a report in the *County Times* for 2 April 1903. It reads: *Canvassing for the District Council election next Saturday is being carried on with vigour. On Monday morning one of the candidates thought to steal a march on his opponents by attending at the Talyllyn Railway Company's station to interview the workmen going up with the early morning train* (This would have been around 6am). *To his surprise, however, he found, that one of the other candidates was there on the same errand.*

Potential Closure

With leases at Bryneglwys nearing their end it is clear that W.H. McConnel was looking for a possible alternative venture. In March 1904 he leased Braich-y-rhiw Farm with 'the intention of developing a slate quarry'. This was a site above Rhydyronen on the opposite side of the valley from Bronbiban quarry. However, the lease was short-lived and R.B. Yates reported in the October that the company's interest in the site had ended.

Next, at a public meeting on 29 December 1905 it was stated that the McConnels proposed ending quarrying at the conclusion of the existing leases, the first of which would expire in 1907. This obviously caused deep concern in the area. Happily by July 1906 some agreement on, at

History

least a temporary extension, seems to have been reached, and the quarry was reported to be back on a five-day week.

Production at Bryneglwys even continued after a major rock fall that month when some 25,000 tons of rock were said to have caved in. This was in part probably caused by the quarrymen now cutting away at the supporting slate pillars rather than opening up new chambers.

On 18 December 1909 the McConnels ceased quarrying slate at Bryneglwys. According to a subsequent letter by R.B. Yates in the *Cambrian News* this was not due to any unwillingness by the landlords to negotiate new leases. Instead it was probably that the family had simply had enough, and decided that it was time to move on. In the letter Yates also stated that the desire of the family was that a new owner should be found, in the meantime the quarry and business would be wound down.

Preparations for the closure of the railway were also in hand. In April 1909 Yates had written to the Board of Trade asking what procedures needed to be followed in order to close the railway. The Board seemed unconcerned, one file note read that it was 'a narrow gauge one ... running from Aberystwyth (sic) to Talyllyn (sic). Probably its passenger traffic consists largely of tourists'. Yates was advised that if the company wished to simply cease operating there were no procedures, but if it wanted to apply for a warrant to abandon the line it needed to be aware of relevant legislation.

The local community, though, did not wish to lose their railway. In August 1910 Samuel Edmunds also wrote to the Board of Trade to ask what notice the company might have to give if they were to cease operating. On Wednesday 12 October a public meeting was called at the behest of the Clerk of the Council, Richard Barnett. This was reported in the *Aberystwyth Observer* the following day; it is worth noting this in some detail, as the similarities with a meeting held forty years later in Birmingham are striking. It was said that:

If a committee were formed to take over the railway, they could not expect a big profit; in fact, they might run it at a loss unless some industry were opened ... The probable time of the closing of the railway would be November 15th ... Mr R. B. Yates assured the meeting that Mr McConnell (sic) would let or sell the concern at the most reasonable price possible, as he was extremely anxious to keep the line open, but he would only do so if guaranteed from actual loss. If the meeting would offer a nominal rent, he believed Mr McConnell would be ready to accept.

... proposed... the meeting express the opinion that in the interests of Towyn and its residents the railway should be kept open. ... This was carried unanimously. It was further proposed that the following gentlemen should form a committee to approach Mr McConnell as to his terms for letting or purchase of the railway: Messrs C. Garland, R. J. Morgan, Daniel Edwards, J. C. Edwards, Haydn Jones, R. Jones M.R.C.V.S., with power to add.

In the end, rather than a committee, it was Henry Haydn Jones, newly elected Liberal Member of Parliament for Merionethshire, who was to become the saviour of both the quarry and the railway.

Above: A train at Abergynolwyn probably c. 1910. R.B. Yates, the manager, is seen looking out from the brake van. On the ground to the left of the locomotive is Jacob Rowlands, who was the guard for many years, and Dick Price, the driver, is on the right. Note the siding on the left, this was relaid some time later further away from the platform. (Photo: John Alsop Collection)

History

History Part Two
The Haydn Jones Years

Henry Haydn Jones

The new owner of the Talyllyn Railway and the Bryneglwys quarry was the recently elected Liberal M.P. for Merionethshire, Henry Haydn Jones. Today we are very cynical about our politicians, but in the case of Haydn Jones' acquisition of both the quarry and the railway the motive seems to have been quite altruistic. He purchased both in 1911 after the election was over, and, as will be seen later, kept the railway running after standing down from Parliament in 1945. All of this indicates that he was a man of principle acting out of a genuine concern for the well-being of the people of the area.

He paid £5,250 for the assets of both quarry and railway, much of which he reportedly had to borrow. To run the quarry he established the Abergynolwyn Slate and Slab Company with himself as sole director. New leases were negotiated for the quarry and production recommenced. On the railway there does not appear to have been an interruption of services due to the change of ownership.

Above: Sir Henry Haydn Jones M.P.   (Photo: TR Collection)

By 1912 the quarry was back in production with 120 men in employment there. On the railway jobs were also preserved, although the former General Manager, R.B.Yates, had left the company during the changeover. The General Manager now being listed as Richard Barnett, who was also the Secretary of the Abergynolwyn Slate and Slab Co.

Passenger figures had fallen from 22,598 in 1908 to 20,719 in 1910, but then increased to 22,173 in 1911, with a sharp increase to 28,166 in 1912. The shutdown of the quarry meant that the total of coal and minerals carried also fell from 3,972 tons in 1909 to 332 tons in 1911. Most of the latter was probably coal. However, when slate production recommenced goods traffic increased again.

It has been reported that Haydn Jones' original intention was to keep the quarry and railway for ten years and then sell them on. Despite this he did invest in both ventures, even though the loss on the railway was running at £337 by 30 September 1912. The outbreak of war in 1914 could also have changed with his original plans.

A Potential New Locomotive

One possible development was the acquisition of a new locomotive. It seems that the firebox on *Dolgoch* needed replacement, and it could have been that Haydn Jones was evaluating the costs of repair versus replacement.

There was a quotation from W.G. Bagnall for one of their *Mercedes* class 0-4-0 saddle tank locomotives at £440 dated 10 May 1912. Another quote from Bagnall was for either an 0-4-2 saddle tank of their *Forward* class, or an 0-6-0 saddle tank. These were priced at £470 and £480 respectively.

There were also two quotes from Kerr, Stuart. The first, dated 28 February 1913, was for an 0-4-2 *Tattoo* saddle tank for £458. This design was the same type as the one later supplied to the Corris which became Talyllyn No.4 *Edward Thomas*. The second quote from Kerr, Stuart was for an 0-6-0 side tank locomotive, including a copper firebox and brass tubes; this was estimated at £528.

In the end it seems as if Haydn Jones decided he could not afford the expense of a new locomotive. As a result *Dolgoch* was returned to Whitehaven for the necessary work to be done at a cost of around £243.

The First World War and Beyond

On the outbreak of war the railway was not taken into Government control, a decision that was to have a bearing on later events. At the time there was a severe slump in the North Wales slate trade. In fact only a few weeks previously Haydn Jones had led a delegation to see the then Chancellor of the Exchequer, Lloyd George, about securing some tax concessions that would aid the industry.

Rails Along The Fathew

History

Above: An indication of the date of the transfer of the railway to Haydn Jones comes from this share certificate for £400 (nominal value) worth of shares owned by Richard Barnett. He was listed as the Secretary of the Talyllyn Railway Company between 1911 and 1917. The certificate is signed by R.B Yates, W.H. McConnel and possibly John Wanklyn McConnel on 25 March 1911.

During the war the quarry suffered from a shortage of labour as men both joined up and also took higher paid jobs elsewhere. By September 1918 Haydn Jones wrote that there were only forty men employed in the quarry 'mostly old, infirm and long past their best, and a few lads over 14'. One wonders what the men concerned would have made of Haydn Jones' description of them. Clearly any reduction in the output of the quarry would have had an effect on the railway, but there are seemingly few surviving records from this period on which to draw.

After the War and Into the 1920s

In 1919 there is evidence that Sir Haydn was again investing in the railway. During the year £393 was paid out for the upkeep of the Permanent Way, £100 of which was in materials. This would have been enough to purchase 1,000 sleepers, sufficient for half a mile of track.

Locomotives were also under discussion. This time it seems that it was *Talyllyn* that was in need of an overhaul. Therefore, once more Haydn Jones enquired about a replacement locomotive this time from the Hunslet Engine Company of Leeds. On 6 January 1919 they sent details of a 4-6-0 tank locomotive of the type supplied by themselves to the War Department.

Unfortunately the paperwork does not indicate whether this was a new or a 'war-surplus' locomotive, nor is there any indication of the price. However, the type of locomotive under consideration would have been too large for the Talyllyn's loading gauge. This also explains why the Talyllyn did not follow the lead of the Glyn Valley or Welsh Highland Railways in obtaining an ex-War Department locomotive, as again it would have been too big to pass through the line's bridges.

Therefore, Haydn Jones once more chose to repair rather than replace. The railway's return for 1919 shows that nearly £426 was paid out on materials for locomotive repairs, although whether this was just on *Talyllyn* or both locos is not clear.

Around the end of the war Haydn Jones had begun a long drawn out battle with the North Wales Quarrymen's Union. In 1920 this came to a head with Haydn Jones unilaterally closing the workings on 31 January 1920. The *Cambrian News* reported that discontent had been stirred up among the workforce for political ends, but how true this was is unknown. Haydn Jones had previously threatened to close both quarry and railway, the latter he stated he would sell for scrap in order to recover his losses. In the end the Union backed down and the quarry reopened in the March.

History

Above: A well known postcard of *Dolgoch* at Wharf station reputedly taken in September 1916, Jacob Rowlands is stood on the footboard of carriage No.3, and Hugh (Old or Gas) Jones is by the locomotive cab with Dick Price on the right. The overbridge has been rebuilt once, but will be rebuilt again around 1917. The others are possibly two of the slate loaders, the one on the left is apparently reading *The Daily Telegraph*. (Commercial Postcard)

The post-war recovery helped to improve the financial situation along with a large fare increase. Second Class was abolished in July 1920 and fares became either First or Third in line with the practice on the main line. *Talyllyn* evidently returned to service in 1920. Later in the year it was repainted, reportedly being turned out in a red livery. The carriages were also repainted at a cost of £102. By the end of 1920 the railway had carried 33,895 passengers during the year, a record since 1899, and the following year conveyed 2,641 tons of goods. The operating deficit in 1921 even decreased to £176.

These early years of the 1920s could well be said to be the heyday of the Haydn Jones era. Demand for slate was high, the tourist trade was developing and there was little competition for the railway. There was a programme of renewal on the Permanent Way with 3,000 sleepers replaced between 1921 and 1924. Wagons were repaired or renewed and the locomotives also seem to have been regularly maintained.

We also have several eye witness accounts of the railway during this time. A.C. Waine's father was a friend of Haydn Jones' brother Daniel Lincoln, and the family holidayed in Tywyn between 1917 and 1922. He recalled the guard, Jacob Rowlands, and the booking office in the brake van. At Abergynolwyn he stated that the carriages were shunted into a siding and the locomotive would set off to Nant Gwernol with maybe a dozen empty slate wagons.

Haydn Jones would also ride up to the quarry sitting in the time-honoured fashion on the floor of the brake van with his feet resting on the running boards. Apparently the children took delight in putting footprints on his coat tails!

One practice that was remembered by many was hiring a slate wagon for a party to ride back down the valley to Tywyn by gravity after the last train. Mr Waine recalls that the cost was half a crown (12½p) paid to Jacob Rowlands. The last recorded hiring of a wagon was in June 1942 for seven people at 6d per person.

Of course many railways at that time were being absorbed into the 'Big Four' as a result of the Grouping of 1923. Those included in this process were principally those lines that had been brought under government control during the Great War. As the Talyllyn was not in this category it was not affected, and so did not become part of the Great Western Railway (GWR).

In 1926 an article about a recent visit to the line by H.G.W. Household and O. Elsdon appeared in *The Railway Magazine*. This notes that there was now a motor charabanc which connected the trains at Abergynolwyn to the lake. At this time the booking offices at Pendre and Abergynolwyn also seemed to be used, although they were opened by the guard when the train arrived at the station. The colour of the coaches is described as crimson lake, but unfortunately no mention is made of the locomotive livery.

History

All this paints a picture of a railway that was doing well, serving its community and also the needs of holidaymakers. By 1925 the annual deficit was even down to under £100. Sadly this would soon begin to change.

The Start of the Decline

The post-war boom in the slate market began to wane. Output from Bryneglwys peaked in 1926 and then began a steady decline, and with it the numbers of men employed also decreased. Between 1926 and 1930 the workforce had more than halved. This is also reflected in the passenger figures for the railway, which went from 19,128 to 8,807 over the same period.

Economies were made on the railway with nine employees leaving between 1925 and 1930 with only one replacement. In addition, long-time guard Jacob Rowlands died on 18 December 1928. These economies helped reduce the operating deficit from £404 in 1926 to £93 in 1931, the lowest it would be during the inter-war period. The situation was also not helped by the great depression of the early 1930s.

According the Annual Returns no money was spent on the repair of locomotives or carriages between 1929 and 1935. But it is known that work was done on *Talyllyn* in 1932. Certainly a new smokebox door and saddle tank was fitted at this time and it is likely that work was done on the boiler. Where this expenditure appears in the Annual Returns is a matter of conjecture, possibly under miscellaneous.

Permanent Way costs were also seemingly reduced to simply paying wages. H.C. Casserley visited the line in June 1932 and recalled that the track was already beginning to get in a poor state, and that there were very few other passengers, 'if any at all'.

During the 1930s there was a major up-grade to the valley road to Abergynolwyn and the lake, ironically championed in part by Haydn Jones, using one of the government's schemes to aid employment. This doubtless led to the increasing numbers of motor cars taking traffic away from the line. There was also the introduction of a bus service.

In 1932 the staff consisted of two clerks, an engine fitter, an engine driver, a fireman, two platelayers, two goods' loaders and a goods' agent, a total of ten men. By 1935 this had become seven with the loss of one clerk, the engine fitter and a goods' loader. This was to remain the staffing level until the outbreak of war.

Economies were also made in the level of service offered. From 1932 First Class fares were abolished and only Third Class was available, although the First Class carriage was reportedly often available for Third Class passengers. In 1934 the winter service was reduced to three days a week with trains operating on Tuesdays, Thursdays and Saturdays. That year the Monday morning quarrymen's service was also withdrawn.

The following year the days of winter operation were changed to Mondays, Wednesdays and Fridays. However,

Above: *Talyllyn* is being serviced at Pendre c. 1925.

(Photo: TR Collection)

History

a six-day a week service was still run in the summer. Combined with other timetable changes the total mileage of trains operated was halved to an annual total of 5,684 by the end of 1935.

Renewals and Replacements

In 1935 *Dolgoch* was in need of some major work that was beyond the capabilities of the workshop at Pendre at the time. It was therefore sent to Britannia Foundry at Porthmadog for the work to be done. Again there is no separate entry for the costs of the repair listed in the Annual Return for the year.

Haydn Jones also purchased some rail from the then defunct Glyn Valley Tramway in 1936. This was laid up Cynfal bank between 1938 and 1939. The delay was reportedly due to the need to acquire new nuts and bolts to replace those burnt off by the contractors when the rail was lifted.

Between 1936 and 1939 some £200 was spent on Permanent Way materials, roughly equally spread across the years. In 1939 it is also recorded that the railway received 11s 6d for the sale of old rail, which was presumably some of the rail that had been replaced.

Around 1939 the station building at Abergynolwyn was replaced with a slate-built structure. There were also monies paid out for work on the locomotive and carriage sheds and other buildings over the two years.

Into the Second World War

Although isolated from the main impact of the outbreak of hostilities nevertheless the war brought changes to Tywyn. An army camp was built at Morfa and by 1943 the army had taken over the promenade establishing a large NAAFI, military hospital and even a cinema. Here they practised amphibious landings including preparing for D-Day.

Of course food production was important during the war, and so the farmers were to play a key role in the war-effort. Meanwhile on the hills around Abergynolwyn plantations of fir trees appeared. None of this seems to have brought significant extra passenger traffic to the Talyllyn, which once again was not regarded as strategic enough to come under government control. There was an indirect benefit to the quarry and railway during the war, however, and that was a rise in demand for roofing slate in order to repair bomb damage.

Surprisingly we have a plethora of eye-witness accounts of the railway during the war. This was because a number of enthusiasts encountered the railway at various times during the conflict and recorded their experiences for posterity. These help to give a picture of the railway during these years. Among these was a writer called Tom Rolt. We will be hearing more about him, and the role he was to play in the Talyllyn story, later.

As part of the wartime restrictions the winter passenger timetable of running twice daily three days a week was

Above: A 'guest' driver, a Mr Riding, on *Talyllyn* at Wharf in 1933. As usual the train is mixed with some wagons coupled at the back. It is worth noting that the south-side doors have been removed on the brake van, but it still retains the running board and guard's ducket on that side.
(Photo: E.J. Riding/TR Collection)

History

Above: This photo probably dates from 1943 with Hugh Jones on the right with a mixed train consisting of the First Class carriage (although First Class fares were no longer charged) and two wagons. One of these is loaded with some sacks, possibly of flour, and the other with coal. It is possibly the train James Boyd describes below, but with the third wagon yet to be added.

(Photo: J.I.C. Boyd)

imposed year round from September 1939. This was reduced to Wednesdays and Fridays only from January 1942. The service was increased to three days a week from June 1942, and remained at that level until January 1943 when again it became Wednesdays and Fridays once more until 2 August 1943. Occasional slate trains were run on other days as Graham Teasdill and his mother discovered unexpectedly in the cutting between Tywyn Wharf and Pendre stations one day.

When long-time company employee Hugh Jones retired in 1973 he commented on the state of things during the war years, particularly when some of the other employees left for better paid jobs with the army:

"Many a morning train ran with me as driver, fireman, and guard: Edward Thomas booked the tickets at Wharf, but then had to stay in the office, so if there were any passengers at the intermediate stations, I had to leave the engine, issue their tickets from the van, and then return to the engine. The train would be left unattended at Abergynolwyn while I took the locomotive to the foot of Alltwyllt Incline for any wagons of slates there might be; ... all this was on wages of £2 a week, with no paid holidays."

In 1943 there were also two periods when the passenger service was suspended. Between 23 June and 20 July and then some weeks in November, only resuming on 31 December. Why this was is unclear, there was some general goods traffic on four dates during the latter hiatus, but otherwise the railway seems to have been shut down completely. When services resumed it was again only on Wednesdays and Fridays (except for Bank Holiday Mondays when services would be run) a situation that would remain until 1946.

One of these periods could have been the result of a serious derailment to *Dolgoch* near Fach Goch. This was recalled by Dai Jones on his retirement. Apparently the locomotive derailed so badly it ended up at ninety degrees to the track. Quarrymen needed to be summoned to get the locomotive back on the track, but then it was found it could not move under its own power.

Therefore Herbert and Dai, who had been summoned from school, went down to Pendre and lit up *Talyllyn*. In order to plug the leaks on the locomotive they had to pour oatmeal into the boiler, before taking it up the line to rescue *Dolgoch*.

Certainly *Dolgoch* seems to have been in poor condition at the beginning of 1943, as observed by James Boyd on a visit to the line. The up train consisting of *'one four (sic) compartment First Class coach'*, along with three wagons, one loaded with coal, one with flour and the third with Permanent Way materials. The driver was Hugh Jones, and Boyd was the only passenger. Two loaded slate wagons came down with the return trip plus five extra passengers. *Talyllyn* was in the workshop for repairs at the time, and the brake van was not in use either.

Rails Along The Fathew 33

History

Left: One of the last known photographs of *Talyllyn* in steam before preservation. It is seen at Abergynolwyn in September 1940 in very poor condition.
(Photo: J.W. Sparrowe/TR Collection)

The informality of the railway is illustrated by the fact that Boyd was invited to drive the locomotive on the down trip. Graham Teasdill records how the guard used to carry a gun in the van in case he saw any rabbits to supplement his rations. One driver, Teasdill recalls, even stopped to pick up some eggs that had been laid on the side of the track.

Boyd's report mentioning the wagon of Permanent Way materials highlights the fact that maintenance work did continue during the conflict. However, obtaining materials could be a problem as witnessed by an exchange of letters that took place between Sir Haydn (he received his knighthood in 1937) and the Railway Executive in March 1941 over the supply of sleepers.

During the exchange Sir Haydn states that the railway had not had a supply of secondhand sleepers from the GWR since the outbreak of war, and that the situation with the track was now so bad the railway might be forced to close. This was, he pointed out, at a time when slate was in high demand due to enemy action.

In the end a supply of a hundred ex-GWR sleepers seems to have been secured to deal with the immediate needs. These would doubtless have been sawn in two to produce two hundred sleepers for the line. This was for the spot replacement of rotten sleepers along the line.

A Locomotive Crisis

In 1945 the war in Europe was drawing towards its close, but on the Talyllyn a crisis was about to occur. *Dolgoch* was becoming increasingly unreliable. Trains were cancelled between Wednesday 24 January and Friday 2 February, and then between 9 and 14 March. On 16 March 1945 the last passenger train was to run until Good Friday 19 April 1946. The winter passenger service would not operate again until after the Preservation Society took over.

The near year-long shutdown between 1945 and 1946 was because during 1944 an assessment was carried out on *Talyllyn*'s condition by the Atlas Foundry in Shrewsbury. It did not make good reading and indicated that the locomotive was in need of extensive repairs. Therefore, it was decided to send *Dolgoch* off for overhaul to the Foundry and to suspend the passenger service in the interim. *Talyllyn* was steamed for a limited goods service, but by now the quarry was running down.

By this time too Sir Haydn must have decided that he would be retiring as an M.P. at the General Election that was held in the July. Therefore, it does say something for his commitment to the community that, although he was unable to save the quarry, he did keep the railway running. The repairs to *Dolgoch* did not come cheap, the returns of 1945 indicating that they must have cost around £655 including transport. Overall the railway made a loss of over £1,000 for the year.

Dolgoch returned to service in September 1945, but the passenger service remained suspended until the following Easter, only goods trains being run. However, it is reported that soon after *Dolgoch*'s return it derailed badly and *Talyllyn* had to be steamed to affect a rescue. This was the last known time that *Talyllyn* was steamed before its overhaul in the late 1950s.

History

Above: *Dolgoch* at Wharf c.1938. (Photo: Cozens Collection/TR Collection)

During 1946 the three-day summer passenger service resumed from 12 August, but without the brake van. This had previously been intermittently out of use due to the state of its tyres, which were now ruled unsafe. The van was to remain out of use until 1949. During this period trains operated with little braking power as the brakes on *Dolgoch* were almost ineffective.

Given the state of *Talyllyn* it is not surprising that Sir Haydn again looked for alternatives. In September 1946 an enquiry via Atlas Foundry was again made with the Hunslet Engine Co. about a refurbished steam locomotive. They responded by recommending a new diesel locomotive. At the same time an enquiry was made with Andrew Barclay about the regauging of Barclay works No.1454, a sister *Light* class locomotive to what would later be No.6 *Douglas*. The response can be seen overleaf along with a quotation for a *Caledonia* class locomotive, slightly more powerful than the *Light* class.

The quarry closed on Boxing Day 1946 following a heavy rock fall. However, the mineral extension remained in use to clear stocks of slate from Bryneglwys. It would not be for several months that the last slate train would run.

Nationalisation

On the wider front Nationalisation of the railway network was now being considered, and the question has been asked why the Talyllyn did not become part of British Railways. To this a number of answers have been given including that the Ministry of Transport had 'forgotten' about it, or they thought it to be closed.

One myth that has persisted is that Sir Haydn did not make any Annual Returns to the Ministry. This is patently untrue as a nearly full set exists at the National Archive. These include returns for the war years, although some of the revenue account information is missing for the years between 1940 and 1943. In addition, as has been seen, Sir Haydn was in correspondence with the Railway Executive over the supply of sleepers in 1941.

The reason why the Talyllyn was not in the Nationalisation Bill lies with the process by which the list of those railways to be included was drawn up. This was initially based on the lines that had come under Government control during the world wars with extra 'strategic' lines added. As the Talyllyn did not come into either category it was omitted.

A number of smaller independent lines wanted to be included in the Nationalisation Bill. They saw it as a means of survival, and so a meeting between representatives of the Ministry and the Association of Light Railways was held. At this it was stated that 'a line had to be drawn somewhere'. In other words the Ministry did not want to take on what it perceived as 'lame ducks', but there was a mechanism for railways to appeal to be purchased by the British Transport Commission to become part of the Nationalised network.

History

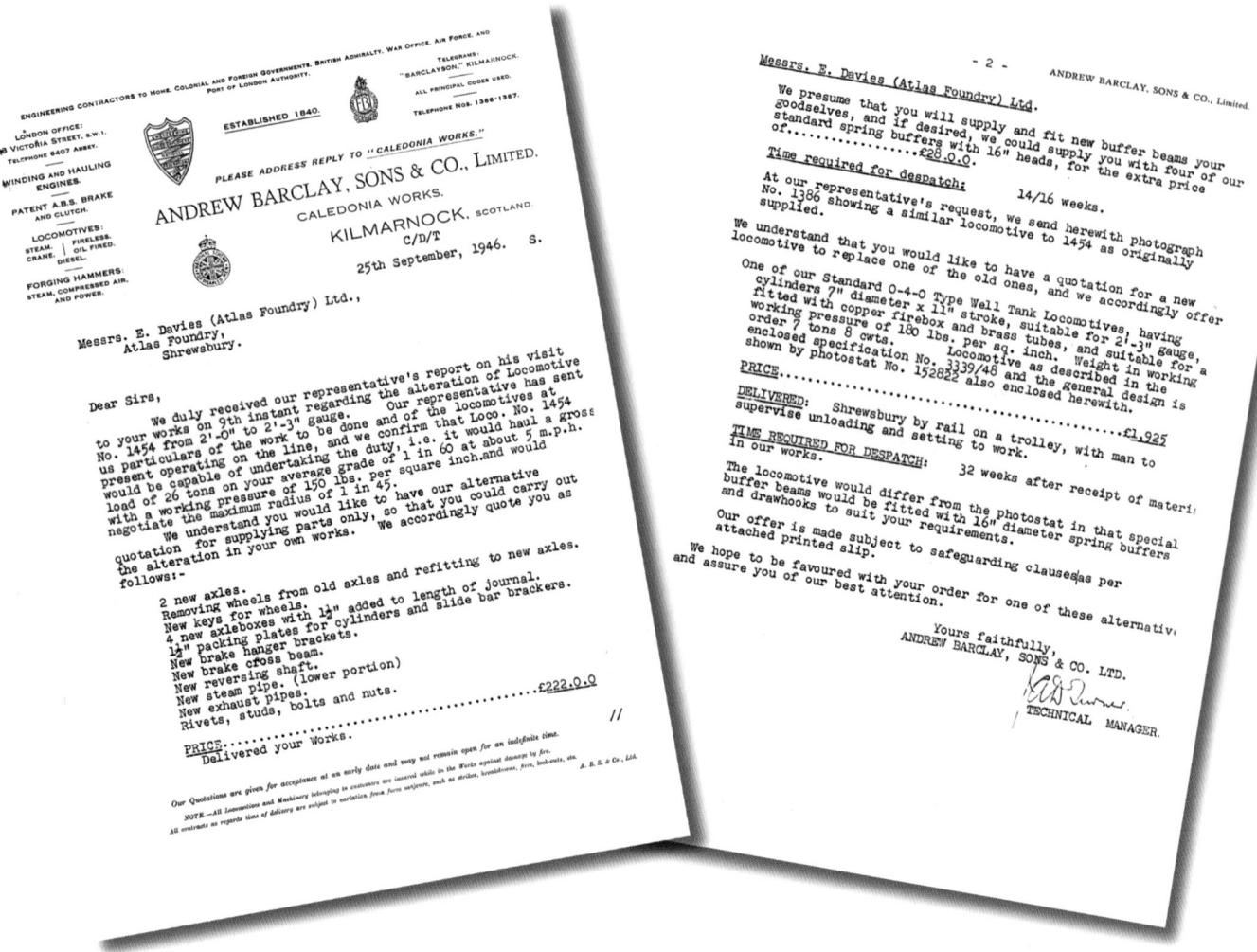

Letter 1:

ANDREW BARCLAY, SONS & CO., LIMITED.
CALEDONIA WORKS.
KILMARNOCK, SCOTLAND.
C/D/T

25th September, 1946. S.

Messrs. E. Davies (Atlas Foundry) Ltd.,
Atlas Foundry,
Shrewsbury.

Dear Sirs,

We duly received our representative's report on his visit to your works on 9th instant regarding the alteration of Locomotive No. 1454 from 2'-0" to 2'-3" gauge. Our representative has sent us particulars of the work to be done and of the locomotives at present operating on the line, and we confirm that Loco. No. 1454 would be capable of undertaking the duty, i.e. it would haul a gross load of 26 tons on your average grade of 1 in 60 at about 5 m.p.h. with a working pressure of 150 lbs. per square inch, and would negotiate the maximum radius of 1 in 45.

We understand you would like to have our alternative quotation for supplying parts only, so that you could carry out the alteration in your own works. We accordingly quote you as follows:-

2 new axles.
Removing wheels from old axles and refitting to new axles.
New keys for wheels.
4 new axleboxes with 1¼" added to length of journal.
1¼" packing plates for cylinders and slide bar brackers.
New brake hanger brackets.
New brake cross beam.
New brake shaft.
New reversing shaft.
New steam pipe. (lower portion)
New exhaust pipes.
Rivets, studs, bolts and nuts.

PRICE...£222.0.0
Delivered your Works.

Letter 2:

- 2 - ANDREW BARCLAY, SONS & CO., Limited.

Messrs. E. Davies (Atlas Foundry) Ltd.

We presume that you will supply and fit new buffer beams your goodselves, and if desired, we could supply you with four of our standard spring buffers with 16" heads, for the extra price of.................£28.0.0.

Time required for despatch: 14/16 weeks.

At our representative's request, we send herewith photograph No. 1386 showing a similar locomotive to 1454 as originally supplied.

We understand that you would like to have a quotation for a new locomotive to replace one of the old ones, and we accordingly offer One of our Standard 0-4-0 Type Well Tank Locomotives, having cylinders 7" diameter x 11" stroke, suitable for 2'-3" gauge, fitted with copper firebox and brass tubes, and suitable for a working pressure of 180 lbs. per sq. inch. Weight in working order 7 tons 8 cwts. Locomotive as described in the enclosed specification No. 3339/48 and the general design is shown by photostat No. 152822 also enclosed herewith.

PRICE...£1,925

DELIVERED: Shrewsbury by rail on a trolley, with man to supervise unloading and setting to work.

TIME REQUIRED FOR DESPATCH: 32 weeks after receipt of material in our works.

The locomotive would differ from the photostat in that special buffer beams would be fitted with 16" diameter spring buffers and drawhooks to suit your requirements.

Our offer is made subject to safeguarding clauses as per attached printed slip.

We hope to be favoured with your order for one of these alternatives and assure you of our best attention.

Yours faithfully,
ANDREW BARCLAY, SONS & CO. LTD.

TECHNICAL MANAGER.

Letter in response to an enquiry to Andrew Barclay from Atlas Foundry about re-gauging works No.1454 for use on the 2 ft 3 in gauge.

TYPE No. 152822
CALEDONIA TYPE LOCOMOTIVE, IN ALL USUAL SIZES.

ANDREW BARCLAY, SONS & CO., Limited,
CALEDONIA WORKS, KILMARNOCK, SCOTLAND.

Rails Along The Fathew

History

Above: *Dolgoch* waits at Tywyn Wharf with its train in June 1950. (Photo: The Elliot/Dan Quine Collection)

Some railways, such as the Derwent Valley Light Railway, did this. There is some evidence that the Talyllyn also made such an appeal, because the British Transport Commission carried out an assessment of the Talyllyn in 1948. It concluded that it was doubtful the railway could be made a paying proposition and that its acquisition was not recommended. Therefore the railway remained an independent operation, and, as we shall see, this actually allowed the Talyllyn to become the World's First Preserved Railway.

The Final Haydn Jones Years

In 1948 while most other railways were adapting to being part of the new nationalised railway, the Talyllyn was continuing to try to survive. For the start of the new season fares were raised by at least 50%, with a Tywyn to Abergynolwyn return increasing from 1s 8d to 2s 6d. This certainly generated more income with passenger revenue increasing by around a third over the year. At the same time discussions were being started on the long-term future of the railway as will be seen later.

The following year the brake van returned to service, its wheels having been re-tyred. The closure of the Corris Railway the previous year also gave the opportunity for the purchase the remaining locomotives and rolling stock. An inspection was made, but it was decided not to proceed. Eventually, however, they were all destined to end up on the Talyllyn. Sir Haydn did though buy some eight tons of Corris rail intending to use it as an extension of the Glyn Valley material, but it was not laid until the Preservation Society took over.

Towards the end of the season there was another break in the service when on Friday 26 August 1949 *Dolgoch* cracked its frame while hauling a train near the viaduct. Staff from Atlas Foundry were called in to weld the frames, and trains resumed on Monday 19 September. However, the break in the service led to an article appearing in the *Birmingham Post* for 5 September. It was entitled *Breakdown on the Talyllyn Railway*, and if any single event led to the preservation of the railway this was probably it.

Sir Haydn had promised to keep the railway running throughout his lifetime, which was a commitment he kept until his death on 2 July 1950. Apparently he even sounded out members of his family to see if anyone would take on the railway on after his death, and had been looking at options for a replacement boiler for *Talyllyn*.

Described as being well-respected rather than well-liked, Sir Haydn had done everything that could have been asked of him in terms of both the quarry and the railway. It needs to be remembered that he also took over the Aberllefenni quarry, and in so doing provided sufficient traffic to keep the Corris Railway running for many years longer than might otherwise have been the case.

Maybe coming over as high-handed at times, but none the less seemingly a man of his word, he was responsible for the 'preservation' of the Talyllyn Railway long before any official organisation was established. Without him the railway would not have survived, and without him a world-wide railway preservation movement might never have been born. Perhaps this is his greatest legacy.

Rails Along The Fathew

History

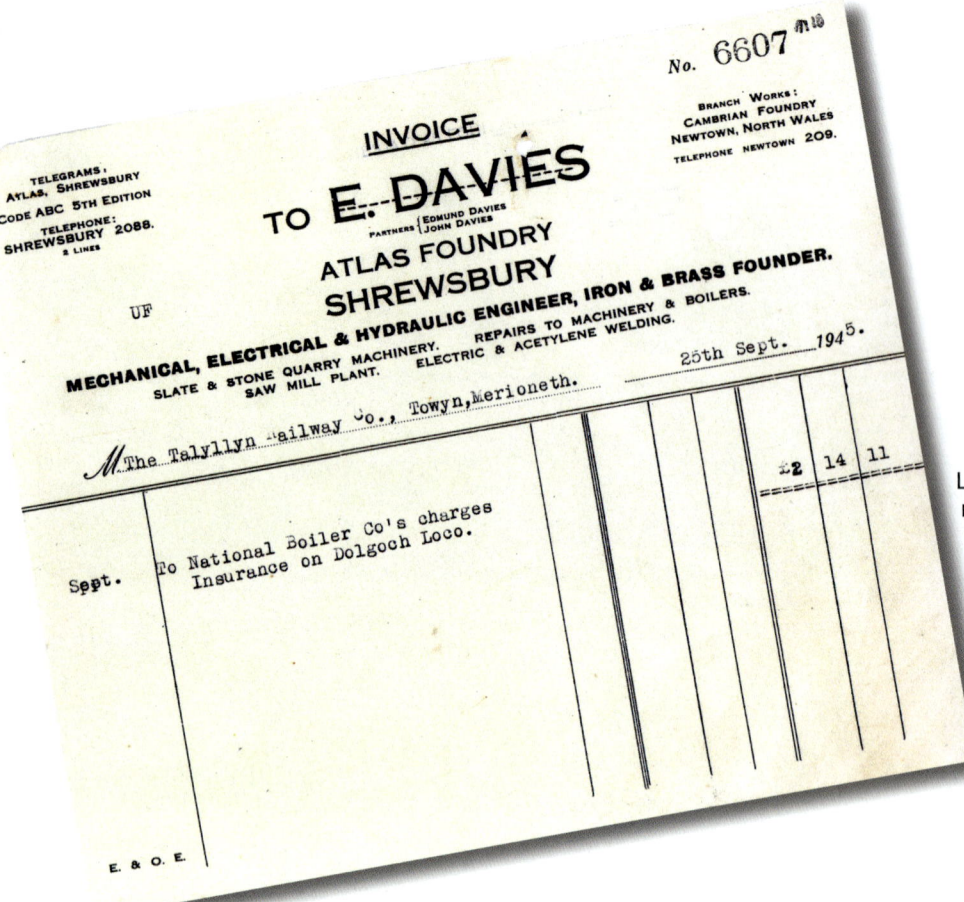

Left: One of the myths that has done the rounds about the Haydn Jones years was that the locomotives were not insured. However, as can be seen from the receipt to the left, they were. In addition, many of the fragments of the company's accounts that exist include a sum for insurance, although exactly what this covered is unknown.

Above: A pre-preservation colour view of *Dolgoch* at Pendre on 30 June 1950. Note that by this time the locomotive boiler had been painted black.
(Photo: S. Bragg / TR Collection)

Rails Along The Fathew

History

History Part Three
The Preservation Era

Above: Locomotive No.2 *Dolgoch* stands at Wharf station in 1951. For the first season of operation by the Preservation Society *Dolgoch* remained in its post-Atlas Foundry overhaul livery, except for the addition of nameplates from about July 1951. It was repainted the following winter into 'standard' Talyllyn Green. (Photo: The Elliot Collection)

The Origins of the Preservation Society

The story of the preservation of the Talyllyn has its origins during the Second World War. In January 1941 a letter was written to *The Modern Tramway* by an Arthur Rimmer, who was concerned that the rails of the Welsh Highland Railway were about to be lifted. He felt that re-opening the line would aid the war effort and that possibly rail-minded clubs and societies might combine to undertake the task.

Later on during the war the author Tom Rolt was staying at Talyllyn and decided to visit the railway. This he described in his book *Railway Adventure* when he famously encountered the sign, 'NO TRAIN TODAY'. Nevertheless he walked up the line and on to his lodgings at the lake, just a short walk of ten miles.

It was the publication of the White Paper for the nationalisation of the railways that sparked Tom Rolt's interest again. He noted the absence of the Talyllyn's name from the list of those railways which were to be nationalised, the reasons for which we have already touched on. He became concerned about the fate of the line, and discussed it with two ex-railwaymen friends, Bill Trinder and Jim Russell.

Trinder and Rolt made their first trip together to Tywyn to see the railway at Easter 1948. Although the railway was not operating on the day they visited they explored the line and met Edward Thomas. On another visit Bill Trinder met Sir Haydn, the two got on and there was a subsequent meeting involving Rolt as well.

Over the course of the next few months Rolt developed a scheme which he believed would give the line a future. This was to follow the example of the Ravenglass and Eskdale Railway and convert the line to a miniature railway on a 15 in gauge track. The original locomotives would either be placed in a museum, or the track between Wharf and Pendre would be retained for the original stock to run over. He viewed this as the only option if the railway was to have a commercial future.

Rails Along The Fathew

History

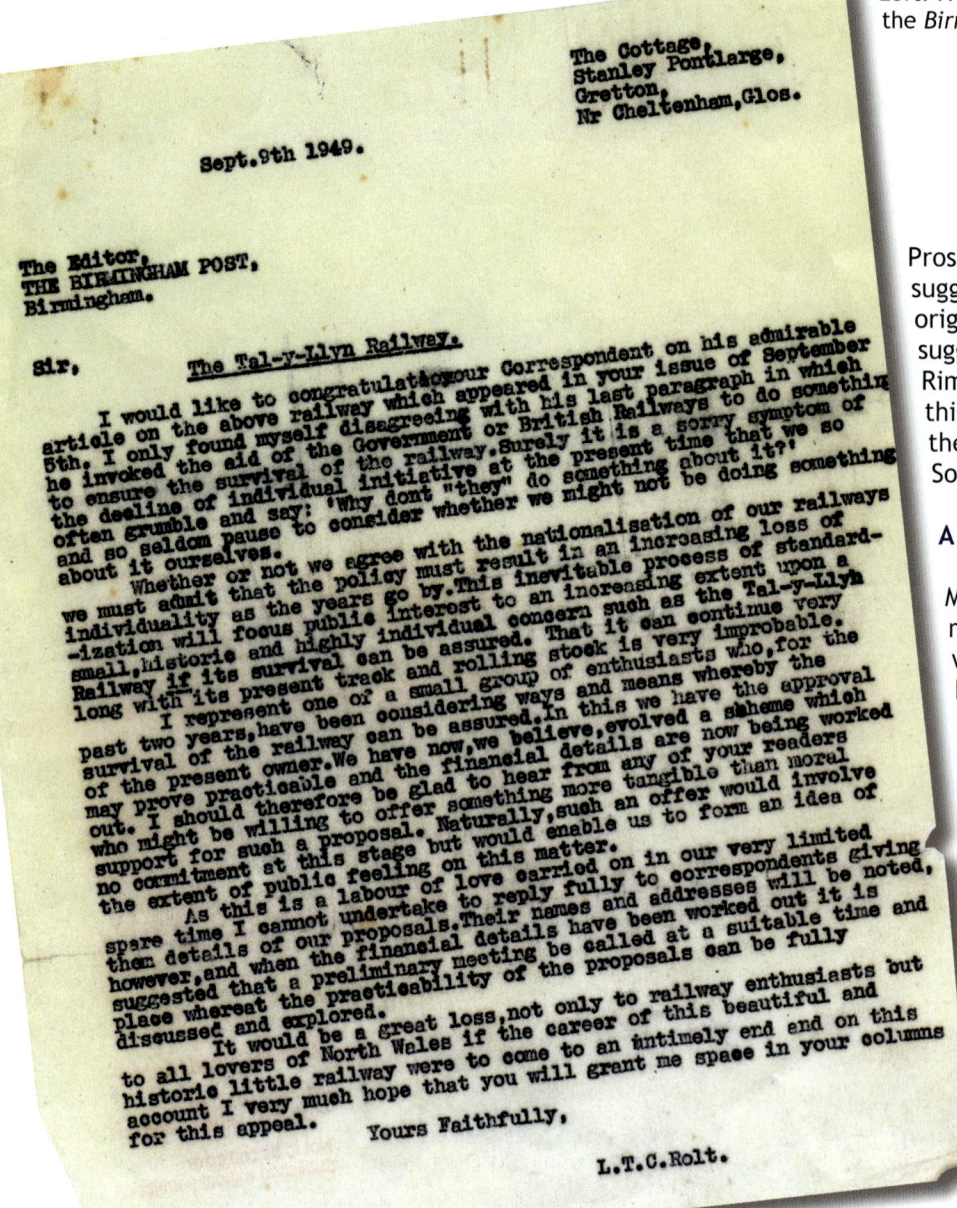

Left: A copy of Tom Rolt's original letter to the *Birmingham Post*.

Prosser was not happy with the suggestion of ripping up much of the original line, instead he made a suggestion inspired by Arthur Rimmer's idea from 1941. It was in this correspondence that the name the 'Talyllyn Railway Preservation Society' was first mentioned.

A Society is Formed

Meanwhile Trinder had been very much acting as the go-between with Sir Haydn, who was obviously keen to see the railway continue. However, he was more than aware of the poor state of the line.

On 9 July 1950 Sir Haydn died, and it was clear that if things were not done quickly then the likelihood was that the railway would die with him. Hurried meetings were arranged with Trinder, Rolt, Prosser and Edward Thomas all involved. Letters were exchanged between Rolt and Sir Haydn's solicitor which resulted in the reassurance that it was Lady Haydn's wish to see the railway continue 'if at all possible'.

The upshot of this was that a meeting was arranged at the Imperial Hotel, Birmingham for Wednesday 11 October 1950 at 7.15 pm. Attendance was not large, numbering fewer than forty. Bill Trinder took the chair, sharing the platform with Tom Rolt, Jim Russell and Edward Thomas.

Bill Trinder gave a brief summary of the events so far. He also emphasised the wishes of Sir Haydn and his widow that the railway should continue to run. Tom Rolt then stated that the purpose of the meeting was to establish a committee to look into the viability of saving the line. Finally Edward Thomas outlined the current state of affairs with the railway.

After a number of questions had been asked a committee of fifteen was elected. These included not only Trinder, Rolt, Russell and Prosser, but also Patrick Whitehouse, who was elected Secretary and Patrick Garland, who, despite thinking he had not heard such a 'crack-pot scheme' in his life, agreed to be Treasurer. Among the

Wider Publicity

At the same time the railway was getting attention through other channels. The autumn of 1949 brought two major articles about the railway, the first appeared in the *Picture Post*, while the second was the *Birmingham Post* article previously mentioned. This consisted of a description of the line coupled with the news of the breakdown to *Dolgoch*, and also voiced the fears of what would happen when Sir Haydn died. 'Could not the government or British Railways do something?' it asked.

This brought a response in a letter from Tom Rolt published on 14 September to the effect that rather than expecting someone else to do something he and others had acted. This was the point when Rolt and another Talyllyn pioneer, Owen Prosser, entered correspondence.

Rails Along The Fathew

History

Above: Ex-Corris locomotive No.4 in the workshop at Pendre in September 1951. Its saddle tank has been removed, which can be seen on the left. No.4 was later transported to Hunslet's works in Leeds for overhaul, returning in May 1952.

(Photo: TR Collection)

others elected were names that were to become synonymous with the railway in the years ahead. The committee's first meeting set the annual subscription at £1 for which members would be entitled to free travel on the railway. The Talyllyn Railway Preservation Society was born.

Preparing for re-opening

An inspection train was organised in Tywyn for some of the committee members to view the railway. This was the last train operated by the 'old' company, but things did not go according to plan. *Dolgoch* and the train made it to Abergynolwyn, but on the return trip the locomotive was derailed east of Brynglas, one of the most inaccessible spots on the railway. The passengers were forced to walk back leaving the stricken locomotive behind.

Events continued to move forward. An agreement was reached in February 1951 with the executors of Sir Haydn's estate for the Society to take over the running of the railway for a trial period of three years. It was also agreed that all the shares in the TRCo. would be transferred to a new company, Talyllyn Holdings Ltd. In the meantime five directors of the TRCo. were appointed, three by the Society, and two by the Haydn Jones family, with Patrick Whitehouse as Secretary.

The Directors asked Tom Rolt to become the General Manager in succession to Edward Thomas, as he was 'self employed', but also had an engineering background.

Meanwhile there was a lot of work to be done, not least solving the problem of additional motive power, as well as dealing with the condition of the Permanent Way.

As already stated Sir Haydn had enquired about the former Corris locomotives, now stored at Machynlleth, after the closure of the Corris Railway in 1948. In March 1951 Rolt, Russell and David Curwen, whom Rolt had met when researching his plan for the miniature railway, and who had now been appointed the Chief Mechanical Engineer for the railway, went to inspect them. This showed that the former Corris No.3 was in better condition than previously believed, but the condition of No.4 was much worse. Nevertheless they offered the best opportunity for the railway to acquire new motive power.

Therefore, a visit was made to the appropriate authorities at Swindon by Trinder, Rolt and Russell. The result of this was that the locomotives were offered for less than their scrap value of £25 each, an offer the Society gladly accepted. They also purchased a number of Corris wagons, while the former Corris brake van which had been acquired privately was also donated to the Society, becoming Van No.6.

Back at Tywyn other work was proceeding. *Dolgoch* had gone into the works to have as many of its ailments dealt with as possible. This included a full-boiler inspection. It was believed at the time that *Dolgoch* still had its original boiler, which would have been eighty five years old. There was therefore much relief when it passed. The locomotive was put back together and first steamed in

History

mid-April 1951. It was used to bring the two Corris locomotives up from Wharf station to Pendre plus twelve wagon-loads of coal. No.3 had been named *Sir Haydn* by the committee, while No.4 had been named *Edward Thomas*.

In the evening *Dolgoch* was taken up the line towing the ex-Corris brake van that had been delivered. All went well until Dolgoch was reached where it was discovered that the water tank there was empty, and the locomotive had to dash back to Tywyn finally coming to rest in the middle of the road crossing at Pendre. It was manually manoeuvred into the platform and abandoned for the night.

At the same time work on the Permanent Way continued. Some rail from the Corris Railway along with a quantity of sleepers had been purchased. This was used to relay one of the worst stretches of line between Fach Goch and Cynfal halts. As *Dolgoch* was being tended to in the works, it was necessary to push the materials from Wharf to the site by hand. Even with the use of wagons this would have been heavy work. Rail was also lifted from the Abergynolwyn village incline for use on the main line.

By this time the resources of the Society were growing. At the end of April 1951 some £1,440 had been donated. In addition a pool of volunteers had come forward ready to help with the many practical tasks that needed to be undertaken.

The New Era

It had been decided that the line would formally reopen on Whit Monday 14 May 1951, but that passenger trains would only run as far as Rhydyronen. *Dolgoch* did take a train up to Abergynolwyn on the Saturday filled with volunteers and supplies to be dropped off at the stations en-route.

By the Monday everything was ready, the novelty of a railway being run by volunteers had attracted considerable interest, and so there was a gathering of people, many with cameras ready to record the occasion.

A tape was strung across the track in front of *Dolgoch*, which Bill Trinder cut after giving a short speech. The first train departed for Rhydyronen with David Curwen at the regulator and John Snell firing. John was then between school and university and would spend his summer on the railway.

At Rhydyronen the absence of a loop meant the train had to be hand shunted in order to get it ready for the return trip. In total, five return workings were run that day, carrying over 300 passengers. The World's First Preserved Railway was in business, nearly eighty-six years to the day since *Talyllyn* had first been at work on the line.

Tom Rolt recorded many of the events of the first two years of the preserved railway in his book *Railway Adventure*, which has served to inspire many to visit and work on the line ever since. Unfortunately some gained the impression that Rolt alone was responsible for saving the Talyllyn. This was far from true, as Rolt himself makes clear in the book, many people were involved, not least Bill Trinder. Patrick Garland many years later stated that Rolt and Trinder were the joint founders of the Preservation Society. To them and those other pioneers, many of whom have gone unnamed, we owe an enormous debt of gratitude.

A Learning Curve

The first year of the railway's operation under the auspices of the Society proved to be a steep learning curve. One of the urgent priorities was to get locomotive No.3 into service to aid *Dolgoch*. This was achieved on 20 July 1951 when No.3 made its first journey on the railway under its own steam. However, problems rapidly became apparent.

The long rigid wheelbase of No.1 *Talyllyn* had led to the practice of the track being laid slightly wide to gauge. Neither No.1 nor No.2 *Dolgoch* had problems with this, but No.3 had much narrower tyre treads. This resulted in a series of derailments. No.3 was not able to be used in regular service until the track was improved. As a result the railway effectively had only one operational locomotive, *Dolgoch*, nicknamed *The Old Lady*, for its first season.

Nevertheless despite various alarms and excursions the railway survived and during the year 15,628 passenger journeys were made, the highest number since 1927. The winter saw a number of improvements being carried out. These included a loop at Tywyn Wharf, to eliminate the use of gravity shunting to run round trains, as well as a platform and buffer stop. This was to prevent runaways over the wharf edge such as had happened in 1886.

Left: As part of the preparations for the re-opening in May 1951 the stations were 'spruced up' with new nameboards.
(Photo: O. Prosser/TR Collection)

Rails Along The Fathew

History

Most importantly, locomotive No.4 *Edward Thomas* had been overhauled at Hunslet's works in Leeds, and was ready to assist No.2 *Dolgoch*. The first official train of the new season was on Whit Monday 2 June 1952 and the train was to be double-headed with Nos. 2 and 4. To add to the occasion the BBC was there to record the event, such was the publicity the railway was attracting.

The line was now being featured in all sorts of articles in the railway, local and national press. This was excellent for publicising the railway and bringing in extra passengers, but also meant that the Talyllyn was no longer a forgotten backwater far from the corridors of power in Whitehall.

In 1952 the Ministry of Transport invited representatives from the Talyllyn to a meeting in London. This took place on 18 April 1952 at which various issues were discussed about the safe running of the line. As a result it was 'suggested' that Colonel McMullen of the Ministry should be invited to perform an informal inspection. This was arranged for 12 June 1952. Tom Rolt recorded that he anticipated it with considerable trepidation.

In the event the Colonel proved very sympathetic to the railway's cause. He also evidently had a considerable liking to the lodgings that Patrick Whitehouse had arranged at the Tyn-y-Cornel Hotel by Talyllyn Lake.

The result of his inspection was not as onerous as was feared. His main concerns were the track and the state of some of the bridges. Plans were immediately put in place to rectify the worst of the issues highlighted. However, the state of the bridge at Tywyn Wharf, and also of 'School Bridge' between Wharf and Pendre, led to a lengthy correspondence between Patrick Whitehouse and the County Council as to whose responsibility they were.

Left: Bill Trinder cuts the tape to signify the beginning of the preservation era at Tywyn Wharf station on 14 May 1951. (Photo: TR Collection)

Right: At Rhydyronen because there was no run-round loop it was necessary to hand-shunt the coaches to move the locomotive to the other end of the train. (Photo: R.D. Butterell)

Left: One of the opening day trains returns to Tywyn and is about to pass under Tŷ Mawr bridge. (Photo: R.D. Butterell)

Rails Along The Fathew

History

Increasing Maturity

With locomotive No.4 available, and the experience gained from the first season; 1952 was a much less eventful affair. This was probably just as well as David Curwen was unable to fulfil the role of engineer, and so Rolt had to fill in. Many of the office responsibilities were taken over by Sonia Rolt. She, with Barbara Curwen, had also become the first recorded female guards in the railway's history. Extra trains were run and passenger journeys increased to 22,866.

The winter of 1952/3 saw more changes at the railway. First was the appointment of a new General Manager in succession to Tom Rolt. The new man was Ken Marrian who came with a railway background. In the autumn of 1952 the railway had also acquired its first internal combustion engined locomotive. No.5 was a motor tractor constructed by David Curwen. Unfortunately it was not a success, only lasting in service a matter of months.

In spring 1953 it was announced that another steam locomotive had been donated to the railway. This was an Andrew Barclay 0-4-0 well tank built in 1918, which had seen service with the RAF. It had been donated by the Birmingham firm of Abelson and Co., and was given the number 6 on the Talyllyn roster, being named *Douglas* after Abelson's Managing Director, Douglas Abelson. The locomotive was 2 ft gauge, and so had to be re-gauged before it could run on the Talyllyn.

One of the highlights of 1953 was the running of two decorated specials on 2 June in honour of Queen Elizabeth the Second's Coronation. Locomotive No.4 and all the original carriages were decorated for the trains and children were conveyed free of charge. The event attracted the attention of the BBC who sent a cameraman along for the occasion. Sixty years later the BBC came back in order to film a re-enactment of the trains in honour of the Diamond Jubilee of the Coronation.

By this time the track had been improved sufficiently to allow locomotive No.3 to operate safely. In addition, the railway had acquired the first new passenger coaches since 1867 with the first being, somewhat perversely, carriage No.8, which had been converted from an ex-Penrhyn coach. This was followed by carriage No.7 also converted from a former Penrhyn coach, which had had a roof added.

Increased Capacity

In June 1953 the Territorial Army came to re-lay a substantial section of the line east of Brynglas as a training exercise. In order to give total track occupation to the troops the passenger service was terminated at Brynglas, where the siding was converted into a loop, and new train staffs, to ensure only one train could run on a section of line at a time, were introduced. But all this was done without Ministry approval, a fact Colonel McMullen reprimanded the directors for shortly afterwards. By working 24 hours a day the Territorials re-sleepered 600 yards of track east from Brynglas and 1,300 yards west of Quarry Siding. Unfortunately the quality of some of the work left something to be desired. The new loop did allow two-train-set working to be introduced for the summer peak service, which increased capacity.

The Talyllyn was also to be celebrated on celluloid. That year saw the release of *The Titfield Thunderbolt*, inspired by a visit by the screenplay writer T.E.B. Clarke to the railway in 1951. Although the railway itself was not featured many elements of the Talyllyn story were included in the script. Even one of the Society's Vice-Presidents, the actor Hugh Griffith, was

Left: The first known publicity poster for the preserved railway, issued in 1951.

History

featured playing Dan. That June a Canadian, Carson Davidson, was also filming on the railway, although it wasn't to be for another decade that his work, *Railway With A Heart of Gold*, was completed. Nevertheless it encapsulated the early years of the railway.

With increasing passenger numbers there was an urgent need for new carriages to be introduced, and the railway's first bogie coaches, Nos. 9 and 10, made their debut during 1954. At the end of May that year a more mundane, but nonetheless important, piece of progress was made with the completion of the first telephone line between Tywyn Wharf and Abergynolwyn stations. The Talyllyn had entered the 20th century! Another Territorial Army camp saw more track improvements west of Abergynolwyn.

On 19 July 1954 locomotive No.6 arrived having been regauged, overhauled and repainted at Hunt Bros. The same transport was used to take No.2 *Dolgoch* away for a much needed overhaul. That summer the Talyllyn also acquired another internal combustion locomotive, No.7. This was a 'Mercury Tractor', which was converted to run on rails and proved moderately successful in service.

During 1955 further progress was made. A large quantity of secondhand rail from a quarry near Nuneaton arrived. This enabled the first full relaying, rather than re-sleepering, of substantial lengths of the line since 1952 to get under way. The railway also acquired a motor trolley to aid the work of the Permanent Way gangs.

One feat, typical of the Talyllyn of the period, was the construction of a 'new' carriage in two days. Assembly of carriage No.11, using another Penrhyn body, started on Sunday morning 31 July 1955, and it made its first journey to Abergynolwyn on the Bank Holiday evening 1 August.

The following year the emphasis was once more on the Permanent Way, although another open carriage, No.12 also entered service. By the end of that year passenger numbers had reached 36,928. They were to rise again by over 50% during 1957. This was because the railway featured in two live outside broadcasts by the BBC on 22 and 23 May that year. The first was part of the programme *Now*, while the next day the railway was also featured in its children's programming. Broadcasting took place between Dolgoch and Abergynolwyn using a complicated series of relays to get the signal down the valley.

Presenting the *Now* programme were Huw Wheldon and Wynford Vaughan-Thomas, the latter becoming a member of the Preservation Society as a result. During the course of the broadcast they interviewed a number of volunteers and members of staff, including the Society's President Lord Northesk. The dangers of live television were though evident when the set was 'invaded' by a flock of sheep. Nevertheless the publicity generated brought many new people to the railway.

There were other developments during the year. Open carriage No.13 entered service and two former Glyn Valley Tramway (GVT) coach bodies were recovered from separate sites. In order to house the additional stock construction of a new carriage shed began at Pendre on the site of the old barn. The re-sleepering of the entire Permanent Way was also completed during the year.

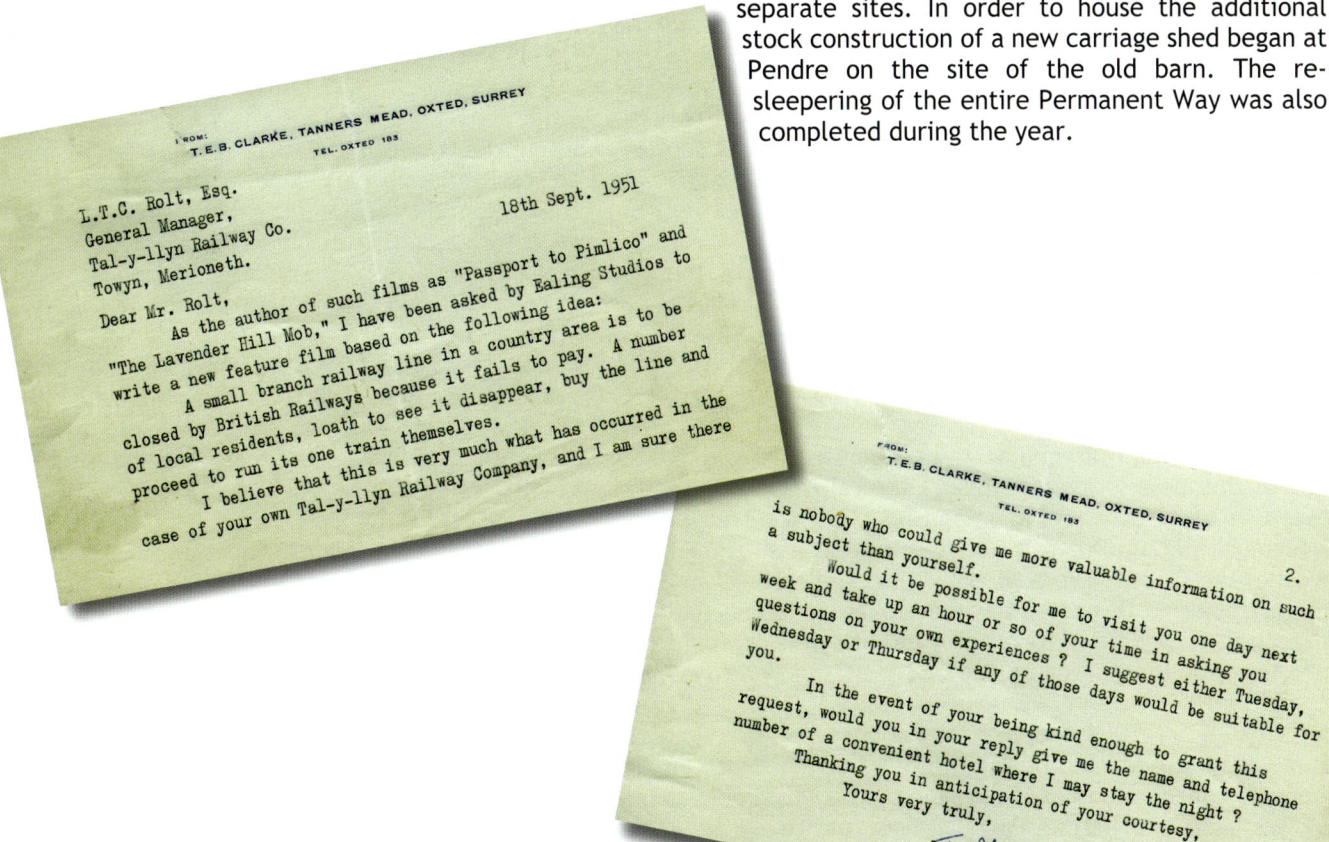

Above: The Letter to Tom Rolt from the screenwriter T.E.B. Clarke, which eventually led to the film *The Titfield Thunderbolt*.

Rails Along The Fathew

History

Coronation Day 2 June 1953.
Above: One of the original leaflets.
Left: The morning train departs (top) and arrives back (bottom). (Both Photos: J.J. Davis/TR Collection)

On the locomotive front another internal combustion locomotive arrived on the railway, this time of more conventional design, a Ruston-Hornsby four-wheel shunter. It was given the number 5 in the locomotive fleet and named *Midlander*, after the Midland Area Group which had arranged its purchase and conversion to 2 ft 3 in gauge.

The same group then undertook to perform the restoration of the rusting hulk of *Talyllyn*. On 24 March 1957 *Talyllyn* was moved to the works of Gibbons Brothers Ltd. at Lenches Bridge, Pensnett. It would return in working order the following year.

Unfortunately all this good news was counterbalanced by one of the most serious challenges the railway has ever faced in its history, a major landslip. This occurred in November 1957 in Dolgoch woods just under half a mile west of the station. The cause was a blocked culvert, and major repair work had to be undertaken including pile driving the foundations for a new retaining wall. It would not be until the winter of 1959/60 that the work was completed.

Sadly 1958 also started badly with news of the death of General Manager Ken Marrian in January. He was replaced by his assistant Harold Parker. More positively No.1 *Talyllyn* returned from the West Midlands on 14 June, and was soon back in service. Another piece of publicity was gained for the railway with the fitting of an experimental *Giesl* ejector to locomotive No.4 in the September. This was claimed to produce better coal consumption, and resulted in the 'fish-tail' chimney No.4 sported for a number of years.

In addition, the two former GVT carriages (Nos.14 and 15) entered service during 1958. A new source of rail had also been found from the former 3 ft gauge system at a quarry at Crich, which would later be the home of the National Tramway Museum.

Meanwhile a Corris Railway carriage body was found at Gobowen and purchased for £100. It was in near-derelict condition and was delivered to Tywyn on 2 May 1959. In 1960 the new 'North' Carriage Shed came into use, while the old 'South' Shed was subsequently dismantled to be re-built with a steel frame.

The end of 1960 was a time of reflection for many in the Society. Over the course of the ten years since the Society's foundation the railway had been transformed. Much of the track had been completely relaid, and instead of one barely serviceable locomotive the railway now had five, although only one was then in service.

This was, however, No.1 *Talyllyn* which would have seemed a pipe-dream back in 1950. In addition there were more carriages in service, a new carriage shed had been built and many other improvements made. Passenger numbers had also quadrupled over the ten years. It truly was a decade of remarkable achievement for the Society.

History

Above: Locomotive No.6 *Douglas* poses at Quarry Siding with a short train on 24 September 1955. (Photo: J.H.L. Adams)

The Early 1960s

As indicated above, in January 1961 only locomotive No.1 was operational. This was due to Nos 2 *Dolgoch* and No.3 *Sir Haydn* still undergoing major overhauls. In addition, No.4 *Edward Thomas* needed work done, and No.6 *Douglas* had been damaged in a derailment the previous August. Subsequently No.6 was discovered to need a new firebox. Happily, No.4 was completed for the Easter service, and No.6 returned for the high peak season.

Another positive was that both carriages 16 and 17 entered service. No.16, referred to as *The Stanton*, the original carriage having been purchased from a quarry at Stanton-in-the-Peak, was still not completely finished. However, No.17, the ex-Corris coach, had been completely restored and finished in Corris livery. Despite having 'Third Class' emblazoned on it a one shilling supplement was charged for travelling in the coach, although this did not last long.

During 1962 work began on what was intended to become the first of the 'standard' bogie coaches (No.18) with the construction of a 30 ft underframe. This was the culmination of a long development process to determine the future needs of the carriage stock.

That year though saw the first substantial fall in passenger traffic (just under 10%) since the Society had taken over. This was attributed to the bad weather throughout the summer.

The winter of 1962/3 is notorious as being one of the coldest on record. At Quarry Siding an avalanche of snow blocked the line to a depth of 4 feet. Nevertheless some work was achieved. Work had commenced at the end of 1962 on a 45 ft extension to what was now entitled the 'North Carriage Shed', constructed in the late 1950s.

A major change in the way things were managed on the railway was the appointment of John Bate to the paid post of Chief Engineer. In the summer of 1963 No.2 *Dolgoch* returned to service after its overhaul. It had been substantially rebuilt with a new boiler and there was much rejoicing at the return of *The Old Lady*, as the locomotive had become known.

If the year began with a feeling of chill, it also ended on a downward note with the news of the death of Society President Lord Northesk in November 1963. He had been a very visible figurehead of the railway for many years, and through his many connections had undoubtedly assisted its development. The feeling of gloom was compounded by the news that traffic numbers had suffered another fall of nearly 10% by the end of the year.

With the Centenary of the railway coming up the following year a number of projects were underway in 1964. Chief among these was carriage No.18 which was being constructed. Over the summer the railway operated an experimental connecting bus service to Talyllyn Lake. Passenger figures were also significantly up with a record number travelling during the year.

Above: Locomotive No.1 *Talyllyn* with the morning up train at Abergynolwyn in 1963. (Photo: J.H.L. Adams)

The Centenary

Over the winter of 1964/5 a number of events occurred. First, most of the track was lifted at Wharf station to enable the layout to be completely altered. After this, on 21 February 1965, locomotive No.1 departed once more for the Midlands, only this time on an exhibition tour. This included a spell in Centenary Square in the centre of Birmingham. It returned in mid-May ready for the summer service.

During the course of the year a number of special events took place on the railway to celebrate the Centenary of the passing of the Talyllyn Railway Act. These included the unveiling of a commemorative plaque by John Betjeman on Tuesday 1 June. On the same day there was the first running of *The Centenarian*, which was also the inaugural run of carriage No.18 in service. As well as the various events, the railway featured in a BBC documentary and many other publicity and marketing opportunities were exploited during the year.

The late 1960s

At the end of 1965 General Manager Harold Parker retired; in his place David Woodhouse became Traffic Manager and Bill Faulkner became Managing Director. The increasing traffic also led to the introduction of a new two-train-set timetable in 1966, which was just as well because the railway had over 100,000 passenger journeys during the year.

This increased traffic level, and also the issues with locomotive availability, led to the consideration of a new locomotive. The result of these deliberations was a specification around an 0-6-2 tank locomotive. At the time one of the standard Hunslet or Andrew Barclay designs was under consideration as a 'new-build'. However, the prices quoted were beyond the railway's resources at the time.

There was a milestone on 27 January 1967 when the last piece of original Talyllyn rail in the main running line was replaced, near Brynglas. Another development was the arrival on 30 March 1967 of a new body for carriage No.10, which had been built commercially by Tisdales at Kenilworth. This, and other decisions, represented a new emphasis away from a 'hand-to-mouth' approach towards a more long-term view of expenditure.

The following year started badly with an outbreak of foot-and-mouth disease, which in a rural setting such as West Wales caused a number of issues for the railway. Happily, as the year went on further progress was made. Locomotive No.3 returned to service on 23 September 1968, nearly eleven years since it had previously been steamed.

Traffic also continued to increase, to over 122,000 passenger journeys by the year end. This led to the decision to move to a three-train-set peak timetable for 1969, which was going to involve a considerable amount of work for the Permanent Way gang.

History

The Centenary Celebrations 1965

Above Left: In preparation for the Centenary celebrations, over the winter of 1964/65 the station layout at Tywyn Wharf was substantially altered as seen here on 22 March 1965. (Photo: David J. Mitchell)

Above: John Betjeman (right) officially opens the refurbished station on 1 June 1965 with Tom Rolt on the left. (Photo: J.H.L. Adams)

Left: Another part of the Centenary celebrations was the gathering of classic cars at Tywyn at Whitsun 1965. (Photo: David J. Mitchell)

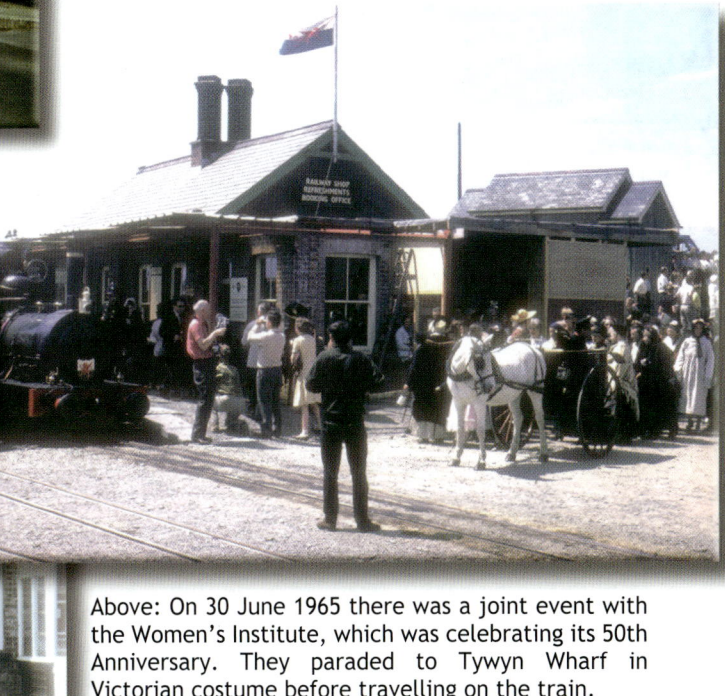

Above: On 30 June 1965 there was a joint event with the Women's Institute, which was celebrating its 50th Anniversary. They paraded to Tywyn Wharf in Victorian costume before travelling on the train.

Left: On 1 June 1965 the railway ran the inaugural *The Centenarian*, which continued to run daily as a named train throughout the season. It is seen here with No.1 *Talyllyn* in charge. Note the temporary canopy on the station building.

(Both Photos: J.H.L. Adams)

Rails Along The Fathew

History

Above: The damage caused to carriage No.1 when a run-away empty stock train hit the buffers at Tywyn Wharf on 6 July 1968. Fortunately no-one was seriously injured and the damage was repaired. With the fitting of continuous brakes in the 1990s such an accident should now be avoided. (Photo: David J. Mitchell)

There were other problems that year too. An accident at Tywyn Wharf on 6 July, due to a coupling failure on an empty stock train, resulted in damage to several carriages. Fortunately there were no injuries. Meanwhile it was realised that the spandrel walls on Dolgoch viaduct were going to need some major repair work, and as a temporary measure tie rods were fitted until the issues could be fully rectified.

Serious preparatory work also began for the extension to Nant Gwernol during the year and two controversial decisions were taken. The first was to demolish the old winding house on the village incline. This was on the basis of an initial visit of the Railway Inspector to assess what would need to be done. The old mineral line actually passed through the middle of the structure, which was in a very dangerous condition, and there was insufficient clearance for bogie carriages. Therefore, with no feasible alternative, it was decided to dismantle the structure. Whether this would have been permitted in today's heritage conscious environment is another question.

The other decision was to demolish the late 1930s station building at Abergynolwyn and build a new larger building with a full café facility. That such a development was necessary is unquestionable, but again there was controversy over whether an alternative could have been found which could have allowed the retention of the former structure. However, once again it was felt there was no viable alternative.

During the winter of 1968 and into early 1969 much work was in progress along the railway. At Abergynolwyn the new station building was being constructed by a contractor. Meanwhile, at Pendre the loop was being extended and at Quarry Siding a new loop was being laid, as part of the preparations for three-train-set service.

With a Herculean effort by all involved the Permanent Way works were completed in time for the 1969 peak season, and the three-train-set service was introduced. There were other developments as well. In the March the railway purchased an Andrew Barclay 3 ft gauge locomotive from the Irish Turf Board. This was to be used as the basis for a major rebuild for what would eventually become locomotive No.7, originally to be named *Irish Pete*. Another three diesel locomotives were also purchased from Park Gate steelworks in Rotherham, although only one, a 1964 Ruston, was to enter Talyllyn service as No.8 *Merseysider*. Meanwhile carriage No.19 entered service on 21 June 1969.

The early 1970s

The early 1970s was to be another period of huge growth for the railway with several notable achievements culminating in the opening of the Extension to Nant Gwernol in 1976. Over the 1969/70 winter much was done on completing various works. Chief among these was the rebuilding of the spandrel walls on the Dolgoch viaduct, which was completed by the end of 1970.

History

Above: No.3 *Sir Haydn* enters the rebuilt Abergynolwyn station building with Hugh Jones at the regulator in August 1970.
(Photo: J.H.L. Adams)

In order to allow more flexible train operation a decision was made to install Miniature Electric Train Staff (METS) machines along the line. This was changed the following year when it was decided to use Electric Key Token (EKT) machines instead. It was to be a number of years before this was completed.

Other items discussed around this time also had a long gestation period. These included the options for providing continuous brakes, and the provision of volunteer accommodation. On a positive note it was decided that volunteers should receive free cups of tea, but not yet coffee.

Another long-term decision was the purchase of the first hardwood sleepers for the railway rather than buying secondhand materials of dubious quality. A further addition to the diesel locomotive fleet was the purchase of two ex-National Coal Board four-wheeled Hunslets, one of which was to become No.9 *Alf*.

In 1970 a joint marketing panel was formed with some of the other narrow gauge railways in Wales to advertise under the title of *The Great Little Trains of Wales*. This has grown since with additional members, and still provides joint publicity and a discount card scheme.

On 3 October 1970 work on the Extension started in earnest, the occasion being marked by the detonation by Tom Rolt of the first series of charges to widen the formation. As this work was to absorb a lot of resources over the succeeding years, it was probably inevitable that there would not be so much progress on the rest of the line.

Nevertheless there were some innovations and new developments. These included the introduction of carriage No.21 into service on 3 August 1971, No.20 having entered service in 1970. Work also started on another new carriage shed at Pendre, to be known as the 'West Shed'.

On 28 May 1972 a notable event happened in the life of the Talyllyn Railway. This was the sight of five locomotives in steam together for the first time following the return of *Talyllyn* after a lengthy overhaul. During this some shortcomings resulting from the rather speedy reconstruction carried out in the 1950s were resolved. It was also transported to London to participate in the Lord Mayor's Show in the November.

In the July Brake Third No.22 entered service, providing a much needed extra brake van. An enhancement to the coaching stock was the provision of electric lighting in the standard bogies.

The year was marred though by the death on 12 April 1972 of Edward Thomas, long time servant of the railway. His role in allowing the Preservation Society the opportunity to take over the railway should not be underestimated.

Work on the Extension and the West Shed continued through the winter and into the following year. Hugh Jones retired on 6 October 1973, after 55 years of service

History

at the quarry and on the railway. The year also marked the 'high tide' of passenger numbers with 185,574 passenger journeys being completed. Despite the high numbers an article by John Snell in *The Economist* that year held that the Talyllyn was the least profitable of the tourist railways. There was heavy investment in new equipment and infrastructure, but a reluctance to raise fares as a means of increasing revenue.

October 1973 had seen the Middle East oil crisis, which had an impact even in Wales. Therefore, 1974 was one largely of maintenance rather than new development, save for continuing work on the Extension. It was also the year the railway lost Tom Rolt, who died on 9 May at the age of 64, sadly before the Extension was completed. The economic climate had an impact on traffic numbers as well with passenger journeys down to 176,996 for the year. The times were beginning to change.

During 1975 increasing resources were directed towards the completion of the Extension. However, on 29 March carriage No.23 entered service. This was to be the last completely new standard bogie coach built for the railway to date.

The Extension

Tom Rolt had long harboured the ambition that one day the railway would be extended along the old mineral line beyond Abergynolwyn. There was even a Christmas card issued in 1951 with a picture of Bryneglwys and the caption 'site for a new terminus'. It was not until the AGM of 1956 that serious noises were being made about the possibility of the Extension. Patrick Whitehouse was asked to write to the Ministry about it, to which the reply was that the Society should not even contemplate this until the original line was in good condition.

Eventually, in 1959, the Society and Company Solicitor George Tibbits was asked to investigate obtaining a Light Railway Order for the section from Abergynolwyn to Nant Gwernol at the limit of locomotive working. This was with the aim of extending services there in time for the railway's Centenary in 1965.

His researches, however, opened a large can of worms. It had been assumed that the railway owned the trackbed for the route, but in fact there was no proof of this. It took Tibbits until September 1964 to establish the landowners and negotiate with them, by which time the aim of opening the Extension for the Centenary had gone.

In May 1964 the Railway Inspector had made an inspection of the mineral line. This showed that the Extension was going to be a major undertaking, with the need to ease many of the curves, particularly with the introduction of bogie coaches. As already mentioned he also indicated that the old winding house would have to be removed.

Following a full survey the railway began the process of applying for a Light Railway Order. This was needed because the mineral line was not part of the original statutory railway. It would take until 21 February 1972 for the Order to be made.

In October 1970 Tom Rolt had detonated the first charges to mark the beginning of the work of widening the trackbed. This was not to be a quick job and for several years the 'Gwerns', as those who worked on the Extension were known, continued the work of preparing the line for passenger trains.

There had been some controversy as well about the facilities to be provided at Nant Gwernol. Rolt had wanted to provide a full set of passenger services, but the narrowness of the site as well as the lack of electricity, or adequate drainage, precluded this. Other options considered included terminating the line at the Winding House site with a footpath to Nant Gwernol, or have a passing loop at the Winding House site. Eventually it was decided to provide a simple station at Nant Gwernol, and instead extend Abergynolwyn station to accommodate two trains.

The work was helped by a 49% grant from the Welsh Tourist Board with the proviso that the Extension was completed by 31 March 1976. However, there were a series of issues and delays, one of which came in late 1974 when it was realised that the line of 'Big Bend' had to be modified. This meant the excavation of an extra 1,500 cu yds of rock. To put this into context the total excavated along the whole Extension to that time was 2,400 cu yds.

Therefore, contractors were brought in to complete the work aided by voluntary help. Over the winter of 1975/6 the track layout at Abergynolwyn was extensively re-modelled, with a new block post and colour light signalling being installed. On 9 May the last length of track was laid on the Extension and the first ballast train ran into Nant Gwernol.

Left: Tom Rolt prepares to detonate the first charges for the building of the Extension on 3 October 1970. Hugh Jones stands immediately in front of the camera on right. (Photo: J.H.L. Adams)

Rails Along The Fathew

History

Above: The official opening ceremony for the Extension to Nant Gwernol took place on 22 May 1976. The platform party included James Boyd, then Chairman of the Preservation Society, Wynford Vaughan Thomas, broadcaster, Bill Faulkner, Managing Director, and Pat Garland, Financial Director of the Talyllyn Railway Co. Note the duffle bag left hanging from the tree! (Photo: J.H.L. Adams)

A Ministry Inspection took place on 11 May. The line was passed to be opened on 22 May, but only for the weekend. It then had to be closed for a week to allow further work to take place. At Abergynolwyn there was a ceremonial driving in of a 'golden' spike (see right) by broadcaster Wynford Vaughan Thomas before the inaugural train, hauled by a suitably decorated *Dolgoch*, headed up the line to Nant Gwernol. The Extension was open, although it was to be some months before the last of the work was completed.

The Late 1970s

Now attention could turn to the backlog of other tasks that had been put to one side. This led to a series of overnight track-laying sessions between Abergynolwyn and Quarry Siding in July 1976. For those involved this was quite an experience, particularly driving back down the valley at 2 am.

That year there was also a significant drought, which led to a number of lineside fires. This resulted in special measures being taken. Trains were followed up the most at-risk portions of the line by the Permanent Way gang motor trolley acting as a 'fire engine'. In addition, locomotive No.1 was fitted with a basic spark arrestor.

The necessity to involve contractors on the Extension put a severe strain on the railway's finances. Combined with the 'flattening' of the passenger figures this led to the decision to defer proceeding with further new carriages, two more having originally been proposed.

Instead it was decided that there would now be a period of consolidation with priority given to completing the Extension, West Carriage Shed, and locomotive No.7. New projects were to be a new messroom at Pendre and the redevelopment of Wharf station. This latter project led to a decision being taken at the 1977 Society AGM to demolish the old station building, but fortunately it was never carried out.

During the summer of 1977 there was a locomotive crisis with a failure of No.3 *Sir Haydn*; this left Nos. 2 and 6 as the only fully serviceable steam locomotives to haul three train sets. Therefore, diesel No.8 *Merseysider* was pressed into service hauling trains from Tywyn to Brynglas. Here it would swap with the steam locomotive on the down train, the latter taking the up train on to Nant Gwernol while No.8 returned with the down train to Wharf. This was the first regular use of a diesel locomotive on the summer passenger services. Meanwhile the workshops performed a small miracle by dismantling No.3, including lifting the boiler off, repairing serious damage to one of the steam chests and associated pipework, and returning it to service in six days.

In 1978 No.3 was transported to the Brush works in Loughborough, where it was originally built, to celebrate its centenary, the Brush Company generously paid for the transportation. There was some optimism as passenger journeys over the year increased to 183,060, but this was to be short-lived.

A New Reality

In the late 1970s and early 1980s a revolution took place in British holiday habits with the advent of the cheap foreign package holiday. In addition the recession during the same period also had a major impact. This drastically affected the number of passenger journeys. These fell to 156,619 in 1979, but by 1987 they were down to 106,055, a decline of more-or-less one third over the period.

This meant that the railway was operating in a completely new environment, and much of the rapid development of the previous years ceased. In turn, many other plans were shelved or postponed. The major redevelopment at Wharf was destined not to happen until the new Millennium. One major opportunity that was not taken was the option to develop a new engineering works on land to the east of Pendre offered to the railway by the Welsh Development Board. This again was due in part to the economic situation at the time.

One has sympathy with those trying to run the railway during these years; through no fault of their own they found money was tight, with little room to develop the line as they would wish. In addition a Society membership which was used to continued good news, suddenly had to come to terms with a new economic reality.

Rails Along The Fathew

History

This did not mean that no progress was made during this time. On 3 May 1980 a new footbridge and full network of paths was opened at Nant Gwernol. Meanwhile construction of a new body for bogie brake No.16 was completed.

On 14 September 1980 the railway lost its other joint founder when Bill Trinder died. Although he had not been actively involved with the Talyllyn for many years his loss was still felt.

During 1981 the decline in passenger numbers continued. The following year started with news of the death of Bill Faulkner, the railway's Managing Director, in the January, David Woodhouse being appointed General Manager in his place.

A controversial development in 1982 was the decision to repaint locomotive No.3 in red and rename it *Sir Handel*, after one of the Skarloey locomotives in the Rev. W. Awdry's 'Railway Series' of books. The effect was completed with the fitting of a face. While some traditionally-minded members disapproved, it did attract useful publicity.

Another source of publicity was the visit to the railway by Prince Charles and Princess Diana on 25 November 1982. They travelled on a special train between Pendre and Rhydyronen stations, with Prince Charles on the footplate of No.2 while Princess Diana rode in carriage No.17.

In January 1983 the death occurred of Herbert Jones, who had been the railway's Locomotive Superintendent for many years. His memory was honoured the following year by the unveiling of a plaque on his former cottage, now part of the locomotive shed at Pendre.

The first visiting locomotive to the line appeared in May 1983 in the form of a Simplex diesel owned by the Corris Railway Society, which was then hoping to open part of the old line. Numbered 5 and named *Alan Meaden* it was to remain on the railway for several months, including hauling some special trains.

Dolgoch had taken part in a special exhibition train organised by the Development Board for Rural Wales (DBRW) in March 1982. It went to various locations across England including Brighton, London and Leeds. A similar train was run in 1984, this time with locomotive No.3. Called the *Mid Wales Express* it visited places including Salisbury, Birmingham, London, Colchester, Windsor, Bristol, Southampton and Portsmouth.

One special event which occurred during the trip was the locomotive's presence at Euston station on 30 April for the naming of British Rail electric locomotive No.86258 as *Talyllyn*. *Sir Haydn* returned to Tywyn on Saturday 5 May and was unloaded a few days later, becoming the last item handled by Tywyn station goods yard before its closure.

Above and right: The railway's first royal visit occurred on 25 November 1982 when Prince Charles and Princess Diana rode between Tywyn and Rhydyronen. Prince Charles accompanied driver Dai Jones and fireman Mike Green on the footplate, while Princess Diana rode in carriage No.17. When they alighted at Rhydyronen an enthusiastic crowd was there to greet them. (Photos: TR Collection)

Rails Along The Fathew

History

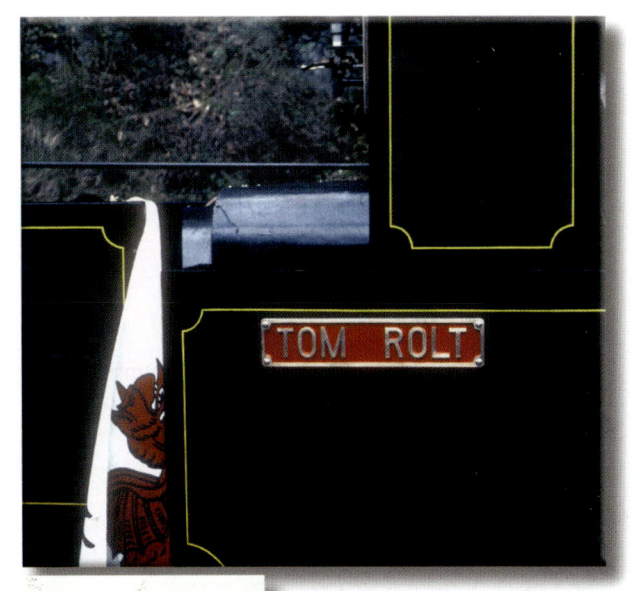

Above left and right: The naming ceremony for locomotive No.7 *Tom Rolt* with his widow, Sonia, doing the unveiling at Abergynolwyn on 6 May 1991.

Left: No.7 *Tom Rolt* is seen at Tywyn Wharf station in 1992. Immediately behind it is carriage No.7 then newly in service after being fitted with a new body to provide accommodation for people in wheelchairs.

(All Photos: J.H.L. Adams)

The Late 1980s

The publication in 1986 of a strategic plan *Twenty Years Ahead* for the future direction of the railway did not produce many immediate changes, but did drive much of the subsequent development into the 21st Century. Decreasing passenger numbers began to be reflected in the timetable with a reduction in the level of the peak service. However, there was also the beginning of an appreciable shift in traffic away from the main holiday season and towards the surrounding weeks and months. These are variously known as the 'off-peak' or 'shoulder' seasons.

December 1986 saw the retirement of Dai Jones, the last remaining employee from pre-preservation days. He described his proudest moment as driving No.2 on the Royal train during the visit of Prince Charles and Princess Diana. Sadly, Dai's father, Hugh, who had started work on the railway in the 1930s, passed away on 18 September 1989.

The Skarloey Railway's *Peter Sam* began a visit to the railway in 1988, with locomotive No.4 *Edward Thomas* being repainted in a suitable livery to emulate the character from the Rev. W. Awdry's books. In 1989 the Queen's birthday honours brought news of an MBE for David Woodhouse for services to Welsh Tourism.

Strategic Development

If the late 1980s had seen relatively little development on the railway, then the 1990s saw a rash of new projects. Many of these were aimed at improving the quality of the 'passenger experience', as emphasised in the twenty-year plan. In addition there was to be the final completion of two long-standing items.

The first of these was the entry into service of locomotive No.7. Work had been resumed on No.7 in 1988, the plan being that it would replace No.6 *Douglas* whose boiler was becoming life-expired. At the Society AGM in 1989 the issue of its name was revisited and *Irish Pete* became *Tom*

History

Left: A handshake to mark the official 'twinning' of the Talyllyn Railway with the Puffing Billy Railway in Melbourne, Australia on 27 September 1992. Taking part are (left to right) Phil A'Vard of the Puffing Billy Railway, John Adams, President of the Talyllyn Railway Preservation Society and Don Marshall of the Puffing Billy Railway.
(Photo: Ed Castellan)

Right: Locomotive No.4 operating as *Peter Sam* crosses Dolgoch viaduct with an up train during the post-Christmas service in 1993. By this time it had been the first to be fitted with an air pump, which can be seen on the driver's side of the smokebox. Some of the components for the air-brake system had been obtained through the links with Puffing Billy Railway.

Rolt. The naming ceremony finally took place on 6 May 1991, when Tom's widow, Sonia, was guest of honour.

Meanwhile the second long-standing project was the provision of accommodation for volunteers. This had been first raised back in the 1960s, and had been looked at on several occasions since. Various suggestions had been made, but these had proved impracticable or, as in the case of the proposed purchase of an ex-BR coach, had fallen foul of planning.

Happily, the solution came when the bungalow *Llechfan* at Wharf station, which had been sold by the Haydn Jones estate, came up for sale. This was purchased by the railway in 1992, partly using the proceeds from the sale of another railway property, *Plas Coch* at Rhydyronen, long-time home of the Jones family. Originally the purchase of *Llechfan* was to deal with the issue of access rights across Wharf station, but it was converted into a volunteer hostel and opened by the actor Timothy West on 25 June 1994.

The decade was also dominated by toilets, with no fewer than three new sets being built. Those at Abergynolwyn, were formally opened in May 1991, at Wharf in December 1992 and at Dolgoch in 1998.

Provision of facilities for the disabled also became a priority. In 1992, the rebuilt coach No.7 entered service. This had been designed as a vehicle for those in wheelchairs. However, it quickly became apparent that there needed to be provision on each of the three sets of coaches run in peak service. Therefore, one end of each of two bogie coaches was converted into an open saloon. Carriage No.21 was modified in time for the 1995 peak service, with No.20 being converted the following year.

During the 1980s there had been growing pressure from the Railway Inspectorate for the adoption of some form of continuous braking. After consideration it was decided to adopt a single-pipe air-brake system and a large number of surplus components were acquired from the Victorian Railways in Australia. An initial short test set consisting of locomotive No.4 along with carriages Nos.16 and 21 was first run on 23 May 1993. Following this air-braking was gradually introduced for all carriages, with air-pumps and control equipment on the locomotives.

Also during the decade there were several changes in senior management. David Woodhouse resigned as General Manager in December 1992, with Maurice Wilson taking over in an acting capacity. He was subsequently appointed Managing Director, with David Leech as Traffic Manager. In 1994 John Bate retired as Chief Engineer, although he continued as Consultant Engineer, with Dave Scotson becoming the Engineering Manager. Finally before the decade closed David Mitchell succeeded Maurice Wilson as Managing Director in November 1999.

Another significant event also occurred in 1992 when a 'twinning agreement' was signed with the Puffing Billy Railway in Melbourne, Australia. In 1993 the railway

History

Above: Locomotive No.1 *Talyllyn* arrives at Nant Gwernol with *The Quarryman* in 2001.

suffered severe flood damage on two occasions. The first occurred at about 6 pm on 10 June when a deluge of floodwater, mud and debris caused extensive damage to the trackbed at Brynglas. The second flood occurred at Cynfal between 6 and 7 December, and resulted in the line being covered with a large amount of debris.

Several new marketing and other initiatives were also undertaken. One innovation was the introduction of the Day Rover ticket in 1995. Initially these cost an extra pound on the full return fare but allowed passengers unlimited travel for one day. Eventually in 2000 the Day Rover became the standard return ticket for passengers travelling the full length of the line.

To provide an attractive potential 'package' for coach parties the 2.30 pm departure (later the 11.40 am departure) was given the name *The Quarryman* in 1995 with special leaflets being issued to passengers. These initiatives, along with other efforts such as the installation of electric storage heaters in three carriages, improved the numbers of coach parties coming to the railway. This led to an increase in overall passenger numbers for several years. As a result an extension was added to the Abergynolwyn station building between 1998 and 1999 to cope with the coach parties. This was later licensed for weddings and civil partnerships.

In 1984 *Race the Train* had been started in partnership with Tywyn Rotary Club, and before the end of the century had developed into an internationally known event with over a thousand competitors taking part. Special events were also developed including *Victorian Week*, an enthusiasts' weekend and two all-night steam events. The Talyllyn was also one of the first heritage railways to have a website from December 1994. *Peter Sam* also made a re-appearance, and continued to delight children of all ages.

Locomotive No.4 revisited its old home at Corris in 1996, while No.6 *Douglas* was fitted with a new boiler, re-entering service in May 1995. A new locomotive was acquired in 1997 in the form of No.10, later named *Bryn Eglwys*. This was an ex-Coal Board four-wheeled Simplex of 1985 vintage.

Into the New Millenium

In 2001 the railway celebrated its Golden Jubilee since preservation. A series of events started in the autumn of 2000, marking the formation of the Preservation Society, and continued into 2001.

The early part of the new Millennium was dominated by the plans for the redevelopment of Tywyn Wharf station. These had first been discussed back in the late 1970s, but now it was agreed that the railway needed new facilities to match the changing expectations of passengers.

Various ideas were discussed. First was the option of developments on the north and south sides of Wharf station. At one point the installation of a traverser to release locomotives at the wharf end of the station was proposed. This would have allowed the installation of a passenger walkway between the north and south sides along the wharf edge to connect the new buildings.

Rails Along The Fathew

History

Another proposal involved the leasing or purchase of part of the former BR goods yard. New buildings would have been erected on the north side of Neptune Road bridge with a car park. Passengers would then have walked through a tunnel underneath Neptune Road onto the old station site to catch their trains.

In the end the decision was to build a new two-storey building on the site of both the café building and Narrow Gauge Railway Museum. The new building would then incorporate both of these as well as much needed office space. This plan also had the benefit that the original building would be retained, and joined to the new building. Even so the estimated cost was of the order of £1 million.

The incorporation of the Museum into the plans enabled an application to the Heritage Lottery Fund to be made for a substantial part of the required amount. In early 2003 it was announced that the Lottery Fund had agreed to a grant of £682,500 towards the project, and this along with other grants and donations enabled work to begin in earnest in January 2004.

It was known that during construction there would be some restrictions on the use of the station, with locomotives being unable to run-round at Wharf. Therefore, in a reversion to pre-preservation practice, trains were propelled to and from Tywyn Pendre where locomotives could run round and be serviced. This practice continued through the summer peak season.

By July 2005 the station building was largely completed and ready for its official opening. This was performed on a return visit to the railway by Prince Charles, this time accompanied by the Duchess of Cornwall, on 13 July. The royal party travelled down the line from Brynglas on a train hauled by locomotive No.7 before alighting at the new station.

Difficult Years

These new facilities brought new optimism, particularly as traffic had been increasing, rising from 89,067 passenger journeys in 2000 to 98,610 in 2005. The new building also led to substantial increases in the takings in both the café and shop. In 2006 a five-year strategic business plan was produced and as part of this a new paid General Manager's post was advertised, with Larry Bridges being appointed in the November.

Unfortunately in 2007 the banking sector began to collapse, and the resulting financial downturn was beginning to effect the railway's finances. This was not helped by some severe flooding in the area during the summer season. Passenger journeys fell to 94,473, and by the end of the summer season in 2008 it was clear that painful decisions had to be made. This was particularly urgent as the railway was facing a £100,000 loss for the second year in succession.

Therefore, after much deliberation, it was decided to make a number of redundancies. This included in the

Above: The new station building at Tywyn Wharf was completed in 2005.

Rails Along The Fathew

History

summer of 2009 the post of General Manager, with David Mitchell coming back in the voluntary role of Acting Chief Executive. It was a difficult time for all involved with the railway.

The continuing international financial crisis did not help matters either, passenger journey numbers continued to fall, to 85,146 for 2010 a decrease of 13.7% over the previous five years. Happily the financial situation began to improve, and in 2009 the railway actually ran at a surplus.

There were also other developments during this period. In 2008 a source of excellent second-hand rail had been found with the dismantling of the 2 ft 6 in line at the ex-Royal Naval Armaments Depot at Trecwn. A substantial quantity of track components was obtained, being lifted from site and transported to Tywyn. In addition, a consortium of Society members purchased three Baguley diesels, two for use on the railway and one for spares. These were stored at Wharf station for a number of years before being taken into railway ownership.

To the 150th Anniversary

In 2011 the railway celebrated its Diamond Jubilee as the World's First Preserved Railway. On 14 May a re-enactment of the first preservation train was run with John Snell, the fireman on the first train, as guest of honour. Sadly this was his last visit to the railway. This was followed by an all-night steam event over the first weekend in June. Later in the month another anniversary was celebrated, that of the Centenary of the birth of Rev. W. Awdry.

In the October the railway had its first 'visiting' steam locomotive in the form of No.7 from the revived Corris Railway. This is based on the Kerr, Stuart *Tattoo* class Corris No.4, which became Talyllyn Railway No.4 *Edward Thomas*. Several special trains and photographic sessions were run to celebrate the event.

It was decided to send carriage No.21 to Boston Lodge works on the Ffestiniog Railway to have its bodywork rebuilt to relieve the pressure on staff and volunteers at Pendre. Meanwhile the major work on the railway was the relaying of the cutting between Wharf and Pendre once more. This involved digging out the trackbed and laying a new drainage system before reinstating 1,501 ft of track.

Rain became the theme for 2012. In April there was historic encounter between No.2 *Dolgoch* and the FR's *Palmerston*, which were present on the Llangollen Railway in steam on specially laid track in the yard at Carrog. However, the occasion was marred by heavy rain, which was to continue over several months. In the June the railway was heavily flooded at Cynfal although trains could still run. Elsewhere in the area flooding caused severe damage that was to affect the tourist trade during the summer.

The railway also suffered a minor locomotive crisis with No.4 requiring a new firebox, No.6 undergoing overhaul and No.3's boiler certificate expiring. This left three locomotives to operate the three train peak service, but there were no cancellations.

Over the winter, construction began on a storage shed at Quarry Siding. This was largely funded by a legacy from volunteer driver Phil Guest, and so it was named *The Guest House* when it was officially opened by Timothy West and Prunella Scales on 5 May 2013.

The year also saw out-of-ticket locomotive No.3 on a publicity tour which included trips on a flat wagon along both the Severn Valley and West Somerset Railways. In July the rebuilt carriage No.21 re-entered service, and in the September Baguley diesel No.11 returned from regauging at Alan Keef's workshop in Gloucestershire. There was also a change in the senior management of the railway with Chris Price being appointed General Manager.

The major news of 2013 came with the Queen's birthday honours list, which coincided with the railway running a re-enactment of its Coronation Day specials. This announced that the Talyllyn Railway Preservation Society had been awarded the prestigious Queen's Award for Voluntary Service, stated to be the equivalent of an MBE (Member of the British Empire) medal for organisations in the voluntary sector.

Left: On the 60th Anniversary of the first train running on the preserved railway, 14 May 2011, John Snell, who was the fireman on *Dolgoch* that day, cuts the same ribbon as Bill Trinder had done sixty years previously while Society Chairman Lis Mann looks on.

Rails Along The Fathew

History

Left: On 5 May 2013 Timothy West and Prunella Scales officially opened *The Guest House* storage shed at Quarry Siding.
(Photo: Andrew Young)

It had been decided to repaint both locomotives for the 150th celebrations, and the livery chosen was the possible Fletcher, Jennings delivery colours of fully lined Indian Red. In order to complete the work in the time available, due to the requirements of the engineering department, a firm of professional heritage painters was brought in to do the work over two weeks. On Christmas Day 2014 the results were revealed to a huge on-line response.

Thus the railway was prepared for its 150th Anniversary. This was celebrated by a series of galas, including visits by the Ffestiniog Railway's *Prince*, the oldest working 2 ft gauge locomotive in the world, and the Welsh Highland Heritage Railway's *Russell*, returning fifty years after it left Tywyn Wharf. They were both in steam at Wharf station over the first weekend in July, one hundred and fifty years since the signing of the Talyllyn Railway Act.

All this was an appropriate precursor for the railway's 150th Anniversary celebrations in 2014. Sadly the year got off to a bad start with news of the death of John Snell, followed in the October with the death of Sonia Rolt.

There was a further problem which was to threaten the official start of the 150th Anniversary, a ceremony to mark 150 years since the completion of *Talyllyn* at Fletcher, Jennings, Lowca Works on 24 September 1864. This was when *Talyllyn* suffered a major mechanical failure in service on 6 April, which resulted in severe damage to its motion. However, following a transfer to the Ffestiniog Railway's Boston Lodge works for repairs, it re-entered service on 18 September in time for its anniversary celebrations.

In the November *Talyllyn* was transported to Birmingham, just as it had been at the start of the Centenary year, this time to appear at the National Exhibition Centre for the Warley Model Railway Show. On its return it and *Dolgoch* were placed into the paint shop at Pendre ready for an amazing transformation.

Left: Also in 2013 the railway recreated the decorated trains it ran for for the Diamond Jubilee of Coronation Day in 1953. It fact it ran them twice, once for a BBC documentary and then on the day itself. In this photo No.4 *Edward Thomas* is departing Tywyn Wharf on 2 June 2013.

Above: On the same day it was announced the Talyllyn Railway Preservation Society had been awarded the prestigious Queen's Award for Voluntary Service, which was presented to Society President Richard Hope by the Lord Lieutenant of Gwynedd, Huw Morgan Daniel, at a ceremony at Abergynolwyn station on 26 July 2013.

60 — Rails Along The Fathew

History

Left: Following its failure in service on 6 April 2014, locomotive No.1 was sent to Porthmadog to be repaired at the Ffestiniog Railway's Boston Lodge workshops. It is seen here at Porthmadog Harbour station with the Ffestiniog Railway's *Linda*, having been unloaded onto a flat truck ready to be taken across the cob to Boston Lodge on 22 April 2014.

Below: In the end both *Linda* and *Talyllyn* were hauled across the Cob by the diesel locomotive *Criccieth Castle*. *Talyllyn* could not run on the Ffestiniog's track due to the difference in the gauge.

Below: Thanks to the work at Boston Lodge *Talyllyn* was returned to Tywyn in time to celebrate its 150th birthday on 24 September 2014. Here Preservation Society Chairman Jane Garvey, on the left, and Society President Richard Hope, on the right, hold a special banner in front of the locomotive at Tywyn Wharf station. This was Richard Hope's final official duty as President of the Society as he stood down at the Annual General Meeting a few days later after nine years. He had previously served as the Society's Secretary for thirty years from 1966 to 1996.

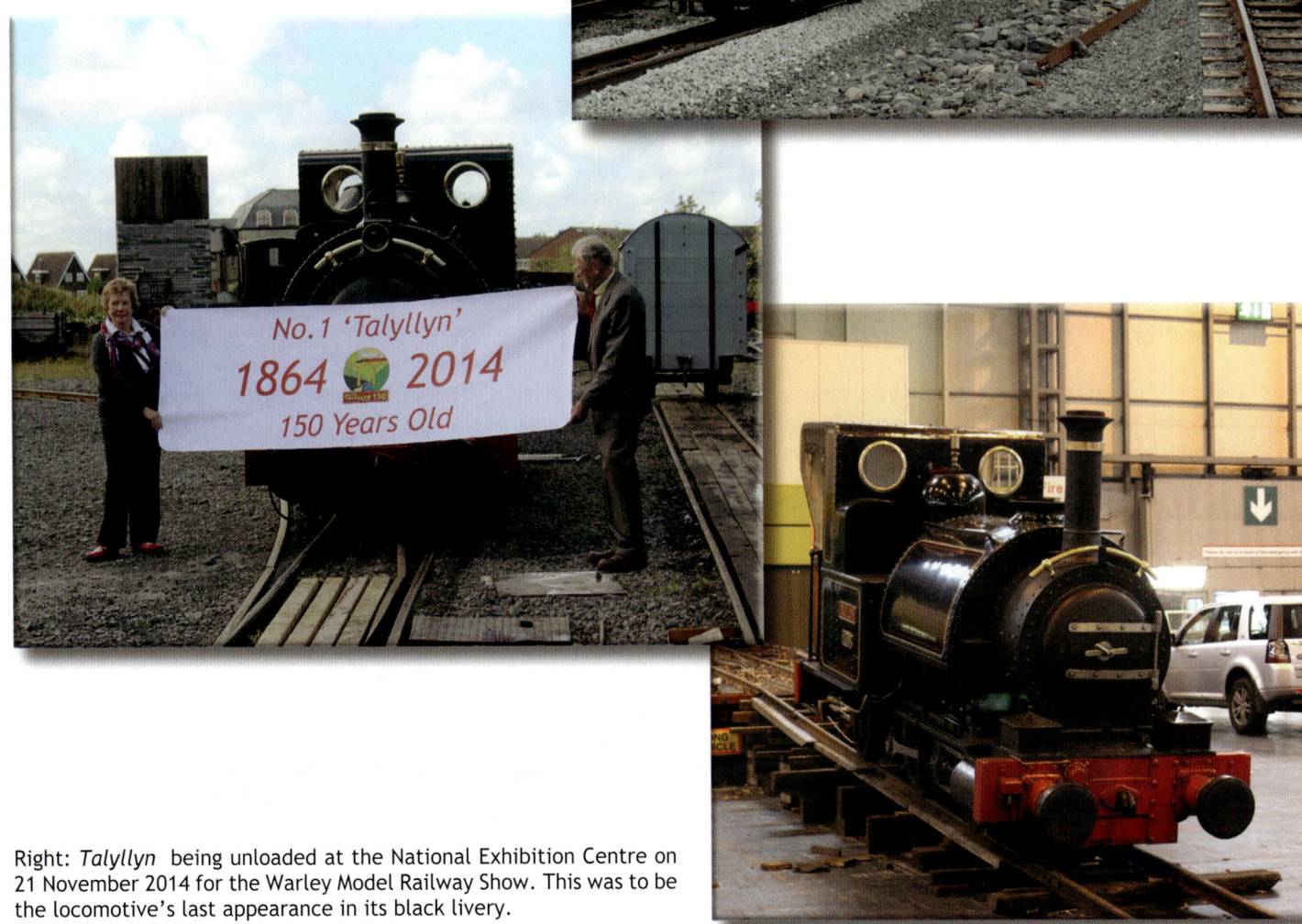

Right: *Talyllyn* being unloaded at the National Exhibition Centre on 21 November 2014 for the Warley Model Railway Show. This was to be the locomotive's last appearance in its black livery.

The Route Described

Tywyn Wharf

Above: A busy scene at Tywyn Wharf station taken from the road bridge at Easter 1960. The original building is in the centre. In the left foreground work is about to start on the new carriage siding. The newly completed Museum building is the background and the Council-built toilet block is at the top of the drive on the right. Meanwhile No.4 *Edward Thomas* prepares to depart with a train consisting of one original Talyllyn carriage, one Glyn Valley carriage, three opens and carriages Nos. 9 and 10.

(Photo: J.N. Slater)

Origins

The origins of Tywyn Wharf (or simply Wharf) station are one of those areas of Talyllyn history that are likely to remain somewhat hazy. In fact had the initial plans of the slate company come to fruition it is unlikely that Wharf station would have existed at all, or at least not in its current form.

This is because the original intention of the slate company was that the narrow gauge wagons would be transported bodily on standard gauge wagons between Tywyn and Aberdyfi. Therefore, their idea at the outset was to run an elevated line into the A&WCR's yard at Tywyn to enable the transhipment to take place.

One possibility was that it was intended to run the railway directly into the A&WCR yard on a northward curve, although no survey of this exists. Instead when the Talyllyn Railway Bill was published in November 1864 Railway No.2 was laid out curving to the south. Trains would therefore have had to reverse before running to the A&WCR station (see plan on page 15).

This line would have been on a 6 ft elevation above the A&WCR line allowing direct transhipment onto the main line company's wagons. Meanwhile it seems that there was to be a small yard at the wharf site.

In the original Bill there was also provision for mixed gauge to be laid down, as well as running powers over the A&WCR. An interesting question is whether originally ithe company intended to run passenger trains into the A&WCR's station, as well as slate trains into their yard.

Even in the final Act, although the mixed gauge had disappeared, there was still the requirement for the Coast line to permit a 'double line of tracks' to be laid by the Talyllyn. Therefore, was one of these to go to the yard and the other to the station? However, if the intention was to run passenger trains from the A&WCR station, why did the eventual passenger service only start from Pendre half a mile away? One theory is that the company only sought official Board of Trade permission to operate passenger services from Pendre station. But then why not bring the site the wharf site up to specification and invite the Inspector back? Clearly they felt the expense was unjustified.

Another question is why did Railway No.2 not get built at all? The TRCo. was still empowered to build it, but only effectively with the co-operation of the A&WCR. One suspects that it was a combination of reasons. The first was probably due to the the A&WCR being 'awkward'. Secondly, it was not worth the expenditure as the amount of slate transported was less than half what was originally envisaged.

The Route Described

Above: The original building at Tywyn Wharf was designed to be a goods and general office, and also housed the scales for the weighbridge. It is seen here in 1951 shortly after the Preservation Society took over. Contrary to some tradition it was not finished before the railway opened, but was completed after the trains were running. (Photo: The Elliot Collection)

As the railway was open for slate traffic a couple of months before the Talyllyn Railway Act was passed in July 1865, the assumption must be that the transshipment arrangement at the wharf site was in place by then. This involved the slate wagons being manoeuvred onto the wharf edge and then the slates were unloaded directly into standard gauge wagons. It is possible that this was seen as a temporary measure, but experience showed it was adequate for the task. Later correspondence reveals that the TRCo. also contributed to the cost of the standard gauge siding at the wharf.

Before the building of the Talyllyn the wharf site had been used by the A&WCR as a 'borrow' pit for gravel for the construction of their line. In order to build a transshipment wharf not only did this need to be filled, but the level raised to enable the slates to be transferred. Fortunately there was a ready supply of 'infill' coming from the cutting between the eventual sites of Wharf and Pendre stations.

King's Station

One theory that has come down through the years is that the main building at Tywyn Wharf was completed before the railway was open, hence its brick construction rather than slate slab. It is likely, however, that while the materials for it had been ordered earlier, building did not commence until the time traffic started on the line. Only the pit for the weighbridge might pre-date the the line's opening. Similar bricks were also used in the construction of ring arches at Hendy Bridge and also the Neptune Road bridge over the Coast line, suggesting a common local source.

A newspaper report from early September 1865 confirms the later building date. It stated that at that time the building, described as being 'a very neat brick building', was nearing completion. While construction of the office continued the railway company used McConnel's house, Brynhyfryd, as its base.

It also seems that the initial layout at what was then known as the 'south' station was developed over several months. Another newspaper report from 31 March 1866 stated that 'the yards and buildings are being enlarged at the south station'. What seems to have developed is a layout as seen on page 64.

As can be seen this had the line splitting into five tracks after it had passed under the road bridge. The southernmost of these probably reflected part of the planned route of Railway No.2. These all now ran to the wharf side where a series of wagon turntables enabled wagons to be run alongside the A&WCR siding.

In the station building there was an office and a set of scales connected to a weighbridge outside. Elsewhere there was a coal yard, a shelter (or caban) for the loaders working on the wharf and at least one wooden shed, which presumably acted as storage and for general goods.

There was no run-round loop, and it is believed that gravity shunting was employed at least for a time. A siding was laid, evidence of which was found in the late 1970s, about hundred yards east of the road bridge where wagons could be stored, and then released to be run into the yard. If this was the practice it seems to have been short lived, as there is no trace of the siding on the 1888 Ordnance Survey map.

The Route Described

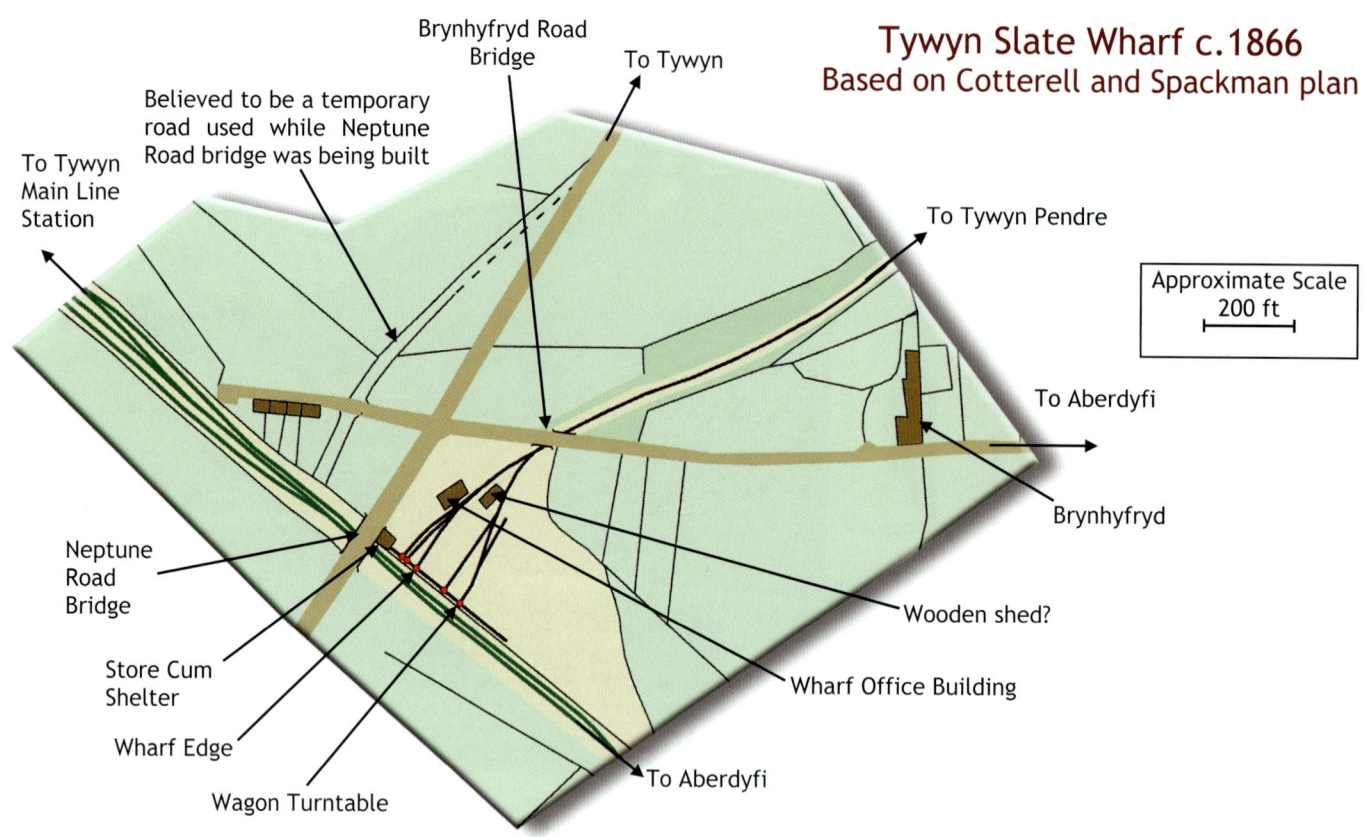

Tywyn Slate Wharf c.1866
Based on Cotterell and Spackman plan

Map labels:
- Brynhyfryd Road Bridge
- To Tywyn
- Believed to be a temporary road used while Neptune Road bridge was being built
- To Tywyn Main Line Station
- To Tywyn Pendre
- Approximate Scale 200 ft
- To Aberdyfi
- Brynhyfryd
- Neptune Road Bridge
- Wooden shed?
- Store Cum Shelter
- Wharf Office Building
- Wharf Edge
- To Aberdyfi
- Wagon Turntable

Left: This view was taken about 1902 and is probably one of the earliest surviving photos of Wharf or King's station. The gunpowder store has been completed, but the road bridge is still in its original form. Note the curve and climb of the track after it passes through the bridge. This is probably one of the last photographs of Hugh Thomas, on the right, while his son, Edward, is third from the right. (Photo: TR Collection)

Right: Wharf station building on 12 June 1920. The centre poster advertises the GWR and Cambrian Railway train times, while on the right is a Talyllyn Railway poster. On the weighbridge line can be seen three two-bar slate wagons and two iron sided open wagons. (Photo: Ken Nunn Collection Copyright NRM/SSPL)

64   Rails Along The Fathew

The Route Described

Above: A well-known photograph of No.2, then named *Pretoria*, at King's station. The rubble on the left could be the result of the construction of the gunpowder store, which would date this photo very early in the twentieth century. Posing on the footplate is John Rowlands. Jacob Rowlands the guard is seen towards the rear. The gentleman in front of the carriage has been identified as Tommy Lloyd, possibly a misidentification, Tommy did not work at the wharf, but his brother John William did.

(Photo: C.H. Young/ TR Collection)

By 1888 the sidings seem to have been rearranged with one of the centre ones removed and others moved. In addition, there is now a siding entering the coal yard next to Neptune Road. The 1901 Ordnance Survey map also shows this arrangement. It also seems as if the 'kick-back' siding on the southern road might have been lifted by 1888, although this might simply have be an omission from the Ordnance Survey maps. Certainly it was re-instated in the early 1900s if it was removed.

For over thirty years passenger trains did not officially serve Wharf station, passengers being directed to Pendre. However, from the earliest days of the passenger service it did feature on timetable posters as being the place that goods and parcels should be taken, being known as King's station. The reason for this name is unclear, the most plausible explanation being that it was the name of a previous owner or tenant of the site.

In July 1900 passenger trains were first advertised as starting from the station. This was in a timetable published in the *County Times* which stated that:

Passengers obtain tickets at Towyn Station, but can enter the train at the Slate Wharf without any additional charge, provided they are there five minutes before the advertised time for departure of the train from Towyn Station.

The suspicion is that this had been the unofficial practice for some time (see photo on page 187). On a timetable poster for 1903 the station was still known as King's, but as we have seen above it was also known as the Slate Wharf, or Slate Wharf station. It does not appear to be until about 1909 that Wharf station became the official starting point for passenger trains. Even so down trains still terminated at Pendre until the 1920s.

During the early years of the twentieth century the wooden parapets on the road bridge were rebuilt at least twice. First, early in the century, the diagonally braced wooden parapets were replaced with rectangular panels. The second time seems to have occurred around 1919/20 when the wooden beams were replaced with steel girders and brick parapets constructed. Between 1900 and 1902 the wooden shed on the south side of the line next to the bridge was replaced with a slab-built gunpowder store.

In June 1915 Haydn Jones got permission from the Local Council to build a bungalow. This is probably the property, known as *Llechfan*, built on the south side of the site. The dwelling was supposedly intended for Meryrick Roberts, the Quarry Manager, but he does not seem to have taken up residence there. With minor changes this was to be the station's layout for the next 36 years until the advent of the Preservation Society.

The Preservation Era

Over the winter of 1951/52 the Preservation Society carried out the first major changes to the track layout at Wharf station for fifty years. This involved the alteration

The Route Described

of the middle tracks to form a run-round loop. In addition a substantial buffer stop was added at the wharf edge, and a platform built. (see plan on page 69)

Another change happened between 1954/55 when the road bridge was reconstructed by the County Council and the road widened. This resulted in a considerable increase in the gradient on the station drive. The County Council also constructed a set of toilets at the top of the drive over the winter of 1956/7.

On the station itself a new building appeared as the old coal yard was converted into a home for the Narrow Gauge Railway Museum in 1959. The following year a carriage siding was added to the layout, as well as an annexe to the station building.

Between 1963 and 1965 there were a series of changes to the track layout at Wharf station and also the buildings. First, the original building had subsidence in the south-west corner, which needed to be dealt with. Subsequently the weighbridge was also removed.

Outside a new curve had been laid by August 1964 giving access to the wharf edge without the need to use the wagon turntables. An extension to the Museum building was also started.

The following winter the track layout was substantially altered with the main platform line being moved much closer to the station building. This in turn meant that the run-round loop could be extended (see plan on page 69). An extension was made to the east end of the station building for an improved booking office.

Other alterations included a new coaling yard, the erection of a temporary steel water tower and provision of an ash pit. All these changes were celebrated during the Centenary by the unveiling of a plaque by the poet John Betjeman, who held the honour of being Society member No.1. This was by virtue of his donation appearing first in Patrick Garland's (the Society's first Treasurer) subscription list.

The next significant change was the digging of a ballast dock between 1971 and 1972. This enabled wagons to be run down below ground level and top-loaded with ballast. Spoil from the excavation was transported to Fach Goch to be tipped.

In 1975 the official spelling of the town was changed from Towyn to Tywyn, and the railway followed suit, so the station became Tywyn Wharf. By now though the accommodation at the station was inadequate for the needs of both the railway administration and passenger provision, and so plans were discussed for a comprehensive rebuilding of the station.

Initially the intension was to demolish the old building and build an entirely new structure. Thankfully, this was never carried out, initially due to the economic downturn. Instead a series of temporary solutions were adopted. The first of these was obtaining a portable office building. This was placed next to the gunpowder store in 1977, and was later moved to the other side of the track, known as the shrubbery area, in 1985. It was subsequently replaced with a larger version in 1989.

In 1990 the need for enhanced catering facilities led to another portable building being obtained. This was placed

Above: This postcard with *Dolgoch* on a short passenger train at Tywyn King's station is worth a second look. The road bridge has been rebuilt from the picture on page 64 and the gunpowder store has acquired a dovecote. In addition, Hugh Thomas is not in the picture which suggests a date post-1903. However, behind the gunpowder store Edward Thomas' house *Trefri* has yet to be built. The mock-Tudor house was constructed in 1906/07 on land sold to Edward Thomas by the railway company, and still stands today. Therefore, we have a date for the picture of between 1903 and 1907. (Commercial Postcard)

The Route Described

at the western end of the platform in front of the Museum building. All this led to a cluttered appearance to the station. Measures were taken to try and enhance the heritage aspect of the location such as the provision of outside gas lighting in 1989, but still it was clear that a more permanent solution was required.

A new brick toilet block was built in the shrubbery area in 1992, with the portable office building being moved to Pendre. One extra benefit of the new toilets was that it enabled the demolition in 1994 of the old Council block at the top of the drive which was an eye-sore.

Meanwhile, a new general office was created in 1992 on the north side of the old station building. That year the *Llechfan* bungalow came up for sale and was purchased to extinguish an access right across the station. It was later converted into a volunteer hostel, opened in 1994.

Wharf Redevelopment

As already stated, previous plans had involved the demolition of the original building while retaining the much more modern Museum building. Later a new set of plans was developed, which retained the old building and instead incorporated the Museum within the new structure.

This plan had several advantages. First it preserved the original building, and indeed enabled the 'mish-mash' of extensions to be demolished. Second, it could be done in phases, and third the incorporation of the Museum opened up the possibility of obtaining grant funding, particularly from the Heritage Lottery Fund.

In the end this was successful and work started on phase one of the redevelopment in 2002, with the main building being constructed between 2004 and 2005. The catering building was moved over by the gunpowder store, and to enable people to access it movable chains were installed across the tracks supervised by what became known as the 'chain gang'. For a considerable portion of the 2004 season trains had to be propelled to and from Wharf to allow locomotives to be serviced at Pendre, and also had to be shorter to fit the reduced length platform.

By 13 July 2005 all was ready for the official opening by Prince Charles and the Duchess of Cornwall. Designed to reflect the ambience of a Victorian railway building, it provided a greatly improved Museum as well as much enhanced catering and commercial facilities. There is also a teaching room named after the long time editor of the *Talyllyn News*, John Slater. It should serve the needs of the railway for many years to come.

Since the completion of the building there have been moves to enhance the heritage aspect of the station. A slate display has been created around the wharf edge, with the restoration of one of the original turntables. Also the water column has been clad with slate slab, and the water tank has acquired timber cladding.

Meanwhile plans for the reinstallation of the old weighbridge have come to fruition with the construction of a replica weigh-house, based on one at Pen-yr-Orsedd, next to the gunpowder store. Work began on this in 2008 and it was formally opened on 19 May 2012, the project being awarded a National Railway Heritage Award that year.

Above: Tywyn Wharf station in April 1949. Edward Thomas is examining the wheel-sets for the brake van before they were sent away to Porthmadog for new tyres to be fitted. (Photo: The Elliot/ Dan Quine Collection)

Rails Along The Fathew

The Route Described

Left: *Dolgoch* propels the empty stock away from Wharf. Before 1952 there was no run-round loop there, and so the stock was either propelled back to Pendre to allow the locomotives to run-round. As an alternative it was sometimes propelled up the cutting and the locomotive uncoupled and run back into a siding. Then the van brakes were released and the carriages trundled back into the station.

In *Railway Adventure* Tom Rolt recalls how this latter practice used to constantly worry him as he envisaged the carriages ploughing over the wharf edge. However, as far is known, this never happened with coaching stock. (Photo: TR Collection)

Right: In 1935 *Talyllyn* awaits to depart from Tywyn Wharf. In the foreground is what is known as the rockery stone. This was reputedly brought down from the quarry for a lady who wanted a stone for her garden. When it arrived she declared that it was too large, and it has remained at Tywyn Wharf ever since. (Photo: TR Collection)

Left: *Dolgoch* stands at Tywyn Wharf in the late 1940s with a mixed train. Conspicuous by its absence is the brake van, that was out of service at this time, but obviously a busy train was expected as all four coaches are in use. At this time *Dolgoch* would have only recently returned from its overhaul at Atlas Foundry in Shrewsbury. (Photo: TR Collection)

Rails Along The Fathew

The Route Described

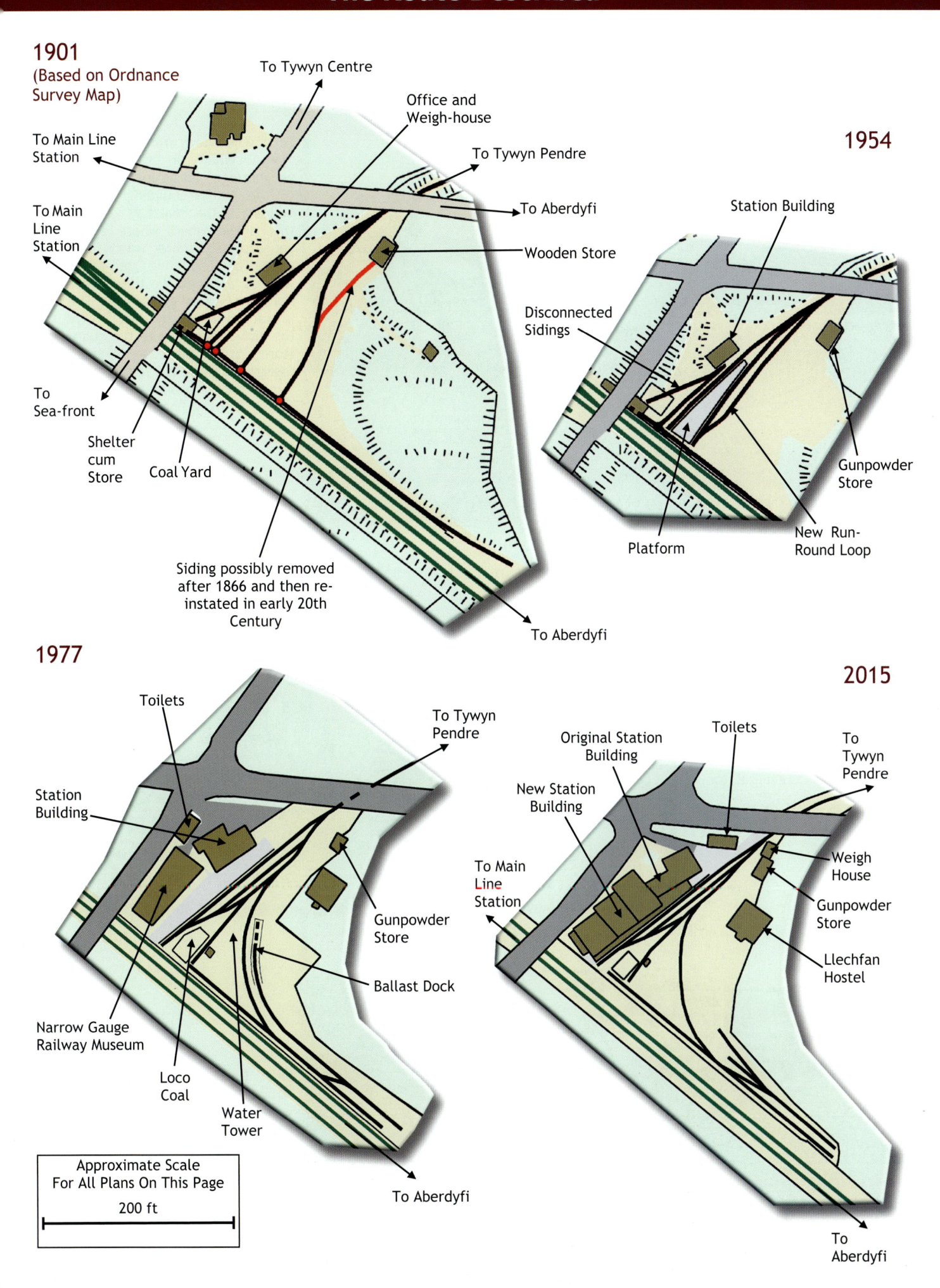

1901 (Based on Ordnance Survey Map)

- To Main Line Station
- To Tywyn Centre
- Office and Weigh-house
- To Tywyn Pendre
- To Aberdyfi
- To Main Line Station
- Wooden Store
- To Sea-front
- Shelter cum Store
- Coal Yard
- Siding possibly removed after 1866 and then re-instated in early 20th Century
- To Aberdyfi

1954

- Station Building
- Disconnected Sidings
- Gunpowder Store
- Platform
- New Run-Round Loop

1977

- Toilets
- To Tywyn Pendre
- Station Building
- Gunpowder Store
- Ballast Dock
- Narrow Gauge Railway Museum
- Loco Coal
- Water Tower
- To Aberdyfi

2015

- Original Station Building
- Toilets
- To Tywyn Pendre
- New Station Building
- To Main Line Station
- Weigh House
- Gunpowder Store
- Llechfan Hostel
- To Aberdyfi

Approximate Scale For All Plans On This Page 200 ft

Rails Along The Fathew

69

The Route Described

Viewed From The Bridge
The changing scene at Tywyn Wharf station as viewed from the Brynhyfryd Road bridge

Left: The view from the bridge at Tywyn Wharf in the 1920s. The weighbridge can be made out in front of the station building. Behind the building is the coal/hay yard. Beyond this is the wharf where a standard gauge private owner wagon belonging to the Tonfanau Stone Quarry stands, as well as a Great Western wagon and Northern Eastern one as well. The slate is stacked neatly by size. On the left the kick-back siding to the gunpowder store is still in place. Meanwhile in the foreground there is a fenced garden.
(Photo: Locomotive and General Railway Photographs Copyright NRM/SSPL)

Right: *Dolgoch* stands at Tywyn Wharf in 1950, during the last days of the Haydn Jones era, with a short train consisting of two Brown, Marshall carriages (the second is probably No.3), and the recently returned to service brake van. By now the line on the left had been disconnected, although the rails were still in place. The station has a general air of neglect.
(Photo: The Elliot Collection)

Left: On 21 September 1954 No.6 *Douglas* stands at Tywyn Wharf station with a train consisting of carriage No.10, two of the original Talyllyn coaches and the brake van. The place still has a slightly neglected feel, but the track layout has changed with a run-round loop having been laid in 1952, and a platform has been built. In the foreground is a point indicator which had recently been installed.
(Photo: J.H.L. Adams)

Rails Along The Fathew

The Route Described

Left: A busy scene at Tywyn Wharf on 25 August 1955. Talyllyn locomotives No. 3 *Sir Haydn* and No.4 *Edward Thomas* are in steam. The train consists of the original Talyllyn brake van, two opens and bogie coaches Nos. 9 and 10. Meanwhile the ex-Welsh Highland Railway locomotive *Russell* is being unloaded in front of the former gunpowder store. This locomotive would stay at the railway until April 1965. However, it was destined to return, now fully restored, as part of the Talyllyn's 150th Anniversary celebrations. (Photo: J.T. Fraser)

Right: Over the winter of 1964 to 1965 there were major alterations to the track layout, the station building and the Museum. Here the work on the track is nearing completion on 22 March 1965 while work on the extensions to the station building continues.
(Photo: David J. Mitchell)

Left: By 1983 there had been relatively little change externally from the mid-1960s as seen above, although the Museum extension was now complete as is the station canopy. The major change was going on in the distance as new housing gradually began to obscure the views of the sea.

Rails Along The Fathew

The Route Described

Left: By May 2001 the platform at Wharf had gained a somewhat cluttered appearance with the addition of a temporary building for the refreshment service at the far end of the platform. It was clear by this point that more suitable premises were required. By now too housing development had more or less completely obscured the sea view. The corner of the toilet block is in the right foreground.

Right: The solution adopted was the construction of a two-storey building housing the Museum, café and offices. By August 2004 construction of the new building was well under way.
(Photo: David J. Mitchell)

Left: A unique view from the bridge on the evening of Saturday 4 July 2015 with every Talyllyn steam locomotive in view, along with visiting locomotives *Russell* (on the left) and *Prince* (in front of the water tower). The latter two locomotives were running on temporary tracks as part of the 150th Party Gala. To the right of the water tower is No.7 *Tom Rolt* with No.3 *Sir Haydn* (which was not in steam) behind. Then on the centre road are No.4 *Edward Thomas* and No.6 *Douglas*. Finally at the head of the train are No.2 *Dolgoch* and No.1 *Talyllyn*. All six Talyllyn locomotives would be attached to the train to haul it up to Tywyn Pendre. It is interesting to compare this view of *Russell* to the one at the top of the previous page.

The Route Described

The View From Neptune Road Bridge

The other bridge at Tywyn Wharf station carries Neptune Road over the former A&WCR or Cambrian Coast line, but it also affords a view over the old slate wharf end of the station.

Left: Locomotive No.4 *Edward Thomas* arrives at Tywyn Wharf with a train from Abergynolwyn on 24 August 1955. The train consists of two original Talyllyn coaches, the Talyllyn and Corris Brake vans, the latter now painted in Talyllyn livery, and two opens. The use of part of the platform as a rail store is interesting. (Photo: J.T. Fraser)

Right: No.5 *Midlander* has brought the coaching stock into Tywyn Wharf ready for the next departure on 21 June 1964. (Photo: David J. Mitchell)

Left: The view from the Neptune Road Bridge in 2001, as No.3 *Sir Haydn* stands at the buffer stop. The 'temporary' refreshment room can be seen in the foreground, along with various other 'temporary' structures.

Right: The view on 30 May 2015 showing the wharf edge tracks as well as the main line, no longer with its adjacent siding, while No.7 *Tom Rolt* runs round its train.

Rails Along The Fathew

The Route Described

Left: *Dolgoch* waits to depart from Tywyn Wharf on 22 August 1949. (Photo: R.D. Butterell)

Right: Tucked in the corner of the station site by the Neptune Road overbridge and the wharf was a shelter used by the slate loaders. However, originally it was built as a back up goods store. (Photo: The Elliot Collection)

Left: No.2 *Dolgoch* at Tywyn Wharf station in 1952. The locomotive had been repainted by this time. (Photographer Unknown)

Right: During the rebuilding of the road overbridge over the winter of 1954/55, Wharf station was effectively cut off from the rest of the railway, as seen in this photo. In the foreground the weighbridge can be seen disconnected from the rest of the track layout. (Photo: TR Collection)

The Route Described

Left: A slightly different view of Tywyn Wharf on 12 September 1959. At this point the County Council had built the toilet block at the top of the drive. This was a case of better late than never, as the Towyn Council's Medical Officer had requested the company to provide urinals at its stations as far back as 1895. (Photo: J.H.L. Adams)

Right: Locomotives No.2 *Dolgoch* and No.4 *Edward Thomas* are replenished at a temporary water tower in August 1965. In the background the Museum extension is still being constructed while the station building still has its temporary awning. (Photo: David J. Mitchell)

Left: Again a different view of Tywyn Wharf station in 2001. In the background on the right is Edward Thomas' old house, the mock-Tudor *Trefri*, while in front of it is the bungalow, now hostel, *Llechfan*. On the wharf edge is the restored covered van and also the newly-built tool van No.29. This was constructed on an ex-MOD chassis.
(Photo: David J. Mitchell)

Right: Two rebuilds: The newly rebuilt diesel No.8 *Merseysider* stands on the curve at Tywyn Wharf on 9 July 2005, next to the ballast dock. Meanwhile the newly rebuilt station building is in the background.

Rails Along The Fathew

75

The Route Described

Left: The new passenger entrance at Wharf station.
(Photo: David J. Mitchell)

Right: The new toilet block as seen after refurbishment in May 2015.

Left: The new-build weighbridge house, with the red Corris mail wagon on the weighbridge, and the old gunpowder store in May 2015.

Right: The water tower was clad in slate and the tank given timber cladding to make a more 'heritage' setting. It is seen here with locomotive No.4, which has been especially 'dirtied' for a photographic charter in March 2010.

Rails Along The Fathew

The Route Described

Tywyn Pendre

Right: *Dolgoch* pauses at Pendre station with a down train in April 1949.
(Photo: The Elliot/Dan Quine Collection)

On departing from Tywyn Wharf the railway passes under the Brynhyfryd Road bridge. The condition of this bridge had given concern since 1952, and the County Council had temporarily reinforced it with some old tram rails that year. This was pending a complete rebuild in connection with a road widening scheme, which eventually occurred over the winter of 1954/55. The bridge then became almost a short tunnel.

The deposited plans show a gentle gradient between the sites of Wharf and Pendre stations. However, when the cutting was dug the gradient leaving Wharf was greatly increased to 1 in 60, probably to reduce the amount of excavation to be done. This then eased to 1 in 200 reaching a summit at the quarter mile post until falling at 1 in 236 to Pendre station.

A major relaying and re-grading project over the winter of 1978/79 eased the climb to 1 in 150 and 1 in 120. In the early days of the Society a signal was erected on the east side of the road bridge, but this was replaced with a Stop Board attached to a signal post in 1955.

In 1965 this was moved 100 yards further east along the cutting and in 1971 it was superseded by a full colour-light signal. It was near the repositioned signal post that the evidence of the gravity siding was discovered during the regrading of the late 1970s.

Just east of the signal a footbridge now crosses the line. Beyond the quarter mile post the line falls, passing under what is known as Ffordd Cadfan or School Bridge. This was named after the British School which had been built in 1860 on what later would be the south side of the line. Until 1955 this bridge carried the main road between Tywyn and Aberdyfi.

It was constructed like the bridge at Wharf with slate slabs resting on wrought-iron girders carried on brick piers, and its condition had also deteriorated. It was therefore also rebuilt as part of the widening of the Brynhyfryd Road bridge in late 1954, to allow it to carry the additional traffic generated when the Wharf bridge was closed. In 1973 the first of a pair of footbridges was added beside the main structure.

At the time the railway was built the cutting lay well outside the main town, and in fact became the southern boundary for the provision of a gas supply in Tywyn in the late 1860s. Up until the 1960s there was little housing along its length and it presented quite a rural scene. However, since then the surrounding land has been built on and the area has been urbanised.

After passing under School Bridge the line enters Pendre yard, still on a descending grade of around 1 in 270. Pendre or Pendref, to give the station its alternative name, literally means 'top of the town'. Today it seems

The Route Described

Left: View of the track up the cutting from Tywyn Wharf towards Pendre in 1951. (Photo: The Elliot Collection)

Below: No.1 *Talyllyn* about to pass under the road bridge at Tywyn Wharf on 9 June 1963. The old signal post fitted with a stop board is still in use in the background. (Photo: David J. Mitchell)

Rails Along The Fathew

The Route Described

Left: Looking west from School Bridge No.1 *Talyllyn* heads up from Tywyn Wharf on 11 April 1982. This shot and the one below give a good indication of the scale of the cutting, all of which was of course excavated by hand.
(Photo: David J. Mitchell)

Right: Looking east from School Bridge *Talyllyn* brings a train down to Tywyn Wharf from the loop at Pendre in the mid-1920s. The barn can be seen in the distance, demonstrating it was in-situ by this time.
(Photo: F.Frith postcard/John Alsop Collection)

Left: During the winter of 1978/79 the cutting between Wharf and Pendre was re-graded to ease the climb away from the terminus. Here the railway's excavator is digging out the trackbed, and loading the spoil into a rake of tipper wagons. These will be hauled away by diesel No.8 *Merseysider* for emptying. (Photo: J.N. Slater)

Rails Along The Fathew

The Route Described

Above: One of the earliest photos of Pendre station and shed known, dating from around 1894. Items of note include the gas lamp mounted on the station building, the 'pipe' chimney on the locomotive shed, and the lack of an ash siding. There was no water column until Society days; instead there was a water tank in the running shed just inside the doors. This constantly leaked, and doubtless encouraged the growth of the ivy on the outside wall. (Photo: H.S. Bristowe J.I.C. Boyd/TR Collection)

right on the edge of the conurbation, but in 1864 Tywyn only really existed in the close-knit area around St Cadfan's Church, and so Pendre was indeed the place that was nearest the heart of the settlement (see picture on page 9).

As stated previously, it is not unreasonable to suppose that this site could well have been the Tywyn base for the construction of the line. Certainly the railway ended up owning a sizeable plot of land here, and with road access and water from the nearby stream it would have been a suitable centre of operations.

The first mention of a structure in the area comes in a newspaper report of May 1865 where the railway is reported as taking a lease on the old malthouse 'at the top of Frankwell Street'. This was stated to be for the

purpose of establishing an enamel works and a show room. It also said that a siding would be laid down to convey the materials to the yard.

On the deposited plans, however, there is no structure drawn on the site, nor is there any mention of an old malthouse in the accompanying book of reference. One explanation could be that the building was a ruin by this time, which is why it was not included.

Whether this was what got rebuilt as the locomotive shed and workshop is a matter of speculation. Instead the next structure to be mentioned is in March 1866 when it is stated that the 'new station at the top of Frankwell Street ... is in the course of erection'. What the report does not say is whether this was the passenger station or the sheds or both.

The Route Described

Right: General view of Pendre in April 1949, from left to right there is the hay barn, the station building, the locomotive running shed and the wooden carriage shed. Behind is the workshop.
(Photo: The Elliot/Dan Quine Collection)

Originally a locomotive shed was situated at Tŷ Dŵr on the mineral extension above Abergynolwyn. This was replaced by the sheds at Pendre, which seemingly were not completed until early in 1867.

The buildings consisted of a two-road hipped-roof slate-built shed cum workshop. Adjoining this on the north side is a single road locomotive running shed which projects out from the western wall line of the two-road shed. At the eastern end of this combined structure was a cottage, originally occupied by William Boustead and his family, part of which used to occupy the eastern end of the running shed. Finally, there is a carriage shed extending from the north door of the two-road shed, originally constructed with half-open wooden sides and a slate roof. (See plan on page 88).

Examining the structure indicates that the two-road shed and running shed were built simultaneously. However, there are some indications that the small cottage at the east end was added when the building was under construction. In addition, there are signs that the running shed was extended westwards at the same time, while the carriage shed as a later addition.

A possible explanation for the additions to the living accommodation at the eastern end was to provide extra rooms for the Bousteads, who were to occupy the cottage. It has also been suggested that the running shed was extended to accommodate two locomotives. Meanwhile, it is likely that the carriage shed was added to allow the two-road shed to be used as a workshop.

The actual station was completed before Tyler's inspection. Originally there was no platform, and the building was a timber structure with a slate roof. It consisted of a shelter open to the platform with a booking office cum store at one end. An interesting question is why the building was not fabricated from slate slab as the line was open for slate traffic by the time it was being built, was this a matter of cost? Another unanswered question is when the platform was added.

The basic track layout in 1901 is shown on page 88. This was to remain largely unaltered until the dawn of the preservation era in 1951. One subsequent addition was the construction of a barn on the north side of the line during the Haydn Jones era. A coaling/ash road was also added by the locomotive shed doors after 1908.

In the early years of the 20th Century there was a dispute over the water supply at Pendre for the tank in the locomotive shed. This had originally been fed from the nearby stream. However, in July 1895 the first water supply was piped to this part of the town and the cottage was supplied with running water.

The railway also made a connection for water to supply the tank. This the railway believed it had done legitimately, but there was no written agreement. In

Right: *Dolgoch* outside the running shed in 1951. The slate wagons are being used for loco coal.
(Photo: The Elliot Collection)

Rails Along The Fathew

The Route Described

1900 it was reported to the Local Council that this had been taking place, and the Council resolved to reclaim the money owed and to make an annual charge.

After much debate the matter was finally settled in 1901 with a charge of £18 0s 7d being made for the unpaid water, and agreement for a meter to be installed at a cost of 10s per annum for five years. It is said that Sir Haydn later got the water supplied free of charge in exchange for allowing a new water pipe to cross the line near Rhydyronen.

The Preservation Era

One of the first actions of the Preservation Society was the renewal of the track between Wharf and Pendre. This included the loop and shed road points, which were refurbished using ex-Welsh Highland Railway materials during the winter of 1951/52. At this time all the points were still individually hand operated. A new water tower was also constructed outside the shed and the ash siding removed.

An ex-LNWR eight-lever frame from Islip was installed to control the points at the west end of the yard in 1958, the ones at the east end still remaining individually controlled. In 1954 some primitive disc point indicators had been erected, but quickly removed again. In 1959 disc point indicators were again installed, this time to the satisfaction of the Inspector.

In 1957 work began on a new carriage shed on the north side of the line west of the station. This was constructed using secondhand roof trusses obtained from a site near Aberdyfi and covered with asbestos sheeting. The new shed was brought into use in 1960.

The old carriage shed was rebuilt between 1960 and 1962. In the latter year a new ablutions block was also completed behind the station. No sooner had the new, now 'North', Carriage Shed been completed than it required lengthening to accommodate the railway's growing carriage fleet. Therefore, a 45 ft extension was completed in 1963.

Above: Another early colour photo of Pendre station looking east in 1951, showing the original station building. On the left in the undergrowth is the body from a gunpowder wagon, while one the shed doors has been replaced with some corrugated iron.
(Photo: The Elliot Collection)

The Route Described

Left: In 1908 *Pretoria* (as *Dolgoch* had been renamed at that point) enters Pendre yard with a mixed train. On the rear are eleven wagons, and the driver is John Rowlands. Standing on the right is R.B. Yates, the General Manager at the time, and on the extreme right is the gunpowder wagon. It is worth noting that the ash siding is still not in place at this time.
(Photo: G.M. Perkins)

Right: Looking west towards Wharf in 1950, certainly a contrast with the photo above.
(Photo: The Elliot Collection)

Left: Early in 1952 *Dolgoch* again heads up through Pendre yard with a short passenger train. By this time the points had been renewed. On the right locomotive No.1 has been moved out of the workshop and is now stored under a tarpaulin on the siding leading to the barn. (Photo: Rod Holcombe)

Rails Along The Fathew

The Route Described

Up until this point Pendre still had a very rural feel, but in 1965 work started on a housing estate on the south side of Pendre yard. Meanwhile on the land to the north of the North Carriage Shed a concrete sectional building was erected. This was to provide extra office and storage accommodation.

In 1966 Herbert Jones and his wife moved out of the cottage at Pendre. The wall between the shed and the cottage was demolished in 1968, to allow the shed to be extended into the former residence. There was a period when locomotives were run into this part of the shed with the wallpaper still on the walls.

Outside there were some changes to the track layout. The ash siding was reinstated in 1967. Then in 1969, as part of the preparations for the three-train-set service, the loop was restored to its pre-preservation 210 ft length so it could be used as a crossing loop. A two-lever frame was also installed to control the east end loop points.

The means of controlling trains on the section between Wharf and Pendre also changed. Divisible Train Staffs were superseded by Miniature Electric Train Staffs (METS) in 1966, and then by Electric Key Tokens (EKT) in 1973. Meanwhile EKT working was introduced between Pendre and Brynglas in 1971. In each case the machines were installed in the locomotive shed. As the west-end points were still controlled from the frame at the other end of the yard, this led to the need for the blockman to be fleet of foot when crossing trains.

This changed when work started on the new West Carriage Shed in 1971. In order to make room for the new shed considerable excavation had to take place, with the spoil again being tipped at Fach Goch. Part of the new facilities was to be a purpose-built block post, which was to be fitted with an ex-LMS 15-lever frame. By December 1973 the paint shop and the first 50 ft of carriage storage in the West Shed were available for use. The new block post was also being completed.

With efforts now being concentrated on the Extension, work on new developments at Pendre ceased. The exception was the acquisition in 1975 of the old slaughterhouse at the north-eastern corner of the site.

Later, after the Extension was open, work resumed on other projects including lengthening the West Carriage Shed by another 30 ft, which was brought into use in 1978. In 1981 the station building underwent a major restoration.

The carriage storage section of West Shed was finally completed in 1982, and a paint store added at the eastern end in 1985. The previous year a portable office was placed next to the North Shed, later replaced by the former General Manager's office from Wharf in 1992. An annexe was also provided to the North Shed in 1986.

During the 1990s there were some discussions with the Railway Inspectorate about the provision of colour-light signalling, with plans being prepared for submission. A dummy signal was even mounted on the north wall of the locomotive shed, which remained in place for some time until the plan was abandoned.

Since then little structural change has taken place to the main buildings. One incident in 2008 led to the need to rebuild the block post. This was when an attempt to 'bump start' diesel locomotive No.9 led to considerable damage to the building and severe damage to the Permanent Way trolley. Since then a substantial new buffer stop has been added to the headshunt.

Above and Right: Two lesser photographed sides of the buildings at Pendre, relatively little altered from their original condition. The front of the old cottage can be seen above, still with Herbert Jones and his family in residence. The porch is obviously a later addition as is the television aerial. To the right the south side of the original shed cum workshop can be seen. Both photographs were taken in 1964.
(Photos: David J. Mitchell)

The Route Described

Left: Pendre station building in 1950. This view shows to construction of the original building, and its dilapidated condition at the end of the Haydn Jones era.
(Photo: The Elliot/Dan Quine Collection)

Right and Below: Two photos which show Pendre yard looking both east and west. The photo to the right looking east, taken in 1965, emphasises the very rural setting of Pendre until the mid-1960s. Locomotives No.2 *Dolgoch* and No.4 *Edward Thomas* are shunting. The North Shed is complete, and the water tower has acquired a square tank.
(Photo: David J. Mitchell)

Left: Looking west from the top of the water tower. Housing is beginning to encroach upon this scene in March 1968. Locomotive No.1 *Talyllyn* is on the left with locomotives No.4 *Edward Thomas* and No.2 *Dolgoch* behind on the main line. On the right is the upturned saddle tank from No.3 *Sir Haydn*, while in the middle-left background is the ground-frame and Bill Faulkner's greenhouse. The ash siding has been reinstated by this point.
(Photo: David J. Mitchell)

Rails Along The Fathew   85

The Route Described

Left: The yard and sheds at Pendre on 24 July 1955 with the station in the background. Locomotive No.6 *Douglas* is on the left, and No.3 *Sir Haydn* is on the right.
(Photo: J.T. Fraser)

Right: On 30 July 1955 locomotive No.4 *Edward Thomas* eases out of the loop with a mixed Permanent Way train for a working party from the London area. This consisted of carriage No.9 and van No.5 with an assortment of wagons behind. The pile of old sleepers on the right were the result of the re-sleepering programme then going on.
(Photo: Keith Stretch)

Left: On 27 July 1955 No.3 *Sir Haydn* stands on the main line beside the water column at Pendre.
(Photo: Keith Stretch)

Rails Along The Fathew

The Route Described

Right: *Talyllyn* slumbers at Pendre in 1947.
(Photo: F.R.Lawrence/ TR Collection)

Left: The sleeper awakes, a somewhat busier workshop, with No.1 *Talyllyn* now restored to service in the background.
(Photo: J.I.C. Boyd)

Right: Father and son team John (left) and Brian (right) Green at work on the final stages of the construction of carriage No.18 in the North Carriage Shed c. late 1964. (Photo: J.I.C. Boyd)

The Route Described

1901 (Based on Ordnance Survey Map)

Labels: Locomotive Shed, Station Building, To Rhydyronen, Workshop, Cottage, Carriage Shed, To Tywyn Wharf

1967

Labels: Ablutions Block, Station Building, To Rhydyronen, Pre-fabricated Building, North Carriage Shed, Extension, Former Cottage, Workshop, To Tywyn Wharf

Approximate Scale For All Plans On This Page — 200 ft

2015

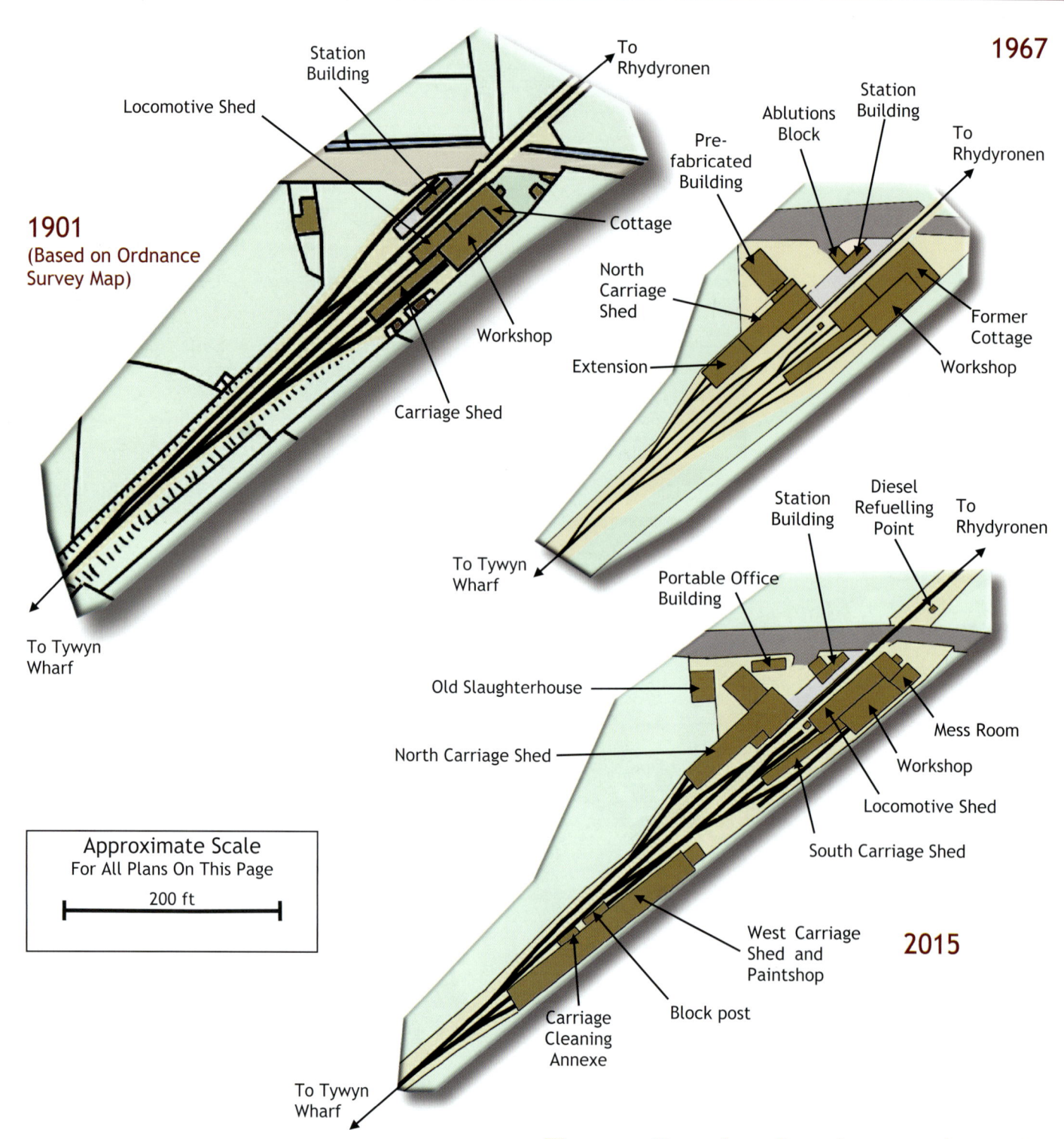

Labels: Station Building, Diesel Refuelling Point, To Rhydyronen, Portable Office Building, Old Slaughterhouse, North Carriage Shed, Mess Room, Workshop, Locomotive Shed, South Carriage Shed, West Carriage Shed and Paintshop, Block post, Carriage Cleaning Annexe, To Tywyn Wharf

Tywyn Pendre Station and Yard Through The Years

Left: Breaking ground for the foundations of the pre-fabricated concrete office and stores building on 6 August 1966. In the background work is being done on the ablutions block.
(Photo: David J. Mitchell)

88 — Rails Along The Fathew

The Route Described

The North Carriage Shed

Left: The last roof truss is put in place on the first phase of the new North Carriage Shed on 27 July 1958.
(Photo: Keith Stretch)

Right: The cladding being applied on 3 August 1959.
(Photo: Keith Stretch)

Left: The completed first phase of the North Carriage Shed, with No.6 *Douglas* at the water tower. (Photo: J.H.L. Adams)

Right: In 1968 the dividing wall between the running shed and the cottage was demolished. The running shed was then extended into this section, while the rest of the cottage was converted for other uses.
(Photo: TR Collection)

Rails Along The Fathew

The Route Described

The West Carriage Shed

Right: The West Carriage Shed under construction on 18 April 1973. (Photo: Keith Stretch)

Left: The block post in April 1974. (Photo: Keith Stretch)

Right: The completed shed in use on 5 September 1986. (Photo: David J. Mitchell)

Rails Along The Fathew

The Route Described

Between Pendre and Rhydyronen

Above: A scene that can now longer be viewed as modern industrial buildings now obscure this vista looking south across Parry's Bank between Pendre and Tŷ Mawr. Locomotive No.1 *Talyllyn* heads back to Tywyn with a down train in August 1979. The object to the right of the locomotive is the crane jib for the 10-RB excavator. (Photo: David J. Mitchell)

Leaving Pendre station the track continues on a falling gradient across the level crossing. When the railway opened the lane here was little more than a track allowing access to Tŷ Mawr and Caeau farms, but was still a public road.

In Captain Tyler's second inspection report he refers to some gates that had been put up near the line at Pendre which needed to be moved back. This possibly referred to some crossing gates although the report is not clear on this point, and in fact neither of his reports mention any road crossings at all. The crossing was provided with gates pre-preservation, being widened in 1959 and again 1984.

After passing over the road the railway then crossed a stream, which was culverted by the railway at the request of the Board of Health in the 1860s. On the south side of the line an electricity sub-station was opened in 1967. In the 1970s light industrial units were developed to the north, one of which was offered to the railway, but the economic situation, along with other issues, meant that the railway was unable to take up the offer.

Right: In *Railway Adventure* Tom Rolt speaks of Peter Williams acting as gate keeper at Pendre Crossing as he lived in the cottage attached to the sheds. Here he is attending to this duties.
(Photo: B. Wilke)

Tŷ Mawr

The line is now on a level stretch of embankment, known as Parry's (or Tŷ Mawr) Bank, formed from the spoil from Wharf cutting past the half-mile post. It now begins to climb and turn eastwards before coming to Tŷ Mawr bridge at the three-quarter mile point.

When the line was originally opened the railway crossed the parish road here on a level crossing, which had caused concern to the Board of Health. However, in October 1865 plans were prepared for a slate-built overbridge, which carried the road on slate slabs supported by cast iron 'T'

Rails Along The Fathew

The Route Described

section beams. This was in use by the time of Captain Tyler's inspection. In 1985 this had a weight restriction placed on it due to the weakness of the construction. The course of the original road can still be seen in the fence boundaries to the east of the bridge.

In 1969 the line of Tŷ Mawr Lane was proposed as the route of a Tywyn bypass, and the fields between Tŷ Mawr and Pendre on the south side were to be given wholly over to housing. Fortunately the rural outlook has been maintained, although industrial units now take up most of the north side of the line.

Above: With an increasing diesel fleet a refuelling point was established just east of Pendre crossing. Here No.8 Merseysider *is being refuelled by Dai Jones on 19 April 1973.* (Photo: Keith Stretch)

Left: Locomotive No.3 is observed approaching Tŷ Mawr bridge with an up train in 1973. The difference in the construction of this bridge, and the one at Rhydyronen, to the others on the line is fairly obvious; these are built of slate slab rather than stone and brick. (Photo: J.H.L. Adams)

Below: Just before Tŷ Mawr a tip was established for ash and material from the North Carriage Shed and its extensions. This was accessed via a 'sliding' siding seen here in spring 1966. (Photo: David J. Mitchell)

Rails Along The Fathew

The Route Described

Left and Below: Two photos taken from Tŷ Mawr bridge over sixty years apart.

Left: No.2 *Dolgoch* approaches the bridge with an empty ballast train from Tywyn at Easter 1952.
(Photo: J.I.C. Boyd)

Right: In 2015 No.4 *Edward Thomas* approaches Tŷ Mawr with the early morning Easter Monday market train on 6 April. The screen of trees on the right masks the collection of light industrial buildings that now occupy the previously open fields.

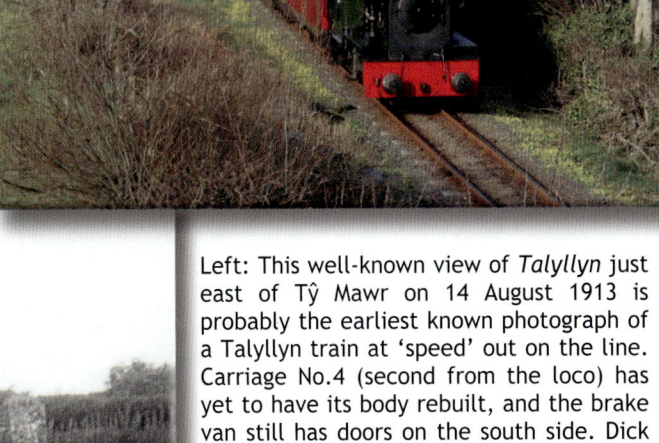

Left: This well-known view of *Talyllyn* just east of Tŷ Mawr on 14 August 1913 is probably the earliest known photograph of a Talyllyn train at 'speed' out on the line. Carriage No.4 (second from the loco) has yet to have its body rebuilt, and the brake van still has doors on the south side. Dick Price is the driver.
(Photo: Ken Nunn Collection Copyright NRM/SSPL)

Right: Tŷ Mawr bridge was a replacement for an earlier level crossing. Looking north over the east side of the bridge in April 2015, the course of the original road is indicated by the line of the hedge running down from the embankment on the right.

Rails Along The Fathew   93

The Route Described

Hendy

The line now goes through a set of reverse curves before resuming its north-easterly course, and the climb stiffens until Hendy Halt (74 chains from Wharf), which serves Hendy Farm, is reached. The line is now on the route of the original parish road, which was rebuilt to the north, but there is little evidence of it today. This was because it was officially rerouted through Hendy Farm to Tŷ Mawr Lane in 1880. Hendy Halt seems to have been a stopping point since the earliest days of the railway, but other than a stile, nothing marked the halt until Society days, nor did it feature in any official timetable. This was true for all the halts along the line.

After the halt the line continues to climb until it passes under Hendy bridge. This was to a different design again to the bridges at Tywyn and Tŷ Mawr, being of arched construction. To allow locomotive No.6 *Douglas* to pass under the bridge the track was lowered in 1953 by hand digging the trackbed and the use of thin sleepers. Subsequently it was lowered again in 1971 when the trackbed was cut into the underlying rock.

Left: Hendy Halt on 21 July 1954 looking towards Hendy bridge. The black and white painted metal poles carried the telephone line.   (Photo: J.H.L. Adams)

Below: On 11 September 1965 the County Show was held at Hendy Farm and a shuttle service was run to Hendy Halt from Tywyn Wharf. Here is the shuttle train 'topped and tailed' by No.2 *Dolgoch* at the front and No.1 *Talyllyn* at the rear with Corris carriage No.17 and van No.6 in between. A small temporary platform had been built at the halt for the occasion.   (Photo: David J. Mitchell)

Left: Hendy Halt as seen from Hendy bridge, as locomotive No.7 *Tom Rolt* slows to stop for passengers on 26 April 2011.

Right: When locomotive No.6 *Douglas* was acquired the track under Hendy bridge had to be lowered in order to allow it to pass safely under. A volunteer gang is hard at work on this project on Good Friday 3 April 1953.   (Photo: J.N. Slater)

94 Rails Along The Fathew

The Route Described

Fach Goch

The line turns northwards again past the one mile post, before easing north-east once more. To the south was the new line of the parish road, now hard to distinguish in the fields. The climb eases and there is a short level section before the track continues on a hedge lined embankment. Near milepost 1¼ there is the remains of a 'borrow' pit used to obtain material for the embankments of the line during its construction.

This was partly filled in the 1970s by spoil from both the new ballast dock at Wharf and the excavation for the West Carriage Shed. This was tipped from a siding brought into use in 1971 200 yards west of Fach Goch Halt just short of a mile and half from Tywyn.

Fach Goch Halt is situated on a northward curve in the track by an occupation crossing serving Fach Goch Farm, and has always been a humble affair. Across the the fields to the north can be seen the gatehouse to the Ynysmaengwyn estate home of the Corbets, when the railway opened, and later of John Corbett, the 'salt magnate' from Droitwich.

As already stated, in 1971 a siding was laid to tip spoil in the old borrow pit. This was known as 'Happy Valley Junction', and in 1979 an intermediate token machine was installed here. This was to allow spoil trains to operate in between passenger services. The siding remained in use until 1982.

From Fach Goch the line turns north before turning north-east again, and the grade stiffens to 1 in 77 up Cynfal bank. It was here that the ex-Glyn Valley Tramway rail was laid in the late 1930s, the only section of track to be fully relaid prior to preservation.

Left: Fach Goch Halt ostensibly served Fach Goch Farm on the south side of the line. In 1978 the halt possessed a nameboard and small platform, installed for an elderly lady passenger, which was removed when she ceased to travel. Near here for some years during the 1970s and 1980s there was a siding leading to a spoil tip.

Right: Photographs of passengers boarding at Fach Goch are rare, but they are seen doing so in this picture taken in 1953. Note the white coats then used by the guards.
(Photo: R.F.G. Overton/TR Collection)

Rails Along The Fathew

95

The Route Described

Cynfal

Cynfal Farm now lies to the south and beyond it are the ancient fortifications of Bryn-y-Castell. The replacement parish road can also be seen close to the line on the south side. Near the top of the bank the line passes over Cynfal stream, an artificial watercourse built to supply Ynysmaengwyn. This has been a continuous source of problems over the years, frequently flooding the line. The stream has been dug out on a number of occasions but the Welsh weather has won out every time.

The line now runs under Cynfal bridge, built to a similar design as Hendy, and comes to Cynfal Halt 1 mile 69 chains from Tywyn Wharf. The Roberts family from Cynfal Farm reputedly persuaded Haydn Jones to build the halt, although it was probably an unofficial stopping place before then. It was the only halt with a platform when the Preservation Society took over, and was rebuilt in 1979.

From Cynfal the line runs straight and briefly level as it approaches milepost 2. This section was considered as a potential site for a passing loop in 1968 as part of the plans for the Extension. The train is now approaching Rhydyronen on a gentle eastward curve, and the guard will signal the fireman if there are any passengers or goods for the station.

Above: Locomotive No.1 *Talyllyn* climbs Cynfal bank with a train for Nant Gwernol in 1999. The diverted parish road can be seen on the left.

Right: Locomotive No.3 *Sir Haydn* heads down towards Cynfal bridge and Tywyn with a loaded ballast train from Quarry Siding on 31 July 1955. (Photo: J.N. Slater)

Left: Cynfal Halt was the only halt with a platform when the Preservation Society took over. It was subsequently supplied with a nameboard. In 2014 the railway's General Manager, Chris Price, served a day here as stationmaster making it one of the smallest manned stations in world. It is seen here on 5 June 1953. (Photo: J.H.L. Adams)

96 — Rails Along The Fathew

The Route Described

Rhydyronen

Left: A rare pre-preservation colour photograph of Rhydyronen station taken in April 1949.
(Photo: The Elliot/ Dan Quine Collection)

Rhydyronen (Ash-ford) was the first intermediate station opened on the line after the commencement of passenger services, dating from February 1867. Initially it consisted of a slab-built building, to a similar design to the timber-built structure at Tywyn Pendre, and also a short loop. It served a small hamlet on a packhorse route to Happy Valley, as well as Tynllwyn Farm.

The railway was always keen to promote any aspect of the line which might generate extra passengers and so in a 1905 advertisement it stated that:

Near Rhydyronen Station (2 miles from Towyn) free trout fishing is obtainable. The most powerful Chalybeate Springs in the United Kingdom are also within easy reach.

Previously the virtues of these springs had been extolled in a letter to the *County Times* in March 1900 where the writer expressed the view that the:

Chalybeate springs, whose medicinal properties only need be advertised properly to bring scores to visit them. An enterprising gentleman could erect a suitable building here, and the Talyllyn Railway Company would surely co-operate by running convenient trains at popular prices.

In reality the springs were reputedly the outfall from an old mine, the health benefits of which were somewhat dubious to say the least.

Earlier the possible development of a slate quarry at Bronbiban in the valley above the hamlet might have had a significant effect on the station. Mr Newton Holder, who was in negotiation to lease it in 1895, proposed to build a branch line from the station to the quarry. It is reported that the route was staked out but nothing came of the scheme.

Originally there was a level crossing here, but as with Tŷ Mawr, this was altered to a slab-built bridge. Again like Tŷ Mawr this was built slightly to the west of the original course of the road.

In the March 1977 *Talyllyn News* a Dr Edward Hughes wrote how as a small boy of eight in 1896, living at Tynllwynhen Farm, he would come down to the station of an evening. He would then push an empty slate wagon out of the siding (sic) about 200 yards up the line and free-wheel back down again. This practice came to an end when a padlocked wooden beam was placed across the 'siding'.

During 1901 a dispute arose with the Local Council involving the alleged blocking of a right of way at the station. This was eventually resolved in 1905 when a suitable diversion to the route was agreed.

One delivery to the station during 1902 was several tons of stone from the Bryneglwys quarry. This was used in the construction of a road bridge over the Braich-y-Rhiw stream, or Nant Rhydyronen, to replace a ford.

The Route Described

By the time the Preservation Society took over the loop had been reduced to a siding with only the east end points remaining. The station does though have special significance as being the terminus for the first public passenger service ever operated by a preserved railway on 14 May 1951.

The loop was restored in 1956, but the west end points were removed again in 1971. During the 1970s the establishment of a caravan and camping park at Tynllwyn Farm led to a large increase in the number of passengers using the station. This led to a booking office being re-established at the station in 1971.

In order to allow passengers to safely board full length trains the platform needed to be extended. Therefore in August 1977 an overnight tracklaying session was held to re-align the track through the station. The siding was removed entirely and subsequently the platform extended.

The road bridge was strengthened in 1985 with steel plates and concrete now carrying the road bed instead of the previous slate slabs. In 1995 the station building was re-roofed.

Left: Herbert Jones is seen on the running board of *Dolgoch* at Rhydyronen on 18 April 1949. (Photo: J.I.C. Boyd)

Below: A short mixed train at Rhydyronen sometime between 1946 and April 1949. Hugh Jones is possibly again peering from the footplate. (Photo: R. Holcombe Family)

The Route Described

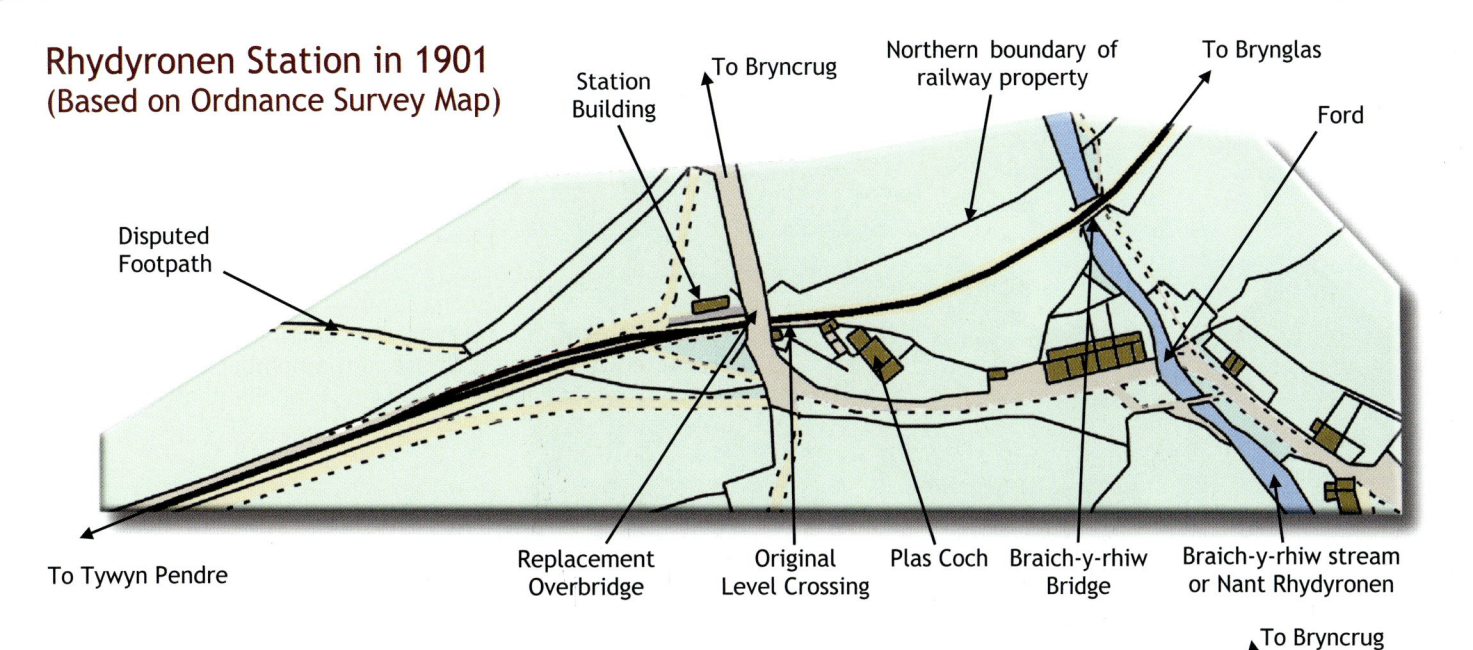

Rhydyronen Station in 1901
(Based on Ordnance Survey Map)

Map labels: Disputed Footpath; Station Building; To Bryncrug; Northern boundary of railway property; To Brynglas; Ford; To Tywyn Pendre; Replacement Overbridge; Original Level Crossing; Plas Coch; Braich-y-rhiw Bridge; Braich-y-rhiw stream or Nant Rhydyronen.

1972 map labels: To Bryncrug; Station Building; To Brynglas; Connection reinstated in 1956 but lifted again in 1971; To Pendre; To Rhydyronen.

Approximate Scale For Plans — 200 ft

2015 map labels: To Bryncrug; Station Building; Caravan Park; Extended Platform; To Brynglas; To Pendre; To Rhydyronen.

Above: In the early 1950s Peter Severn-Lamb supplied a number of cast-iron signs for the railway. One of these was erected at Rhydyronen. In April 2015 it was being 'consumed' by the tree to which it was attached.

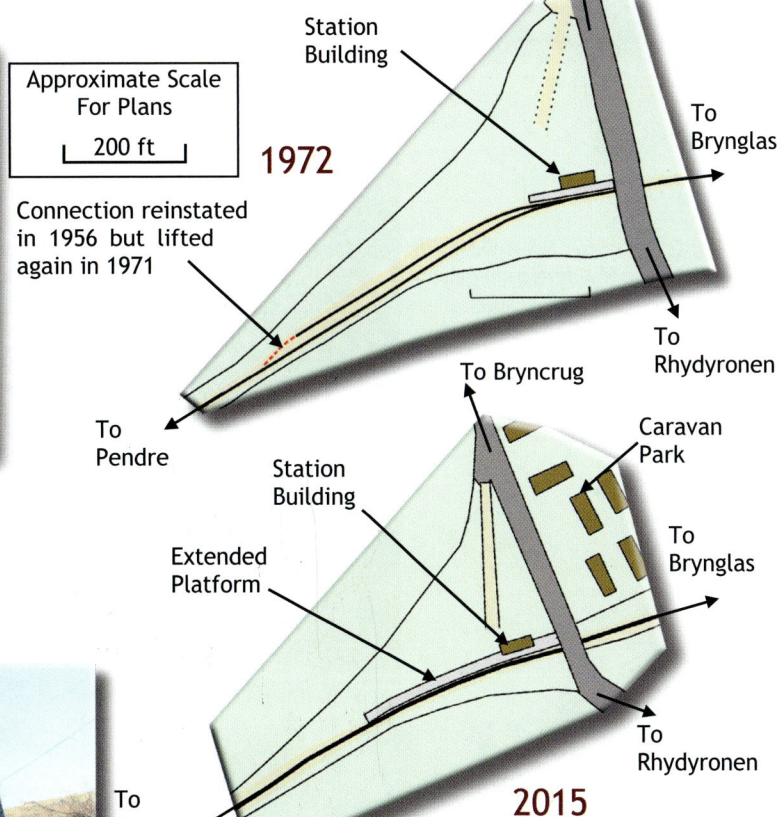

Above: A view of the platform side of the station building in April 2015.

Right: The western side of the road overbridge showing some of the details of the construction.

Rails Along The Fathew

99

The Route Described

Left: *Talyllyn* stands at Rhydyronen in 1941 with a short mixed train. The Second World War seems a million miles away, except that the London blitz had caused a surge in demand for slate and hence the loaded slate wagons at the rear of the train.
(Photo: W.A. Camwell)

Right: In 1952 No.2 *Dolgoch* heads into Rhydyronen with an up train.
(Photo: R. Holcombe Family)

Left: No.4 *Edward Thomas* arrives at Rhydyronen with an up train in the early 1960s, when it was fitted with a *Giesl* ejector.
(Photo: TR Collection)

100 Rails Along The Fathew

The Route Described

Left: In July 1984 No.3 *Sir Haydn*, then painted red and running with its chimney facing west, enters Rhydyronen station with a train from Nant Gwernol. Many will recognise the guard as John Cox and the driver as Viv Thorpe.

Left and Right: Views of the changes at Rhydyronen in the late 1970s. The photo on the left was taken on the morning after an overnight tracklaying session when the track through Rhydyronen was realigned along the course of the former loop/siding in August 1977.
The photo on the right was taken after the platform had been extended.

Right: When it returned to service with its new boiler in 1995 No.6 *Douglas* was repainted briefly in a camouflage livery. It is seen here on 26 May 1995 at Rhydyronen where there was a re-enactment of an army encampment. At the same time Rhydyronen station was having its roof renewed.
(Photo: David J. Mitchell)

Rails Along The Fathew

The Route Described

Left: No.4 *Edward Thomas*, which had been turned round and cosmetically weathered for a set of photographic charters, pauses at Rhydyronen with a short goods train on 16 March 2010.

Right: On 17 October 2011 No.2 *Dolgoch* is in charge of a special train, *The Rolt Explorer*. This looked at the history of the railway as part of celebrations of the 60th anniversary of its preservation.

Left: Previous to this the Diamond Jubilee celebrations had begun with a re-enactment of the first preservation train to Rhydyronen. One of the guests was John Snell the original fireman in 1951. He is seen here once more on *Dolgoch* at Rhydyronen on 14 May 2011, sixty years after the first train.

The Route Described

From Rhydyronen to Brynglas

Above: After leaving Rhydyronen station No.4 *Edward Thomas* passes *Plas Goch* cottage on 16 May 2015. The southern deviation the railway took here is clear as the northern boundary of its property is off to the right of the picture. (Photo: D. Turner)

When entering Rhydyronen station the track curves sharply south-eastward, continuing under the bridge before the curve reverses sharply and the line heads north-east again before crossing the Braich-y-rhiw bridge all on a gradient of 1 in 91. Quite why it does this is not entirely clear. If the line followed the original northern boundary of the railway's land (see plan top of page 99) then it would be much straighter, so why the deviation?

Much discussion has taken place about the route of the line at Rhydyronen. The received wisdom is that it does so to be further from Tynllwyn Farm. Certainly this was one of the parcels of land said not to be occupied by the tramroad in November 1864, when the deposited plans were submitted. However, the plans indicate that the southerly route was the preferred option, so this could indicate there was an agreement with the landowner.

An alterative suggestion has been that the southerly route was chosen because of some engineering issue(s) with the original course. However, there is no clear reason why this would have been necessary.

What is certain is that it brought the line much closer to hamlet and the cottage *Plas Coch*. This was possibly first acquired by the company to provide accommodation for a keeper for the level crossing, but when a bridge was substituted it was retained as accommodation for one of their platelayers.

When Colonel McMullen made his first inspection of the preserved line in 1952, one of his major concerns was the state of the bridge over the Braich-y-rhiw stream. This needed immediate repairs.

From the bridge the line falls until easing to almost level. It was on this section that returning picnic parties, free-wheeling down the line in the evening in hired slate wagons, usually had to get out and push. The line now turns east-north-east and passes the halt at Tynllwyn-hen, nearly two and a half miles from Tywyn.

Like the halts at Hendy and Fach Goch, this was not advertised until after the Society took over. It then acquired a nameboard, but had been a recognised stopping point for many years previously. It serves Tynllwynhen Farm and associated cottages.

Now the climb has resumed and the Bryn Erwest Bank is encountered at a gradient of around 1 in 179. This continues to milepost 3, where to the north can be seen the Afon Fathew stream. Now the vista of the Fathew (or Mathew) valley opens up and on a good day Cadair Idris can be glimpsed over the hills. There is now a series of reverse curves until the line reaches what is now Brynglas passing loop, and then crosses the road on the level before entering Brynglas station at 124 ft above sea level.

Right: The course of the old road, which was replaced by the bridge as seen in April 2015. *Plas Coch* is on the right.

Rails Along The Fathew

103

The Route Described

Left: No.2 *Dolgoch* departs from Rhydyronen on the climb to Abergynolwyn c. 1937 with either Hugh (Old) Jones or Peter Williams at the regulator. In earlier years it had been believed that the gradient here was as steep as 1 in 40, but in fact it was nearer 1 in 91.
(Photo: Locomotive and General Railway Photographs Copyright NRM/SSPL)

Below: Originally Tynllwyn-hen Halt was named Tyn-y-llwyn as seen here in this photo taken on 21 July 1954. Later the term 'hen' meaning 'old' was added, and the 'y' lost.
(Photo: J.H.L. Adams)

Left: Looking east: a potential passenger waits at Tynllwyn-hen halt on 29 August 1957.
(Photo: Keith Stretch)

Rails Along The Fathew

The Route Described

Above: One of the joys of the Fathew (or Mathew) Valley is to see it in different lights and at different seasons. In this photograph the lighter tones and bare trees of March that can be seen as No.2 *Dolgoch* approaches Brynglas with a heritage goods train on a photographic special in March 2008. The scene is not much altered from when the railway first opened. (Photo: David J. Mitchell)

Above: Now it is the deep greens of September as No.6 *Douglas* heads up Brynglas bank in 1968 with the first train of the day, including the Abergynolwyn Tea Van and bogie carriage No.18. Cadair Idris is in the distance. (Photo: J.H.L. Adams)

Rails Along The Fathew

The Route Described

Brynglas

Above Left and Right: Two pre-preservation views of Brynglas in 1949. On the left looking east from the road crossing the platform and station building can be seen, while in the foreground is the old underbridge cum cattle creep. Meanwhile on the right is the view looking west from the same spot showing the siding disappearing into the grass. (Photos: The Elliot Collection)

Brynglas station was built to serve the hamlet of Pandy on the south side of the line, the station name actually coming from the nearby Brynglas Farm, meaning 'Blue (or Green) Hill'. Into the 1940s Pandy had active fulling and weaving mills, while down the lane to the north was the Dolaugwyn flour mill. This was the last of the intermediate stations to be opened before preservation, first appearing in *Bradshaw's Guide* in July 1872.

Before the station opened there were other issues. When McConnel wrote to the Board of Trade in July 1866, he requested permission for a bridge to be replaced by a crossing, because of objections from the landowners and tenants. The response was that the Board had no power; "to authorise the substitution of a level crossing for a bridge to carry the railway over or under a public carriage or turnpike road".

This raises the question then comes as to where such a substitution might have been requested. At Tŷ Mawr and Rhydyronen clearly the pressure had been in the other direction, with bridges being substituted for crossings. Where could a crossing have been requested instead of a bridge?

The only likely location is Brynglas. Today the railway crosses the road on the level, but to the east of the crossing is a low underbridge, now largely filled in, but originally it had only about 6 ft headroom. If this was the bridge that was requested to be changed, it seems unlikely in the light of the Board of Trade's response that it was done before Tyler's inspection.

This raises the question of whether the crossing was ever officially sanctioned. However, Colonel McMullen during his inspection in 1952 did require the local authority to erect appropriate stop signs there.

One thing that is certain is that the track was moved to the south-east at some point. This was possibly due to the underbridges needing replacing, but it also allowed the station to be built. New bridges were constructed parallel to the original underbridge, as well as the bridge over the stream, and the track slewed over. Then the station was erected on the original trackbed, although whether this was all done at the same time is unknown.

The design of the station was different as well. Originally it appears to have been simply a semi-open shelter smaller than the other station buildings. However, subsequently the western end of the building was enclosed to form a store cum Permanent Way hut, complete with a fireplace.

In addition, a siding was in-situ by 1888 on the western side of the crossing, presumably for the wool and flour mill traffic. This was to remain until the Preservation Society took over.

Preservation

As already stated on page 44 in 1953 Brynglas became one of the bases for the Territorial Army's re-laying exercise, and the siding was made into a 'temporary' loop, which was extended in 1954. The loop was at first unauthorised, but permission was given for it retrospectively, along with two new train staff sections, Pendre to Brynglas and Brynglas to Abergynolwyn.

The Route Described

Above: The old mill buildings at Pandy as seen from the railway bridge over the stream. (Commercial Postcard)

Between 1960 and 1962 the loop was extended and re-laid with a four-lever frame installed for point operation. On 28 July 1966 there was a derailment at the east end of the loop when a point was changed under a moving train. Fortunately there were no serious injuries or damage.

A replacement five-lever frame was installed in 1967 which is still in use. Up until this point the frame was out in the open on the west side of the road crossing, with the unfortunate blockman having to seek shelter in the station building during inclement weather. Relief arrived in 1968 in the form of a hut constructed from timber salvaged from the old cottage at Pendre.

Early in 1970 there was correspondence with the Ministry about the possibility of erecting manually operated barriers at the road crossing during the high summer season. The Inspector felt this was unnecessary as the road traffic was light, but that further stop signs might be in order. Somewhat ironically, that summer there was a collision with a car at the crossing, but this did not change the Inspector's opinion.

In 1971 the Electric Key Token system was extended to Brynglas and to accommodate the block instruments an enlarged cabin was supplied. A siding was added on the south side of the loop in 1975, and extended in 1977.

There had also been additional traffic across the occupation crossing east of the station in the summer months. This led to an indicator disc being mounted on the south-side gate in 1987 to warn locomotive crews if it was fastened. In 1990 there were even discussions about signals at the station, but these were not pursued.

On 10 June 1993 heavy rain caused a deluge of floodwater down the Afon Cwmpandy. This swept down mud and debris causing extensive damage to the trackbed at Brynglas. Train services were restored fairly quickly, but the loop was unable to be used for crossings until 28 June. One remarkable survivor of the event was the local farm cat, which was rescued from the blockpost where it had hidden to escape the onslaught. Aside from being hungry it was remarkably unhurt.

Over the years a number of volunteers had had their ashes scattered on the railway after their death. It was decided that this needed to be regularised and a suitable place of remembrance provided. Therefore, a memorial garden was established opposite the station platform in 1998.

There was another collision at the crossing on 1 February 2006 between the Permanent Way trolley and a Post Office van. More recently the station building was re-roofed in 2007, and in 2009 the front of the blockpost was modified to give train crews a better view of cars at the road crossing, and vice versa.

The Route Described

Above: In 1941 *Talyllyn* stands at Brynglas station with a short up train. (Photo: W.A. Camwell)

Above: A rare view from about 1948 of local traffic at Brynglas before the Preservation Society took over. (Photo: R. Holcombe family)

The Route Described

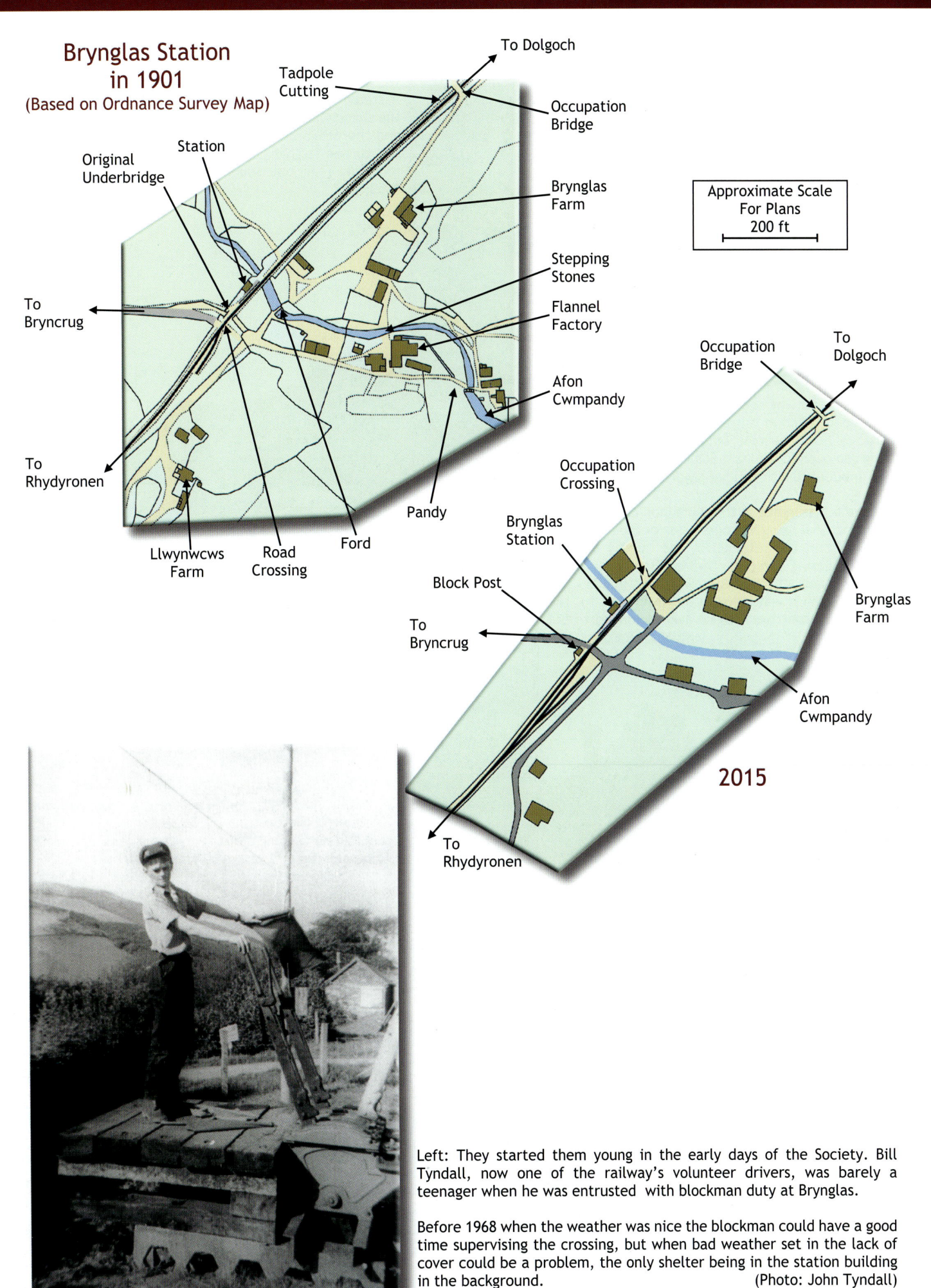

Brynglas Station in 1901
(Based on Ordnance Survey Map)

Map labels: To Dolgoch, Tadpole Cutting, Occupation Bridge, Station, Original Underbridge, Brynglas Farm, Stepping Stones, Flannel Factory, To Bryncrug, Afon Cwmpandy, To Rhydyronen, Llwynwcws Farm, Road Crossing, Ford, Pandy

Approximate Scale For Plans 200 ft

2015

Map labels: Occupation Bridge, To Dolgoch, Occupation Crossing, Brynglas Station, Block Post, To Bryncrug, Brynglas Farm, Afon Cwmpandy, To Rhydyronen

Left: They started them young in the early days of the Society. Bill Tyndall, now one of the railway's volunteer drivers, was barely a teenager when he was entrusted with blockman duty at Brynglas.

Before 1968 when the weather was nice the blockman could have a good time supervising the crossing, but when bad weather set in the lack of cover could be a problem, the only shelter being in the station building in the background. (Photo: John Tyndall)

Rails Along The Fathew

109

The Route Described

Left: A rare view of No.3 *Sir Haydn* on the line in 1951. Due to the problems with the track gauge and No.3's wheel treads, the locomotive was rarely photographed in steam during 1951. It is seen here at Brynglas, next to the siding with a train consisting of one original carriage and the brake van, probably for a working party. No.3 was turned so that its chimney faced down the line the following year, but it did not enter regular service until 1953. (Photo: TR Collection)

Right: The railway seems to have acquired a 'new' semi-open coach in this photograph, as the door on carriage No.3, nearest *Dolgoch*, is missing having been removed for repairs. Something that would not pass modern Health and Safety procedures.

The train is standing in the short loop created when the Territorial Army had possession of the line to the east of here, but retained by the railway to cope with increasing levels of traffic. This photo dates from not long after the loop was built in 1953 and the blockman is waiting with the train staff for the down train to arrive. The caravan belonged to Bill Faulkner. (Photo: TR Collection)

Left: Here a crossing is taking place and the train staff is being passed to Bill Faulkner on No.4 *Edward Thomas* on the up train on 24 September 1955. No.4 still had no running plate at this time, and also seems to be painted in a very dark shade of green. (Photo: J.H.L. Adams)

Right: In 1968 the blockman was provided with some shelter in the form of a small wooden hut. This was replaced by a larger building to accommodate the Electric Key Token instruments in 1971. No.3 *Sir Haydn* is entering the loop with a down train in around 1970. (Photographer Unknown)

Rails Along The Fathew

The Route Described

Left: On 10 June 1993 heavy rain caused a flash flood at Brynglas, bringing down mud and debris from the hills above. As can be seen from this photograph taken on the following day, the tracks were completely covered and it required a large amount of work to get trains running again.
(Photo: David J. Mitchell)

Right: Locomotive No.4 *Edward Thomas* stands on the main line with a 'Driver Experience' train on 3 June 2006 waiting for the down train to pass it on the loop on the left. Such trains are increasingly popular with locomotive No.4 often being employed for these duties, because of its suitability for inexperienced drivers.

Left: On 15 March 2015 the repainted locomotives No.1 *Talyllyn* and No.2 *Dolgoch* meet at Brynglas, with *Talyllyn* on a photographic charter.
(Photo: David J. Mitchell)

Rails Along The Fathew

111

The Route Described

Left: The 'filling-in' of the left-hand side of the building at Brynglas can be clearly seen in this photograph. In addition a blocked-up window can just be made out on the left-hand side in this view taken in February 2015.

Right: The interior of the waiting area at Brynglas, the room seems to have been used as a store cum Permanent Way hut rather than a booking office.

Left: Replacing the brick arch on the original bridge across the stream at Brynglas. This would have carried the original track alignment. (Photo: TR Collection)

Right: The remains of the underbridge at Brynglas in February 2015 now nearly completely filled-in, but obviously of limited headroom when first built. The process of infill was aided by the flood of 1993, when a considerable amount of material was washed into it.

Rails Along The Fathew

The Route Described

From Brynglas to Dolgoch

Above: Locomotive No.2 *Dolgoch* departs from Brynglas towards Dolgoch with an engineering train on 2 May 1981. The building in the foreground has been replaced since this photo. The occupation crossing is just in front of the locomotive.

(Photo: David J. Mitchell)

On leaving Brynglas the line continues to climb and enters what is known as 'Tadpole Cutting'. This takes the train under the last overbridge on the up journey, which is an occupation bridge built to the same basic design as Hendy and Cynfal. Tadpole Cutting, as the name implies, has been subject to flooding down the years, but changes to the drainage have improved the situation more recently.

Now the line is climbing up Brynglas bank, crossing another cattle creep before milepost 3½. The current mileposts were put in by the Society in 1952/53. This one of the most isolated sections of the line, running now on a ledge dug into the hillside, on the opposite side of the valley to the road.

There now follows a series of curves collectively known as 'Six Bends', taken on a continuous climb, followed by Doldeheuwydd bank. This is named after the farm which can be seen on the north side of the valley.

The train has now passed milepost 4, and is approaching the four and quarter mile mark. Near here, now buried in the undergrowth on the south side of the line, is the remains of a Permanent Way hut. Another quarter of a mile further on and the train enters Dolgoch woods on a series of curves.

Near milepost 4¾ the railway is on a 20 ft high embankment over a culvert. This was where the major landslip occurred in November 1957 when a 50 ft length of the bank was damaged. It took until 1960 for it to be fully repaired.

Moving on, the line goes through a reverse curve before reaching the major engineering structure on the line, the 51 ft high Dolgoch viaduct. The viaduct itself has three arches faced in brick and stone. It is likely that when the line was built, the viaduct was constructed in isolation from the other works on the line due the large amount of work required.

In 1952/53 the spandrel walls were repaired by the army, but by 1968 it was clear more radical work was needed. Tie rods were fitted to stabilise the structure, and across the winter of 1969/70 contractors removed the spandrel walls down to the arches and rebuilt them. On leaving the viaduct the train enters a rock cutting on a sharp six chain curve and into Dolgoch station at 187 ft above sea level.

Rails Along The Fathew

The Route Described

Two views taken in Tadpole Cutting with a 64-year gap.

Left: The cutting and occupation bridge in 1951 looking west, with evidence of the drainage issues and also the state of the track. (Photo: Martin Fuller collection)

Below: In February 2015 looking east the drainage has improved, but the area is still not completely dry.

Left: Near milepost 4 No.5 *Midlander* hauls a Permanent Way train to Quarry Siding. (Photo: J.N. Slater)

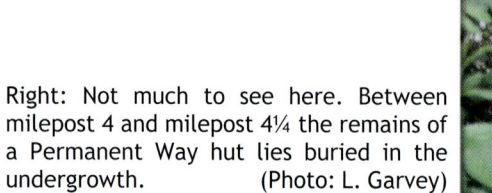

Right: Not much to see here. Between milepost 4 and milepost 4¼ the remains of a Permanent Way hut lies buried in the undergrowth. (Photo: L. Garvey)

114   Rails Along The Fathew

The Route Described

Right: Further up the line on Six Bends the repainted No.1 *Talyllyn* is seen with a mixed photographic charter train on 18 March 2015.
(Photo: David J. Mitchell)

Below: In November 1957 a major landslip occurred near Dolgoch, this left the track on the edge of a virtually sheer drop. (Photo: J.L.H. Bate)

Right: A large retaining wall was constructed at the foot of the embankment. (Photo: J.N. Slater)

Bottom Right: Large quantities of shale from Quarry Siding were then brought in as infill. (Photo: Keith Stretch)

Rails Along The Fathew

The Route Described

Above: A view of *Talyllyn* on Dolgoch viaduct from around 1900. (Commercial Postcard)

Right: From around the same period comes this view of *Dolgoch* with a train on the viaduct. (Commercial Postcard)

Above: *Dolgoch* crosses the viaduct in 1941. (Photo: W.A. Camwell)

Above: In 1968 it was discovered that the spandrel walls of the viaduct needed major work. As an interim measure tie rods were installed (above), before contractors were used to rebuild the walls over the winter of 1969/70. (Photo: David J. Mitchell)

The Route Described

Right: During May 1965 Terence Cuneo came to do some sketches from which he produced a painting of No.2 *Dolgoch* on the viaduct. He is seen here at work.
(Photo: J.H.L. Adams)

Left: In dappled sunlight No.1 *Talyllyn* crosses the viaduct with an up train in July 2001.

Right: In summer it is now difficult to photograph trains on the viaduct due to the amount of vegetation. Therefore shots like this from the ravine floor are only possible in the spring when the green is beginning to return to the trees. This photograph was taken on 12 March 2014 when No.6 *Douglas* had been temporarily repainted into its original livery for the Airservice Construction Corps.
(Photo: David J. Mitchell)

Rails Along The Fathew

The Route Described

Dolgoch

Above: *Dolgoch* arrives at Dolgoch in April 1949. (Photo: The Elliot/Dan Quine collection)

Dolgoch station, whose name means Red Meadow, first appeared in the timetable introduced on 1 August 1867. It was also included in *Bradshaw's Guide*, but for some reason the station then disappears from *Bradshaw* in October 1867 to reappear with Brynglas in July 1872.

The building itself is nearly identical to the one at Rhydyronen, and the station served a nearby farmstead. It seems that the station was opened with a clear eye to tourism. The poster of August 1867 states that:

The waterfall and railway bridge at Dolgoch are to be seen to advantage, and are objects of romantic beauty which require the Painter or the Poet's touch to vividly portray.

How far passengers could access the ravine at this time is uncertain.

There had been attempts to quarry slate in the ravine previously, but in the mid-1870s a serious attempt was made to develop a slate quarry in the ravine near the lower falls. A report in the *Aberystwyth Observer* on 22 January 1876 stated that:

A tunnel, a considerable number of yards long has been driven alongside to the smaller vein and the further the work progresses the better the quality of the slate is shown to be.

Certainly quarrying continued in the ravine until 1880. There was a suggestion that there were plans for a branch from the line at milepost 5 to the workings, but no firm evidence has been found to support this.

In 1902 the ravine was opened to the local community as advised in the *County Times* of 22 May that year:

With great gratification we announce a most munificent gift to the town. This is nothing less than the handing over of Dolgoch Waterfalls, the farm, buildings, and land, which consists of about 245 acres, to the town by Mr R J (Robert Jones) Roberts, chemist. This spot is situated on the Talyllyn Railway, about four-and-a-half miles from the town, and is a favourite resort of visitors during the season. The scenery around the falls is exceedingly picturesque and it forms one of the leading attractions. Until a few years ago the higher portions of the glen were made but little use of, as it meant a stiff climb which could only be indulged in by the more robust. The railway which has a station at this point known as Dolgoch passes over the ravine by means of a very fine three span viaduct. Mr Roberts has, however, during the past two years gone to a very great deal of expense by laying the place out with well made paths along the sides of the glen, which span the turbulent stream below by small bridges, and its most inaccessible heights can now be reached with comparative ease. Its value to the town is incalculable, and we feel sure the handsome gift will be appreciated.

The Route Described

Above: A view of Dolgoch station said to have been taken in 1894. The water tower was probably the original one, and was replaced in the 1920s.
(Photo: H.S. Bristowe/TR Collection)

Strictly speaking the ravine was leased to the Council, and the rest of the land was placed in the hands of a trust. The rents from the farms on the property were used by the trustees towards the upkeep of the ravine.

For many years the access to the ravine was only by an rough path from the station. Over the winter of 1956/57 a new path to the falls was laid out from the western end of the platform, and a footbridge constructed across the railway cutting to allow access to the ravine. In 1973 and 2004 the footbridge was repaired, and between 2003/04 a new path was laid across the meadow to the ravine.

At the station another familiar structure is the old slate water tower. When the first of these was erected is unknown, but a column with a small wooden tank on top appears in the photo above dating from 1894. The column was rebuilt in the early 1920s into the form we see it today. It is fed from a stream in the field to the south. A new tank has since been provided, and the tower is still used regularly by the Victorian Train.

In 1962 with longer trains in service a new water tower was erected. This was made from steel, due to instability in the ground where it needed to be built. At the same time the platform was extended eastwards. In 1977 the 'new' water tower was provided with a larger 600 gallon tank.

Dolgoch has always been a popular stop and in 1966 the booking office was re-established, which also sold drinks and snacks. For many years it was the practice to use the spring opposite the station building to cool bottles of fizzy drinks which were then sold as being 'cool as a mountain stream'. Modern food hygiene regulations have sadly led to this being abandoned.

To cope with the passenger numbers in 1987 the platform was widened. Chemical toilets were provided in 1989 sited in the woods behind the station building. These were superseded in 1998 when waterless composting-type toilets were provided in a timber building.

An electricity supply was provided in 2006, and most recently a third locomotive water tank was erected. This was for down trains, and came into use in 2010.

Right: An interesting sight on 26 February 1956 with the water tower surrounded by icicles.
(Photo: J.N. Slater)

Rails Along The Fathew

The Route Described

Dolgoch Station in 1901
(Based on Ordnance Survey Map)

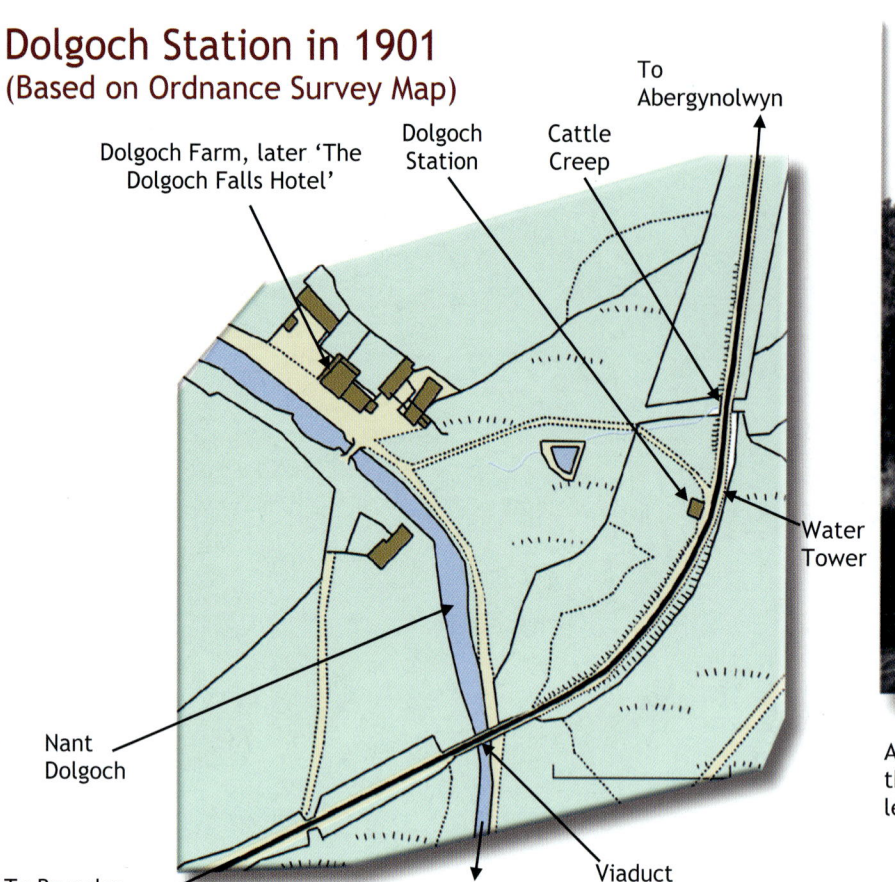

Map labels: Dolgoch Farm, later 'The Dolgoch Falls Hotel'; Dolgoch Station; Cattle Creep; To Abergynolwyn; Water Tower; Nant Dolgoch; To Brynlas; To The Falls and Ravine; Viaduct

Above: The water tower at Dolgoch in 1951, the valve had worn, so there was a perpetual leak of water. (Photo: The Elliot Collection)

Above: A colourised postcard from the 1920s, shortly after the replacement water column was built, with *Talyllyn* taking water. At this time the station had quite an open aspect.
(F. Frith Postcard/John Alsop Collection)

Left: *Dolgoch* taking water in the summer of 1947. Note how the bushes have now grown up.
(Photographer Unknown)

Rails Along The Fathew

The Route Described

Plan of Dolgoch Station in 2015
(Based on plan of 1967 with additions by the author)

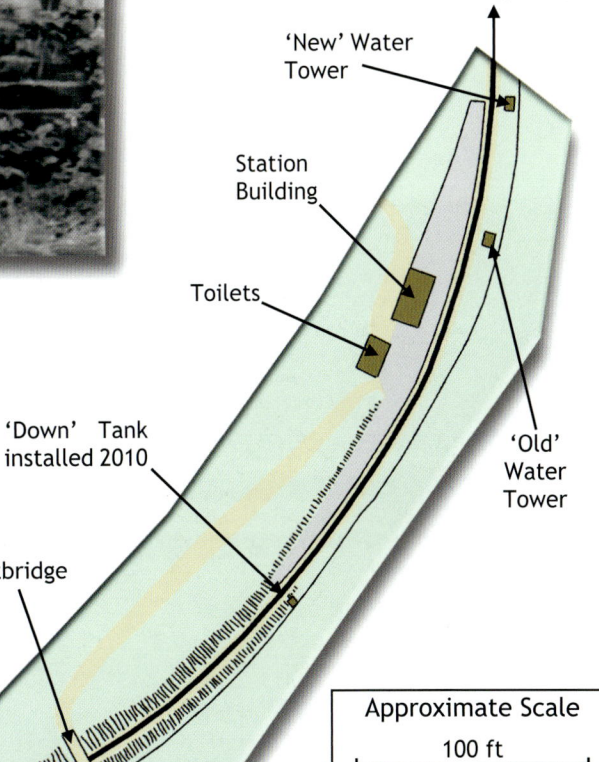

Top Left: *Dolgoch* has finished taking water at Dolgoch in the summer of 1951 with a young Gareth Jones acting as fireman.
(Photo: R. Sansbury/TR Collection)

Above Right: The driver takes a somewhat precarious position on top of *Dolgoch's* cab. Possibly the rod used to pull the valve on the tank had gone missing. This view dates from 22 August 1949.
(Photo: R.D. Butterell/TR Collection)

Above: In 1954 *Sir Haydn* takes water in the down direction at the station. (Photo: N. Rayfield/TR Collection)

Rails Along The Fathew — 121

The Route Described

Right: By 30 October 1955 Dolgoch station was beginning to be tidied up with new signs in place. (Photo: J.N. Slater)

Below: I must admit the main reason for including this photo is that it is among the first that I took of the railway in May 1972. However, my excuse is that it shows the new water tower in use. No.4 is being filled while driver Bill Faulkner looks on. When No.4 was overhauled in the late 1970s it was even fitted with a rack for Bill's pipe!

Right: The new water tower as later fitted with a larger tank. (Photo: Bob Lee/TR Collection)

Left: In March 1972 locomotives Nos. 3 *Sir Haydn* and 6 *Douglas* pause for water at Dolgoch. (Photo: David J. Mitchell)

122 Rails Along The Fathew

The Route Described

Left: In July 2001 the 'old' water tower at Dolgoch was under repair and so looks a little woebegone in this photo of No.2 *Dolgoch* entering the station with an up train.

Right: On 17 March 2010 the locomotive crew take a rest as No.1 *Talyllyn* stands at the now fully restored water tower. If one could lose the pvc supply pipe this would be a timeless view.

Below: In fact with a little digital manipulation we can see how timeless the view has become (with the exception of the widened platform and fencing).

Right: On the return trip the same day the crew makes use of the then newly installed down water tank to replenish *Talyllyn*'s tank.

Rails Along The Fathew

123

The Route Described

From Dolgoch to Abergynolwyn

Left: Tanycoed or Quarry Siding in the early 1920s with a down mixed train when slate output from the quarry was still substantial. Note the apparent lack of a siding at this time. (F. Frith Postcard)

Below: Locomotive No.3 *Sir Haydn* at the same spot in 1954. The course of the now abandoned second siding can be seen to the right of the train.
(Photo J.N. Slater)

Departing from Dolgoch the railway crosses a cattle creep, and is now heading north, still climbing steadily, turning north-east on what was originally a six-chain radius curve. Emerging from the woods the train reaches the occupation crossing at what is now known as Quarry Siding (202 ft above sea level), but in the past was known as Tanycoed. This was the site of the derailment in 1882. Just before the crossing is a platelayer's hut whose roof consists of the remains of *Talyllyn's* second saddle tank removed from the locomotive c.1932.

East of the road crossing there was originally a short siding facing west parallel to the main line. The siding served a small quarry from which the railway dug shale for ballast for many years. As the quarry face receded the siding was slewed further across to allow closer access. It was eventually dismantled, and some time later (certainly after the 1920s) replaced by a siding nearer to the crossing, which again curved into the quarry.

An intriguing possibility as to another use for this site comes from a report of the Urban Council in December 1903. Here the Council Surveyor reported that:

Mr Yates, Manager of the Talyllyn Railway, had, at his request, put in a siding near Towyn, which will enable him to have Tonfanan Macadam (presumably from the quarry at Tonfanau) *delivered in a central place for carting on to Aber Road at a reasonable price. He had not made a start on the widening of the main road near Tanycred.* (mis-spelling of Tanycoed?)... *It was resolved ... Also that stones be put on the Aber Road at once. That the Surveyor make the best arrangements he can with Mr Owens, Tanycoed, as to carting.*

Was the siding at Tanycoed altered for this macadam stone to be delivered, or a temporary siding made? Certainly the site would have been convenient for Mr Owens, who resided at Tanycoed-Uchaf Farm on the other side of the valley to the north-east, and also for the work site on the Abergynolwyn road. Although transporting the stones down the steep track would not have been easy.

Above: *Talyllyn's* second saddle tank, removed in the 1930s, was used as a roof for a Permanent Way hut just before Quarry Siding; whether this replaced an earlier structure is not known.
(Photo: TR Collection)

124 | Rails Along The Fathew

The Route Described

Another option could be that Abergynolwyn station was used as a site for this.

When the Preservation Society took over the quarry was used extensively to obtain ballast material. In order to gain better access to the quarry face a new siding was laid in 1953 on the line of the original one. Over the years the quarry face moved back into the hillside, and various methods of loading the shale were tried. These included a top loading hopper supplied by a conveyor belt.

Quarry Siding Halt existed before Society days, and was at the site of the crossing. It first appeared in the timetables in 1956, and was marked by a nameboard. There was a suggestion in the 1950s that it should be renamed Tanycoed Halt, but this was rejected.

When the passing loop was established here over the winter of 1968/69 the old siding was disconnected, but was reinstated in 1970 when work on the block post was completed. The new passing loop is 200 ft long, and is operated by a six-lever stud lever frame formerly installed at the ex-GWR Watlington station. In 1979 the siding was relaid once again as granite ballast was being obtained from elsewhere, and the siding was then only used for storage.

In 1990 there was a discussion about installing signals here as at Pendre and Brynglas, but again they never appeared. A major change did occur over the winter of 2011/12, when the site of the old siding and quarry floor was levelled and a two-road storage shed erected. This is for Permanent Way equipment and other items requiring long-term storage, and is named *The Guest House* for reasons previously mentioned.

Right: The Platelayers' Hut at Ceunant Coch. Built out of slate slab it would seem to date from not long after the opening of the line. (Photo: L. Garvey)

Above: No.4 Edward Thomas about to depart from Quarry Siding for Brynglas with a ballast train on Sunday 21 February 1954. (Photo: J.N. Slater)

Departing from Quarry Siding on a continuing upward grade the line passes over another cattle creep before emerging onto the open hillside ledge. This is Tanycoed or Bottom Straight with the two farms of Tanycoed-isaf and Tanycoed-uchaf lying on the opposite side of the valley.

At milepost 5¾ this becomes Ceunant Coch or Middle Straight, and the line passes over a cattle creep followed by a bridge over a small stream. Not surprisingly the next section of track is Top Straight which starts after milepost 6. Near here is another platelayers' hut built into the hillside, which appears to be a feature dating from close to the opening of the line.

Abergynolwyn woods are reached six and a quarter miles from Tywyn. During and after the war the Forestry Commission developed the woodlands here, and so there is a fire hazard warning sign to signal crews to take care not to emit sparks from the locomotive chimney. The home signal of the new signalling system is now passed and the train reaches Abergynolwyn station, which now starts at milepost 6½ and is 242 ft above sea level.

Above: Two number fives at Quarry Siding Halt as No.5 Midlander arrives at the halt with Talyllyn brake van No.5 in tow in May 1966. (Photo: David J. Mitchell)

Rails Along The Fathew

The Route Described

Right: The view from the top of the quarry with No.5 *Midlander* about to couple up to another ballast train on 14 March 1964. Hopefully the chap in the truck will realise the locomotive is coming otherwise he could be in for a nasty surprise.

(Photo: David J. Mitchell)

Left: Over the winter of 1968/69 the railway was preparing for the introduction of the three-train-set service. This involved adding a passing loop at Quarry Siding, which is being prepared here as No.4 *Edward Thomas* passes with a down train.

(Photo: David J. Mitchell)

Right: During the winter of 2011/12 the old quarry floor was cleared and a new storage shed erected, as seen here on 2 June 2012. Later named *The Guest House*, the shed is rail connected at the eastern end.

Left: No.6 *Douglas*, driven by Graham Thomas, enters the loop at Quarry Siding on 26 July 2013 with a train for Nant Gwernol.

The Route Described

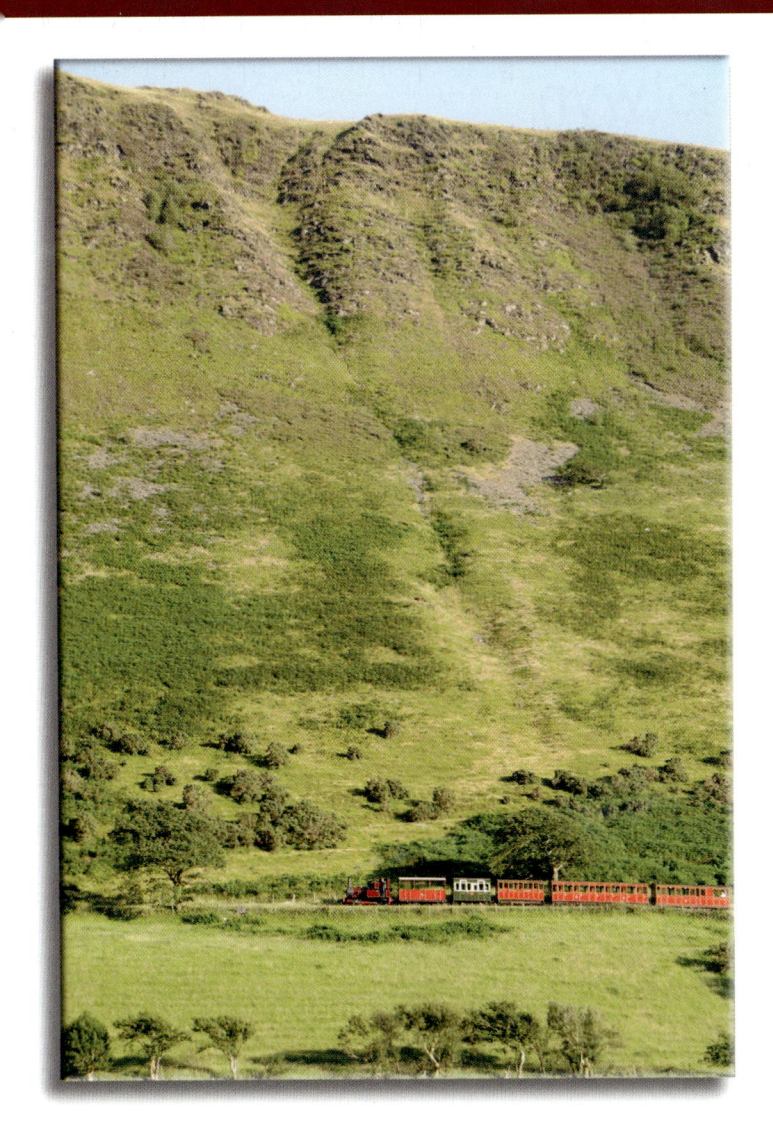

Above Left and Right: Two views that show the scale of the scenery at this point in different seasons. On the left No.2 *Dolgoch* is seen with a train heading towards Abergynolwyn near Ceunant Coch in a view taken from the road across the valley on 27 July 2008. Meanwhile a whole different perspective is seen from Mynydd Rhiwerfa as No.3 *Sir Haydn* takes its train past the ruins of Pentre-maes-trefnant on 23 April 1976. (Both Photos: David J. Mitchell)

Right: *Talyllyn* heads a train consisting of the carriages now numbered 3 and 4 and the original brake van past Llwyn-fynwent in the 1920s. The building is now a ruin in the woods just before Abergynolwyn station.
(John Alsop Collection)

Rails Along The Fathew

The Route Described

Abergynolwyn

Above: Another pre-preservation colour view of Abergynolwyn from April 1949 as Dolgoch *stands at the station with a short train, without the brake van that was still awaiting new tyres to be fitted to its wheels.* (Photo: The Elliot/Dan Quine Collection)

Originally, Abergynolwyn station consisted of a simple short loop. Then a siding seems to have been added between 1888 and 1901. The original building was similar to that at Pendre, and again was of timber construction. According to one source the siding was lifted before the First World War and then reinstated along a different alignment for the loading of timber, with a small slate faced platform added. Certainly the siding was re-laid at some point around this time, and remained until preservation.

The site for the station was doubtless chosen because it allowed easy access to the valley road which led into the village that was then being developed, but it was still some distance from it. When a local eisteddfod was held the bands used to parade down the route to the village.

The station was also publicised as a tourist destination, the timetable poster of August 1867 stating that on:

Reaching Abergynolwyn, the visitor can either pursue his journey to Tal-y-llyn Lake or Caerberllan Castle, called in history Castell-y-Bere

Similarly the *Cardigan Bay Visitor* of September 1892 encouraged the visitor that:

From the terminus (Abergynolwyn) the walk to both Talyllyn, the world renowned fishing station, and to Llanfihangel-y-pennant are wild and romantic, yet easy to travel. The ascent of Cader Idris may be easily made from either place, a feat that may be accomplished by leaving Towyn by the 9.30 a.m. train and returning by the 5.10 p.m. train.

However others were less convinced that the railway was making the best of the area. The following is from the *County Times* of 8 March 1900:

ABERGYNOLWYN. RAILWAY FACILITIES.—Attention has from time to time been drawn to the deplorable state of the railway facilities to this romantic district. Not only are the carriages on the narrow gauge of a primitive description, but the rate of speed is painfully slow, and it takes about 40 minutes to get from Towyn to Abergynolwyn. The morning train leaves at 9-30 and the afternoon at 3-15, whilst there is no evening train at all. On Saturdays more especially the want of an evening train is keenly felt. A little more attention to the passenger traffic would pay the Company. The beauties of the district need only to be known to be appreciated. The waterfall near the second incline to the quarries is worthy of inspection, whilst the panoramic beauties of the Ceunant Walk have been gazed at for hours by interested visitors. The ruins of Bere Castle would engage the attention of antiquarians for a whole day and the district would benefit from the presence of a larger number of visitors. A suggestion is made that the line of

The Route Described

Left: *Dolgoch* with a train at Abergynolwyn possibly in the late nineteenth century. John Rowlands is the driver on the left, Bob Thomas, the fireman, is to the right of the locomotive, and Jacob Rowlands, the guard, is on the extreme right. To his left is William Rowlands the postman at Abergynolwyn, who had come to collect the incoming mail and deliver the outgoing mail for the village.
(Commercial Postcard)

Right: A similar scene taken c. 1913. This time the locomotive is *Talyllyn* with a mixed train. At this point the driver is Dick Price, with Hugh (Gas) Jones on the platform beside the locomotive, while the guard is still Jacob Rowlands, although now somewhat older than in the previous picture and with a new hat. Note in both photos that the brake van still has its doors on the south side.

There is an air of neglect about the station as the guttering is missing and the downpipe broken, while the roof is developing a sag. (Commercial Postcard)

railway should be continued to Talyllyn Lake. If this could be carried out, the passenger traffic of the Company would be increased by some thousands.

Clearly the railway took some of the criticisms to heart and in 1901 it was stated that the shrubs and briars that surrounded the station had been cleared to give it a neat appearance. The exposed position of the station, however, meant that the wooden structure deteriorated faster than its counterpart at Pendre. Therefore, between 1938 and 1939 it was replaced with a slate-built structure similar to those at Rhydyronen and Dolgoch.

During the war the building was used as a sentry post for the home guard. Sniper 'slits' were cut in the western wall of the building to take advantage of its commanding view of the valley. These were filled in during the early preservation years, but help with dating photographs.

Preservation

Like the other stations on the line Abergynolwyn was 'spruced' up before the official opening in May 1951. A train laden with volunteers went up the line on Saturday 12 May 1951 to Abergynolwyn, offloading various items en-route. These included new nameboards.

Over the winter of 1951/52 the loop was relaid and it, along with the platform were extended. From the early days of the Preservation Society refreshments were sold from the building.

The Revd. W. Awdry famously left the lady, who had been selling the refreshments behind when he was a volunteer guard in the 1950s. He used this event in his book *Four Little Engines*, published in 1955. This was the first of his stories to feature the Skarloey Railway, based on the Talyllyn.

The refreshment facilities in the building were limited. Therefore in 1963 a tea van was rapidly built on the remains of carriage No.7, entering service in the August. This was taken up to Abergynolwyn on the first train of each day and returned on the last one. The van enabled a more comprehensive refreshment menu to be offered, including hot tea. Originally it stood next to a wooden platform on the old mineral line, but the following year a special siding was provided.

In 1969 a new 40 ft by 18 ft building was erected at a cost of £6,436. As already alluded to in this book, this was a somewhat controversial development, but the increased facilities were clearly needed. The old tea van siding was also removed. Other needs of passengers were met in

The Route Described

Left: By the late 1930s the condition of the original building had deteriorated, and needed to be replaced with a more substantial structure. Here Dolgoch *stands at Abergynolwyn, while on the right it seems as if a supply of slab has already been brought down from the quarry ready to be used in the new building. (Photo: H.B. Tours/Cozens Collection)*

1973 when a set of public conveniences was built by the County Council in the car park at the bottom of the station drive.

By this time work on the Extension was underway and a tip siding was provided at the western end of the station, using the former west-end Rhydyronen loop points. Later another siding was laid on the eastern side of the building. This allowed the platform to be extended in both directions to permit two trains to stand in the station at the same time.

Over the winter of 1975/76 the layout at Abergynolwyn was entirely revised, and a 650 ft long platform created. In addition, colour light signalling was installed and a new block post built. There was also a siding opposite the Nant Gwernol end of the platform, which was extended in 1977 when the old tip siding was removed. All this certainly altered the feel of the entire station from a country terminus to a busy passing station.

Other developments since have included the widening of the canopy to the platform edge in 1986. In 1990 a new toilet block came into use at the top of the drive next to the station building. Then in 1999 an extension to the refreshment room was opened to cope with coach party traffic.

The same year the opportunity arose to purchase the car park and old toilet block at the bottom of the drive. The area west of the car park was developed in 2002 with the opening of the 'Railway Adventure Playground' as a family facility. The opening ceremony being performed by Lord Faulkner of Worcester.

Left: The replacement 1930s station building. (Photo: TR Collection)

Rails Along The Fathew

The Route Described

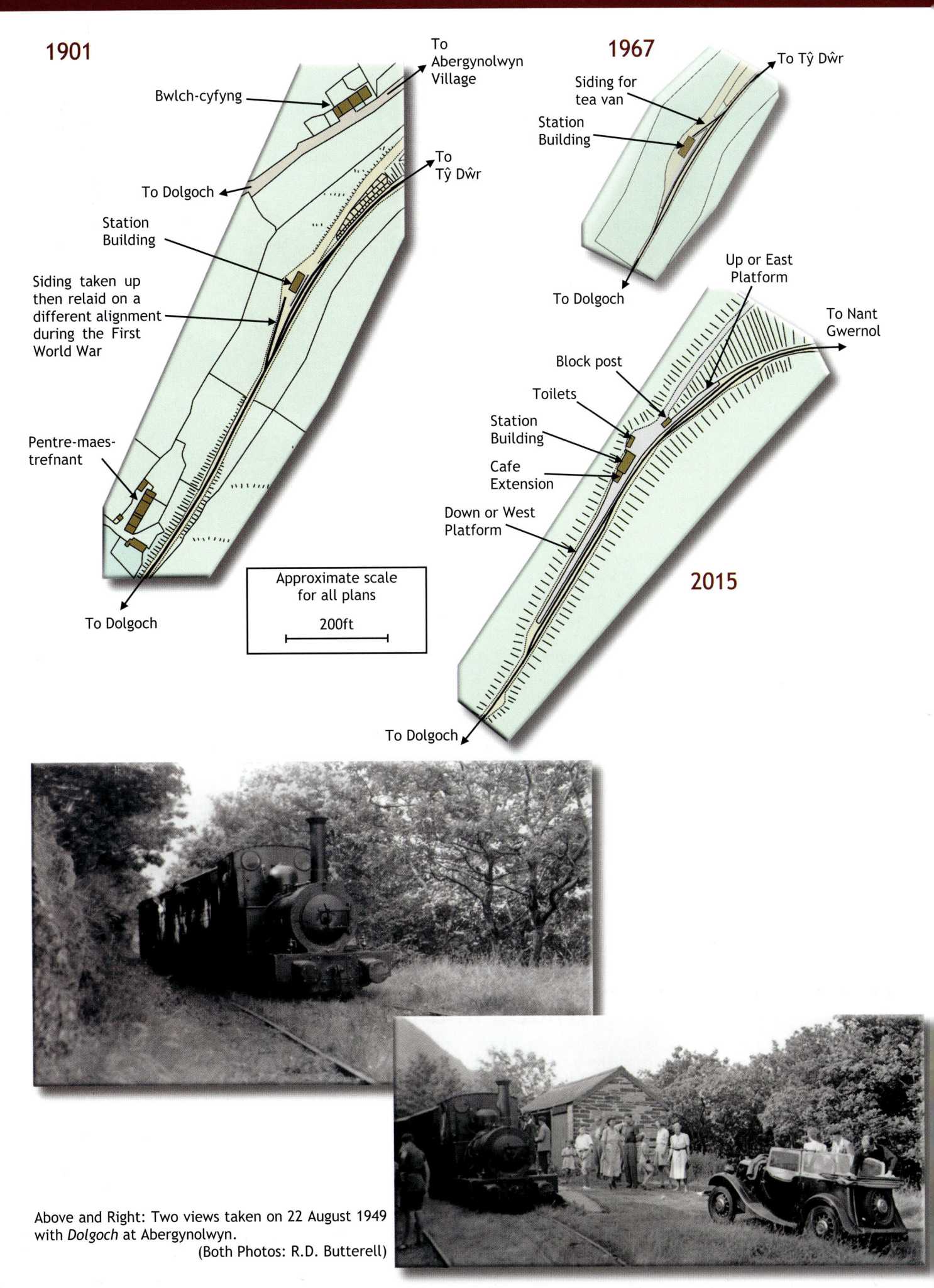

1901

- To Abergynolwyn Village
- Bwlch-cyfyng
- To Dolgoch
- To Tŷ Dŵr
- Station Building
- Siding taken up then relaid on a different alignment during the First World War
- Pentre-maes-trefnant
- To Dolgoch

Approximate scale for all plans
200ft

1967

- To Tŷ Dŵr
- Siding for tea van
- Station Building
- To Dolgoch

2015

- Up or East Platform
- To Nant Gwernol
- Block post
- Toilets
- Station Building
- Cafe Extension
- Down or West Platform
- To Dolgoch

Above and Right: Two views taken on 22 August 1949 with *Dolgoch* at Abergynolwyn.
(Both Photos: R.D. Butterell)

Rails Along The Fathew

131

The Route Described

Above Left: This photo shows reminders of the station's wartime role. Sniper slits were made in the western wall of the station building. In addition, rolls of barbed wire can be seen the left, which were also part of the station's defences. There were also slit trenches and anti-tank obstacles which could be dropped between the tracks.
(Photo: J.W. Sparrowe/ TR Collection)

Above Right: Probably Idris Williams is driving *Dolgoch* as it runs round its train in 1949.
(Photo: The Elliot/Dan Quine Collection)

Right: *Dolgoch* at Abergynolwyn having been uncoupled from a very short train, probably in 1949.
(Photo: The Holcombe Family)

What's in a Name?

The name Abergynolwyn has been something of a mystery as to its exact meaning, however at the local Eisteddfod in August 1877 a young man offered the following suggestion:

The cluster of modern houses which nestle at the foot of the surrounding mountains are known to the inhabitants by the name of Abergynolwyn, and is so spelt by them. Others call the village Aberganolwyn. The young man who won the prize has brought to light publicly a third name—Abergwernolwyn—which, it is said, seems to be the correct one, and that for the following reasons :—On the side of the mountain, not far from the village which is now called Abergynolwyn, there are some springs of water known as Ffynnonau Gwernol. The stream running from these would naturally be called Gwernolwywy, being an old Welsh word signifying a river and the confluence of two streams being termed Aber, the lesser of the two would give the name to the place, as that would be the place where it ended or lost itself in the larger one. Hence the name seems to be Aber-gwernol-wyn, viz., the confluence of the river Gwernol with the stream running from Talyllyn, and called, a little lower down, the Dysynni, or the noiseless stream (Di-sain wy).

The Route Described

Above: A panorama from two photographs showing a train in Abergynolwyn platform in 1951.
(Photo: The Elliot Collection)

Left: *Dolgoch* at Abergynolwyn c.1948. Rod Holcombe is the young man leaning out of the carriage behind the locomotive.
(Photo: The Holcombe Family)

Below Left: No.1 *Talyllyn* stands with a down train comprising carriages Nos. 9 and 10 as well as at least one open on 24 August 1958.
(Photographer Unknown)

Below Right: The newly built tea van was first used at Abergynolwyn on the track just beyond the main platform on what is now the line to Nant Gwernol. Here a temporary wooden platform was built, and it is seen next to this on 17 August 1963.
(Photo: Keith Stretch)

Rails Along The Fathew

The Route Described

Left: Locomotive No.2 *Dolgoch* stands at Abergynolwyn in September 1963 soon after it had returned from being rebuilt.
(Photo: J.T. Fraser)

Right: No.2 *Dolgoch* again, this time waiting at the down end of the platform with carriage No.10 on 31 March 1964.
(Photo: David J. Mitchell)

Left: A controversial decision. The demolished remains of the second Abergynolwyn station building in September 1968. It is easy to be critical with hindsight, but at the time the building was only about thirty years old. In addition, there was an unarguable need the need for increased facilities at Abergynolwyn, and there was not another viable alternative. Nevertheless it was another part of the Talyllyn's pre-preservation heritage that disappeared.
(Photo: David J. Mitchell)

The Route Described

Left: The new station building at Abergynolwyn nears completion in 1969. Some of the slab used for the cladding came from the demolished remains of the former winding house.
(Photo: David J. Mitchell)

Right: Some idea of the extent of the alterations at Abergynolwyn with the opening of the Extension to Nant Gwernol can be seen here on 16 April 1976.
(Photo: David J. Mitchell)

Left: There is a water tank on the bank above Abergynolwyn which is occasionally used to water locomotives. Here the crew of locomotive No.4 *Edward Thomas* are making use of the facility in 1978.

Rails Along The Fathew

The Route Described

The Abergynolwyn Riots

While they did not affect the railway directly, a little known series of events in Abergynolwyn became a matter of national notoriety. They were known as the Abergynolwyn Riots. These seem to have started in around 1876 when groups of men (said to be about twenty to thirty) were seen in and around the village engaged in poaching with blackened faces and dressed in women's clothing.

This seemingly somewhat bizarre behaviour was in fact an echo of the 'Rebecca Riots'. These took place in South and Mid-Wales in the late 1830s and early 1840s over a series of perceived injustices including road tolls. In Abergynolwyn the issue seems to have been about fishing rights. Things came to a head on 10 January 1878 when a policeman was assaulted by a group of these men. This made it to the national press, turning Abergynolwyn into an apparent 'den of iniquity' where policemen could not walk the streets at night. This notoriety upset other villagers who felt that some of the claims of the press were highly exaggerated.

Whatever the rights and wrongs of the situation, extra policemen were deployed to the village during the following winter, and sporadic incidents continued over the next year or so. It certainly gives the lie to the perception that Abergynolwyn was always a sleepy village where nothing much happened.

Left: The extended station building and canopy can be seen on 7 April 2015.

Below: The block post on the same date.

Bottom: The toilet block opened by Ian Allan on 6 May 1991. The publisher was chosen for the task as he had recently written an article bemoaning the poor state of facilities for passengers on heritage railways, and so he was felt to be the ideal person to be asked to 'do the honours'.

The Route Described

The Extension

Left: Just to the east of Abergynolwyn station up until the late 1960s there was a gate across what was christened 'The Road to Adventure' by Tom Rolt. It was thought by many that the gate marked the end of the statutory railway. However, in fact it marked the boundary between the property of two landowners, to control straying sheep. This gate did though mark the beginning of the Extension to Nant Gwernol. (Photo: TR Collection)

Right: After years of not being used, in places the rails on the old mineral line could barely made out. Such is the case in this view of Hendre, now Forestry, crossing. The line of rails can just be made out on the bottom left.
(Photo: TR Collection)

Left: Occasionally trains had ventured up the old mineral line, such as here where No.5 *Midlander* makes its way up to the Winding House site in 1968, but otherwise the tracks lay undisturbed. Note the superelevation, probably to allow *Talyllyn*, with its long wheelbase, to get round the curve.
(Photo: J.N. Slater)

The line beyond Abergynolwyn was not originally part of the statutory railway. Therefore, when the Extension project was started the trackbed had to be considerably widened, with the curves eased in order for bogie passenger stock to traverse it. This sadly meant that a number of pre-preservation features disappeared.

Right: Chief among the artefacts that had to go was the old Abergynolwyn village winding house, as the old 'main line' passed through the building, and there was not sufficient clearance. In addition, the condition of the building had deteriorated to the point where the Railway Inspector recommended its demolition, which is happening here in July 1968. Indeed had the building been left any longer it would probably have collapsed. A young David Mitchell, in 2015 the Preservation Society President, can be seen sitting nearest the camera on the wall. (Photo: J.N. Slater)

Rails Along The Fathew

The Route Described

Plan of The Extension

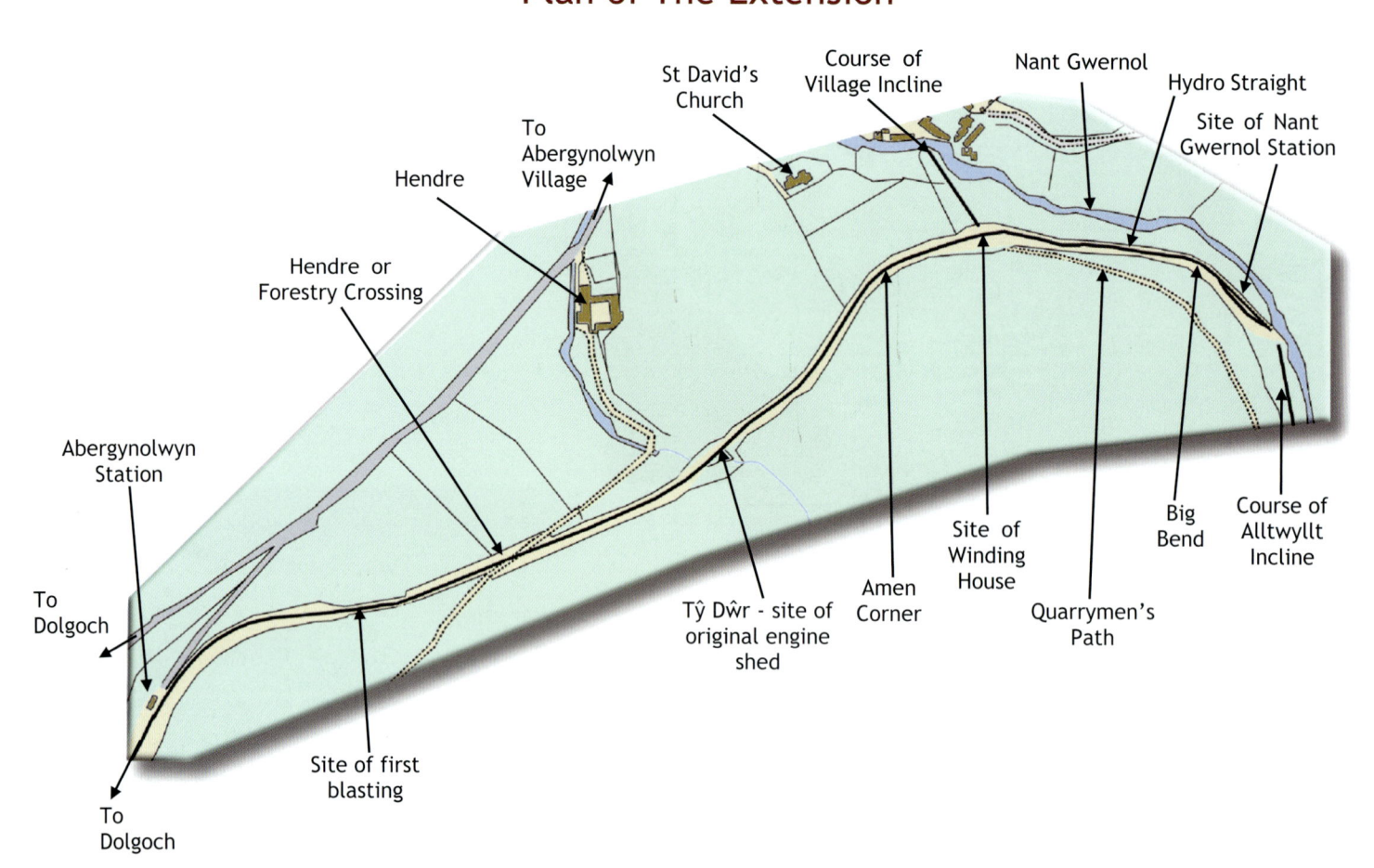

Labels on map:
- Hendre
- To Abergynolwyn Village
- St David's Church
- Course of Village Incline
- Nant Gwernol
- Hydro Straight
- Site of Nant Gwernol Station
- Hendre or Forestry Crossing
- Abergynolwyn Station
- To Dolgoch
- To Dolgoch
- Site of first blasting
- Tŷ Dŵr - site of original engine shed
- Amen Corner
- Site of Winding House
- Quarrymen's Path
- Big Bend
- Course of Alltwyllt Incline

Left: To widen the trackbed blasting was necessary and here project manager Bob Gunn is with Robin Daniel preparing the first charges, which would be detonated ceremoniously by Tom Rolt on 3 October 1970.

Although most of the blasting went according to plan one blast sent a few pieces of debris down onto the village below, fortunately without causing serious damage.

(Photo: TR Collection)

Right: Much of the spoil from the blasting was brought down to Abergynolwyn to extend the embankment and allow the platform to be lengthened. Temporary tip sidings were laid for this. Here some of the 'Gwerns' are unloading one such spoil train in July 1975.

The Route Described

Top Left: The narrowness of some of the original trackbed can be seen here just past the Winding House site in spring 1974. (Photo: David J. Mitchell)

Top Right: Looking towards Big Bend from along Hydro Straight in July 1975. By this time the retaining wall has been built and the trackbed widened.

Left: No.5 *Midlander* departs from Abergynolwyn with another train of empty tippers to be filled with spoil in May 1974. (Photo: J.H.L. Adams)

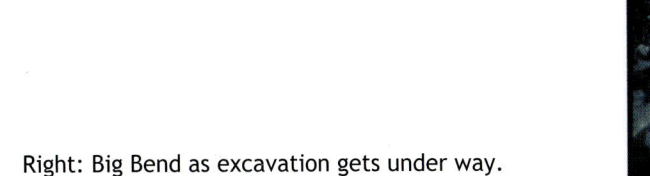

Right: Big Bend as excavation gets under way. (Photo: J.H.L. Adams)

Rails Along The Fathew

139

The Route Described

Left: No.8 *Merseysider* on Big Bend with a train loaded with sand and stone for making concrete at Nant Gwernol on 24 April 1976. The amount of work that has had to be done here to make it suitable for bogie passenger coaches is clear to see. An isolated section of track has been relaid on the original alignment, to demonstrate the excavation that was done at this point. (Photo: David J. Mitchell)

Right: The site of Nant Gwernol station in July 1975.

Left: Hendre or Forestry Crossing in 1977. No.2 *Dolgoch* heads a train for Nant Gwernol. Later flashing red lights were installed to control the road traffic.

Right: The reason why the flashing lights were installed becomes clear when you see the road gradient above the crossing, sometimes used by articulated logging lorries. No.1 *Talyllyn* is in charge of a down train on 25 May 1976. It is worth comparing this view to that on page 137. (Photo: David J. Mitchell)

Rails Along The Fathew

The Route Described

Above: A lovely study of Dolgoch at Tŷ Dŵr. This trough was regularly used by locomotives to take water in pre-Society days. This view is from c. 1949. (Photo: The Holcombe family)

From Abergynolwyn station the line curves sharply east over a cattle creep and a stream. The curve then reverses returning the railway to a north-easterly course past what is now the down home signal. After passing milepost 6¾ the line reaches the occupation crossing at Hendre, now known as Forestry Crossing.

Somewhere beyond this was the site of an accident on 10 March 1902 reported in the *County Times* that week:

ABERGYNOLWYN RAILWAY ACCIDENT.—*An accident occurred on the Talyllyn Railway on Monday, without happily any personal injuries, although there were several narrow escapes. It appears that the locomotive had run on as usual, after bringing up the morning train, past the Abergynolwyn station to the bottom of the first incline; where it hitched on a load of trucks filled with slates from the quarry above. When above Hendre, a very dangerous portion of the line, which is here more or less on the side of the* (sic) *a fairly high precipice, a truck jumped the metals, and the whole set toppled over. Luckily, the coupling between the engine and the first truck snapped, so that the engine remained on the rails, although the engineer and stoker were prepared for the worst. Mr Meyrick Roberts* (The Quarry Manager), *who was riding on the trucks, had a very narrow escape, but fortunately managed to jump clear. The slates were scattered all over the place and the financial loss is rather heavy. No reason has, as yet, been assigned for the occurrence, which created a good deal of excitement in Abergynolwyn.*

Between the end of regular working on the line and the beginning of work on the Extension, there had been a greatly increased amount of forestry traffic across the tracks. This had led to them nearly being obliterated under the mud. After opening to passenger traffic the crossing was eventually equipped with flashing road traffic signals operated by sensors.

Still heading north-east the line now comes to Tŷ Dŵr, the site of the first locomotive shed. A siding was shown to be still in place here in 1888 along with a structure of some kind, but whether it was the old locomotive shed is uncertain. There are later photos which show a smaller wooden building at the site. This was probably a shelter-cum-store or caban for the Permanent Way gang.

Despite the shed's demise, this was the place where locomotives were watered up until the end of the Haydn Jones era. This was achieved by a series of wooden launders on slate pillars which took water from a nearby waterfall, and by use of a removable trough directed it towards the locomotive's tank filler. Unfortunately the the apparatus was demolished between 1952 and 1954.

Rails Along The Fathew

The Route Described

Beyond Tŷ Dŵr the railway now passes high over the village, first curving north and passing milepost 7 before turning sharply eastwards. It is now on what is known as Amen Corner, because of the church below. The curve continues until the track comes to the site of the old village winding house.

Right: Tŷ Dŵr was the site of the original locomotive shed, but this is not it. This wooden structure seems to have been erected later as a store or shelter. The watering point though was original, although the arrangement was changed after the locomotive shed was demolished and the siding removed, as the slate column in the centre stands where the siding would have run. The watering point remained until it was demolished in the early 1950s.
(Photo: TR Collection)

Above and Right: Usually it is *Talyllyn* or *Dolgoch* that is seen taking water here, but No.4 *Edward Thomas* made some trips up the old mineral extension in 1952 and took water at Tŷ Dŵr.
(Above Photo: J.M. Lloyd/TR Collection
Right Photo: J.H.L. Adams)

142 Rails Along The Fathew

The Route Described

The Village Incline

Exactly when the village incline was completed is unknown, but it was in use by October 1869. The mineral line went through the centre of the building, passing underneath the winding drum as it did so. There was also a short loop to the rear, where a large wagon turntable gave access to the incline roads.

The incline itself was double-tracked and 363 ft in length on a gradient of 1 in 2.58, the difference in height being 150 ft from the winding house to the village. In the village the tracks crossed the Nant Gwernol on a girder bridge, and through a set of gates before the lines converged onto a wagon turntable.

From here there was a number of tracks that supplied various parts of the village. This enabled stores and materials to be brought to various commercial premises and residences. It also enabled the removal of the 'night soil' from the cinder privies at the back of the houses at regular intervals. This was then transported by rail to a field near Brynglas for disposal. How long this practice lasted is not known as a newspaper report from 1880 stated that:

A man was paid a sum of about £5 per year to cart it (the soil) *away to the farmers who purchased it at a small cost, while some of the people used the contents for their own gardens.*

But it was said that the 'night soil' was being transported away by rail in 1904, so the practice continued for some time. Abergynolwyn was not connected to a mains sewerage system until well into the twentieth century.

Although not designed for passenger use, some were known to ride in the wagons up and down the incline. They included the Quarry Manager Meyrick Roberts. There were

Top: Careful examination of this photo shows not only the incline and waterwheel in the background, but also the route of the tramway through the village. It can be seen rounding the corner near the Railway Inn (arrowed) then passing through the alleyway between the houses, before coming behind the Jerusalem Chapel at the bottom left of the photo.
(Commercial Postcard)

Bottom: The bottom of the incline as seen from the winding house c. 1903.
(Photo: TR Collection)

The Route Described

also incidents when the incline cable, or a wagon coupling, broke such as the following from the *Cambrian News* of 30 July 1920:

On Friday afternoon while goods were being lowered down the railway incline the wire rope broke and one of the wagons came plunging down at a terrific rate. When it reached fairly level ground, the wagon left the metals, ultimately coming to a standstill about 100 yards lower down. ... Miraculously, as it were, no one was injured as the spot is the favourite playing ground for children.

The last use of the village network seems to have been on 4 July 1946 for deliveries of pig meal to 2 Tan-y-bryn Street and 12 Llanegryn Street. When the Preservation Society took over one of their first acts was to organise working parties to lift rail from the incline. This was because the rail had been more lightly worn, and so could be used to replace some of the more decrepit lengths of track.

Left: The incline as seen from the village. The building on the left was the old smithy.
(Photo: TR Collection)

Right: The old winding house in August 1955. Locomotives used to go straight through the building on the mineral line, and the limited clearances were one of the reasons for its demolition.
(Photo: J.T. Fraser)

Left: Some abandoned wagons in Abergynolwyn village in April 1949.
(Photo: Locomotive and General Railway Photographs Copyright NRM/SSPL)

The Route Described

Abergynolwyn Village and Incline Rail System c. 1901
(Based on Ordnance Survey Map of 1901)

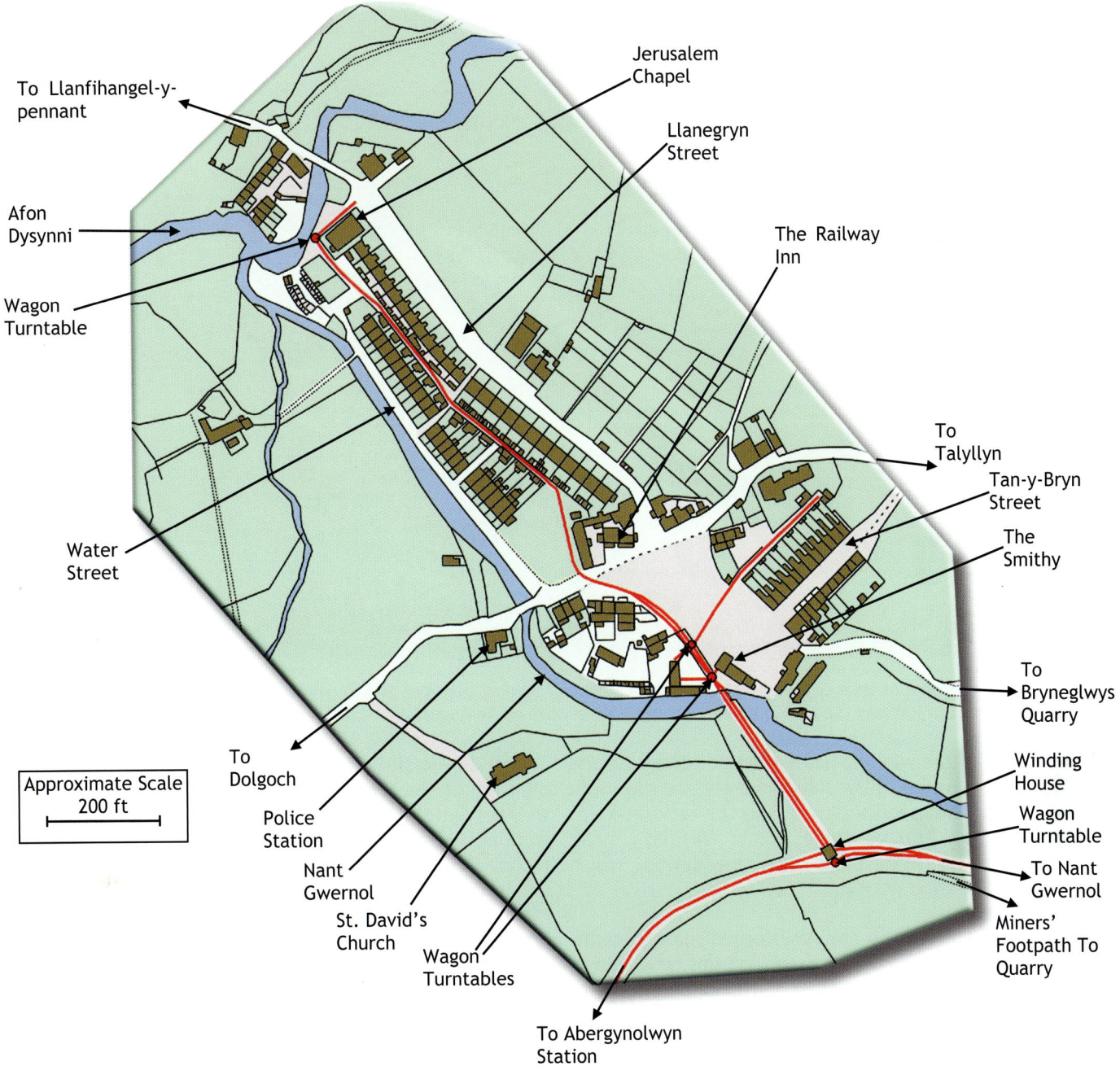

Map labels:
- To Llanfihangel-y-pennant
- Jerusalem Chapel
- Llanegryn Street
- Afon Dysynni
- The Railway Inn
- Wagon Turntable
- To Talyllyn
- Tan-y-Bryn Street
- The Smithy
- Water Street
- To Bryneglwys Quarry
- Winding House
- Wagon Turntable
- To Nant Gwernol
- Miners' Footpath To Quarry
- To Dolgoch
- Police Station
- Nant Gwernol
- St. David's Church
- Wagon Turntables
- To Abergynolwyn Station

Approximate Scale 200 ft

Left: The tracks from the incline can be seen crossing the Nant Gwernol on the left. The smithy is in front of the waterwheel, which powered a sawmill.
(Commercial Postcard)

Rails Along The Fathew 145

The Route Described

Nant Gwernol

Above: A different view of Nant Gwernol station as No.4 *Edward Thomas*, then painted in a GWR livery for the 150th Anniversary of the Great Western Railway the previous year, arrives with a train on 14 August 1986. (Photo: David J. Mitchell)

From the site of the winding house the line turns east and runs straight, parallel to the Nant Gwernol. On the south side of the line between the track and the rock face was a water pipe laid in Haydn Jones' time. This fed a small hyro-electric generating plant at Abergynolwyn, which continued to be used until the 1960s.

Before the Mid-1970s the line now turned sharply southeast. When work began on the Extension this bend had to be eased considerably. As a result it became known as 'Big Bend' where most of the excavation work on the Extension was carried out. A piece of the original track was relaid to demonstrate the change in the line of the trackbed for passengers arriving at Nant Gwernol.

Originally the site of Nant Gwernol station was occupied by a fan of three sidings which converged at the foot of the Alltwyllt Incline. This was the limit of locomotive working. From here the empty wagons were hauled up the incline to the quarry tramway, while loaded wagons were lowered down. As already stated there were several incidences of the couplings between the wagons breaking, or the incline rope snapping, and wagons with their contents shooting over the side of the ravine into the Nant Gwernol below.

One serious incident seems to have occurred either on the mineral extension or possibly on the Galltymoelfre Horse Tramway, between the Alltwyllt and Cantrybedd inclines, on 28 January 1879. The *Cambrian News* of 31 January recorded that:

The tram-road runs along the verge of a precipice, and a truck, in which some children were travelling, ran off the rails and with its contents precipitated into the chasm below. The children are very severely injured, and it is a matter to wonder at that they escaped with their lives.

When the Extension was upgraded for passenger use this became the terminus of the line. A single platform and loop line were constructed, with a timber-built station building echoing the original building at Abergynolwyn.

Left: The future site of Nant Gwernol station on 29 July 1953. The point levers for the siding points are just visible.
(Photo: J.H.L. Adams)

The Route Described

The station was officially opened on 22 May 1976, although various works were still to be completed. In May 1980 a network of paths was inaugurated at Nant Gwernol along with a footbridge across the Nant Gwernol to allow easy access back to Abergynolwyn. Since then the station has been relatively little altered.

Plan of the site of Nant Gwernol station, the limit of locomotive working in 1901. (Based on Ordnance Survey Map)
N.B. The OS Map is slightly wrong in that the retaining wall should be as per the 2015 plan.

Plan of Nant Gwernol Station in 2015

Approximate Scale of Plans 100 ft

Left: The Nant Gwernol station site in December 1975. (Photo: David J. Mitchell)

Right: The completed station at Easter 1979. (Photo: David J. Mitchell)

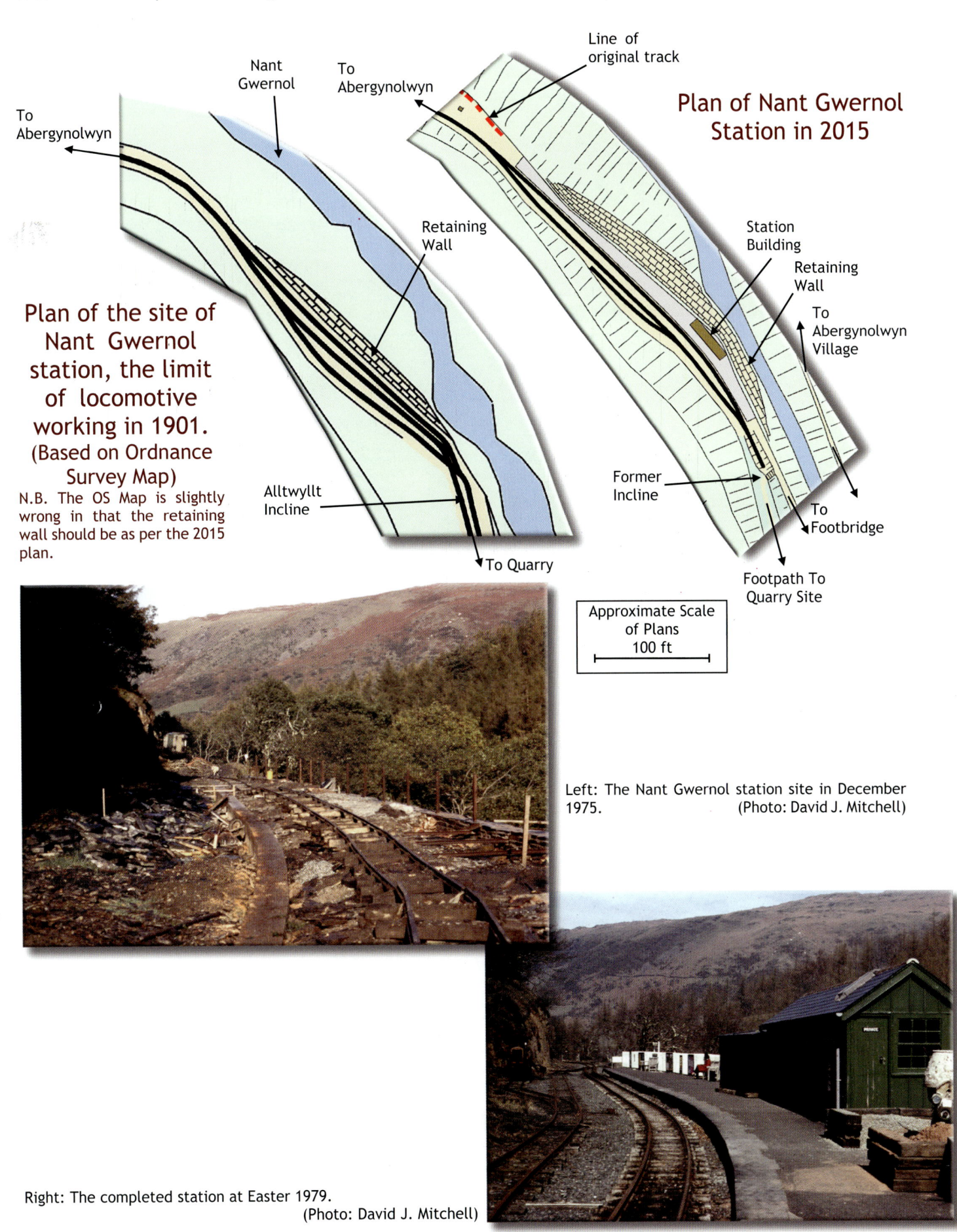

Rails Along The Fathew — 147

The Route Described

Left: Around 1898 the McConnel family made a trip to the limit of locomotive working, now Nant Gwernol station. The locomotive was *Talyllyn* with presumably the First Class carriage, now carriage No.1. The family posed for a photograph along with the guard, Jacob Rowlands, at the rear. Bob Thomas, who was driving that day because John Rowlands was ill, stands by the front of the locomotive. The family were probably Mrs Florence McConnel, with their children Meyrick, Muriel and Eryl. The photographer was William Houldsworth McConnel. One interesting question is who was firing the locomotive?
(Photo: W.H. McConnel)

Above: Nearly 120 years later, on 2 May 2015, the McConnel family were again at the same site for a photograph. Third from the left in the family group beside the locomotive is Mr Roger McConnel, the son of the original photographer William Houldsworth McConnel by his second marriage. On this occasion the driver was David Jones, again standing by the front of the locomotive, whose own family links to the railway almost go back to the date of the original photograph.

Above: The Alltwyllt Incline which rose directly from the end of what is now Nant Gwernol station.
(Photo: TR Collection)

Right: *Talyllyn* shunts some slate wagons at the foot of the incline in 1941.
(Photo: W.A. Camwell)

148 Rails Along The Fathew

Passenger Operations

Pre-Preservation Timetabled Services

As noted previously the first official passenger trains starting running on the Talyllyn in December 1866. Initially these departed from Abergynolwyn station at 8 am and 3 pm returning from Tywyn Pendre at 9 am and 4 pm. This reflected that at least one, or both, locomotives were based at the shed at Tŷ Dŵr. Trains only ran Mondays to Saturdays.

By February 1867 the shed at Pendre seems to have come into use, and a new timetable poster was issued, this time including the station at Rhydyronen. Trains then ran as shown opposite:

The two departure service with an early morning and then a mid-afternoon train from Tywyn was the staple of both the winter and summer timetables, and clearly designed to fill the needs of the local community. There was also an additional service in the early afternoon on Saturdays for the benefit of the quarrymen.

In August 1867 a new summer timetable came into force. As previously mentioned this introduced Dolgoch station, and also had a late morning train running six days a week. This was to entice day trippers up the line.

The following winter the late morning train reverted to Saturdays only. This was to bring the men home who had finished at the quarry for the week, while the afternoon train became a 3 pm departure from Pendre.

During the summer of 1871 the late morning/early afternoon train remained Saturdays only, but instead a 6.30 pm departure was introduced from Pendre six days a week. This did not reappear the following year with the more usual early morning, late morning/early afternoon and mid afternoon pattern being followed.

In July 1872 Brynglas is first mentioned in *Bradshaw's Guide*, and in November 1872 the *Cambrian News* advertised the service as follows:

UP	am	am	pm
Tywyn Pendre	8.30	11.30	3.00
Rhydyronen	8.40	11.40	3.10
Brynglas	8.45	11.45	3.15
Dolgoch	8.55	11.55	3.25
Abergynolwyn	9.10	12.10	3.40

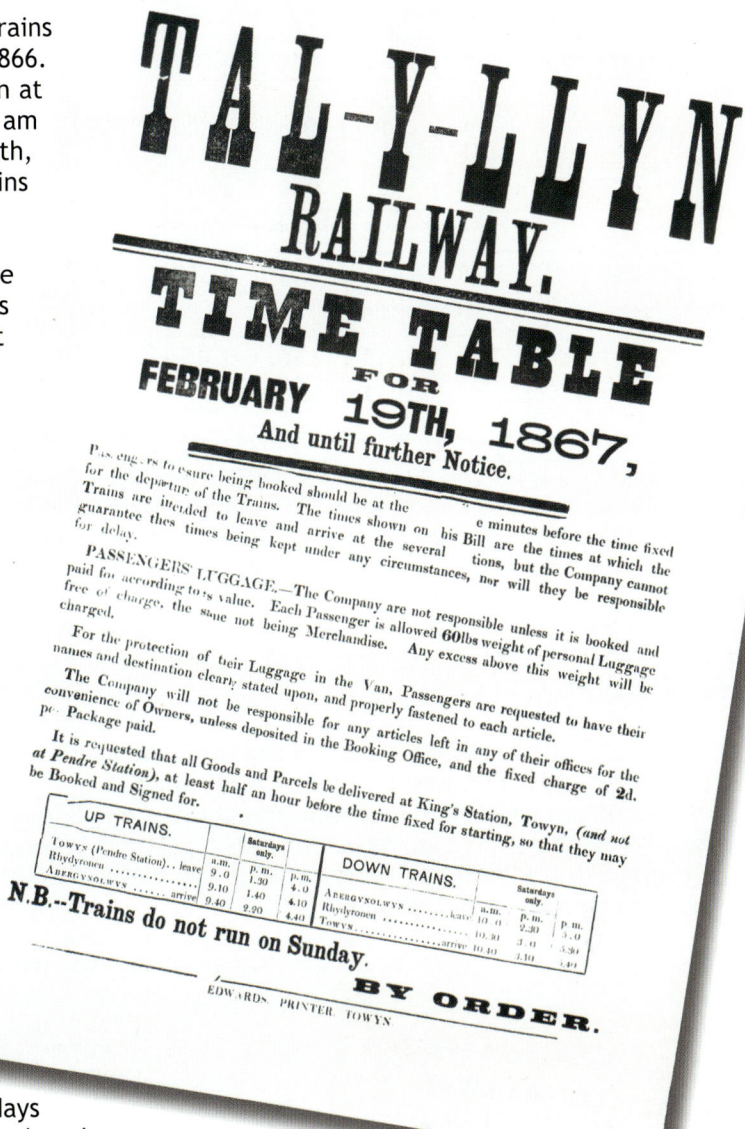

DOWN	am	pm	pm
Abergynolwyn	9.45	1.00	4.30
Dolgoch	10.00	1.15	4.45
Brynglas	10.10	1.25	4.55
Rhydyronen	10.15	1.30	5.00
Tywyn Pendre	10.25	1.40	5.10

In the winter months the 4.30 pm departure from Abergynolwyn would of course return to Tywyn after dark. By the following January the early train was back as a 9.30 am departure from Tywyn. This basic pattern held until April 1876 when the early Monday morning quarrymen's train was introduced (see overleaf). This was for the benefit of the quarrymen who lived at a distance, and then boarded at the quarry during the week.

Passenger Operations

UP	am MO	am	pm SO	pm
Tywyn Pendre	6.00	9.30	12.30	3.20
Rhydyronen	6.10	9.40	12.40	3.30
Brynglas	6.15	9.45	12.45	3.35
Dolgoch	6.25	9.55	12.55	3.45
Abergynolwyn	6.40	10.10	1.10	4.00

DOWN	am MO	am	pm SO	pm
Abergynolwyn	7.00	11.30	1.30	4.30
Dolgoch	7.15	11.45	1.45	4.45
Brynglas	7.25	11.55	1.55	4.55
Rhydyronen	7.30	12.00	2.00	5.00
Tywyn Pendre	7.40	12.10	2.10	5.10

MO - Mondays Only   SO - Saturdays Only

In 1877 the 6.30 pm departure from Tywyn reappeared in the timetable as a Saturdays only service operating in the summer. Between May 1879 and June 1881 the Saturdays only 12.30 pm departure was suspended, due to short-time working at the quarry. When it reappeared it, and the Monday 6 am train, had a note in the timetable to the effect that they would only operate when the quarry was working. This then remained the basic pattern of operation until 1889.

At this point the quarry changed to a five day week and a 5.25 pm Fridays only train was introduced. Meanwhile in 1887 the 12.35 pm and 6.40 pm departures operated on Mondays, Wednesdays and Saturdays. This was a pattern which continued in subsequent years although the early evening train became Saturdays only.

In July 1892 the first known timetable leaflet was issued (see below). This shows that up to five trains could operate during the day. This was a very intensive service, particularly if only one locomotive was in steam, although there could have been more than one crew.

By the summer of 1896 the summer service had become a little less intensive with a maximum of four return trips a day. Train departures from Pendre were then at 6 am (Mondays only), 9.30 am, 1 pm (1 August to 19 September), 3.20 pm, 5.25 pm (Fridays only) and 6.30 pm (Saturdays only during July). These trains continued to run with minor variations in timing until 1900.

As stated previously the first mention of the 'slate wharf' station as a place where trains could be boarded came in July 1900, but only in the summer of 1909 did it become the official starting point for passenger trains. In December 1909 the run down of the quarry and the preparations for potential closure of the line led to a reduction in service. Only the 9.30 am and 3.20 pm departures from Pendre ran, although this was increased the following summer. In July 1912 the service shown on the leaflet opposite operated.

This was to remain the pattern for the succeeding summers until 1916. From then on a late afternoon train was run every day during the summer months. In the 1920s the summer service became a fairly settled pattern of 9.25 am, 2.15 pm and 6 pm departures from Wharf, plus the Monday quarrymen's service.

During the winter months (October through June) things were a little more complicated. The 1 pm departure of the 1912 timetable continued only on alternate Saturdays until 1919 and the 6 pm service became Fridays only. In

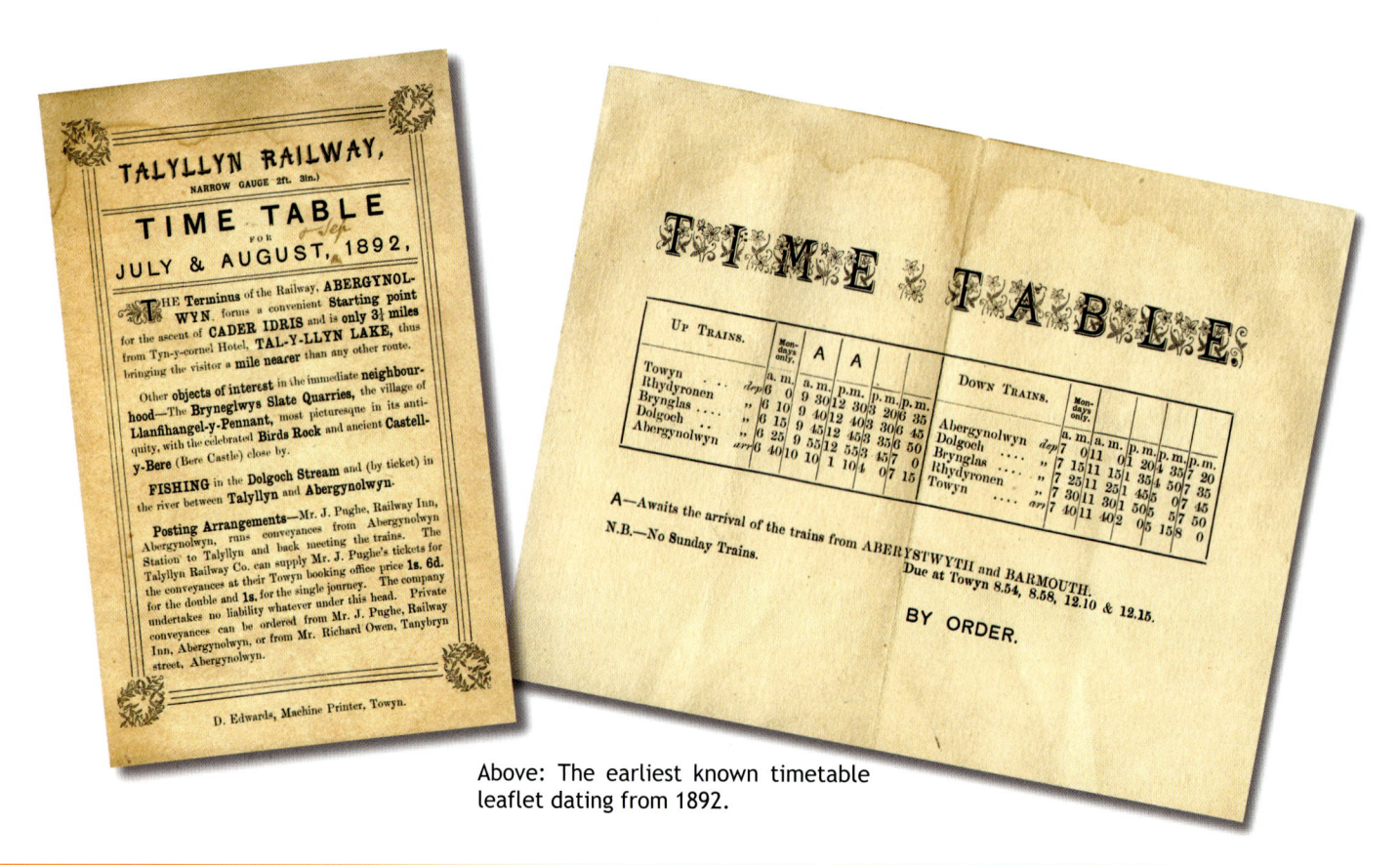

Above: The earliest known timetable leaflet dating from 1892.

150   Rails Along The Fathew

Passenger Operations

the late 1920s there were further minor variations in the services and in the summer of 1927 the timetable was as follows:

UP	am	am	pm	pm	pm
	MO			SX	SO
Tywyn Wharf		9.25	2.15		
Tywyn Pendre	6.00	9.30	2.20	5.50	7.15
Rhydyronen	6.10	9.40	2.30	6.00	7.25
Brynglas	6.15	9.45	2.35	6.05	7.30
Dolgoch	6.25	9.55	2.45	6.15	7.40
Abergynolwyn	6.40	10.10	3.00	6.30	7.55

DOWN	am	am	pm	pm	pm
Abergynolwyn	6.50	11.20	4.15	6.35	8.00
Dolgoch	7.05	11.35	4.30	6.50	8.15
Brynglas	7.15	11.45	4.40	7.00	8.25
Rhydyronen	7.20	11.50	4.45	7.05	8.30
Tywyn Pendre	7.30	12.00	4.55	7.15	8.40
Tywyn Wharf		12.05	5.00	7.20	8.45

MO - Mondays Only   SO - Saturdays Only
SX - Saturdays Excepted

There were major changes in April 1934 when the Monday quarrymen's service was withdrawn. Then from the October only two departures operated from Tywyn Wharf on Tuesdays, Thursdays and Saturdays at 9.25 am and 2.45 pm, except in summer when there were three departures on weekdays at 9.25 am, 2.15 pm and 5.50 pm (5.40 pm from 1936), the latter train departing from Pendre. In 1935 the days of winter operation were changed to Mondays, Wednesdays and Fridays, a pattern which remained until the outbreak of war in 1939.

The war-time service until 1950 has been covered on page 33 including the breaks in operation due to locomotive failures.

Passengers

The quarrymen formed a significant number of the passengers carried by the railway. The early Monday morning and Saturday/Friday return workings were designated as workmen's trains, and special workmen's fares applied.

Right: Summer timetable card from 1912.

Above Right: A hanging timetable card from the early 1930s with alterations to show the Wednesdays and Fridays Only service which operated in the latter part of the Second World War.

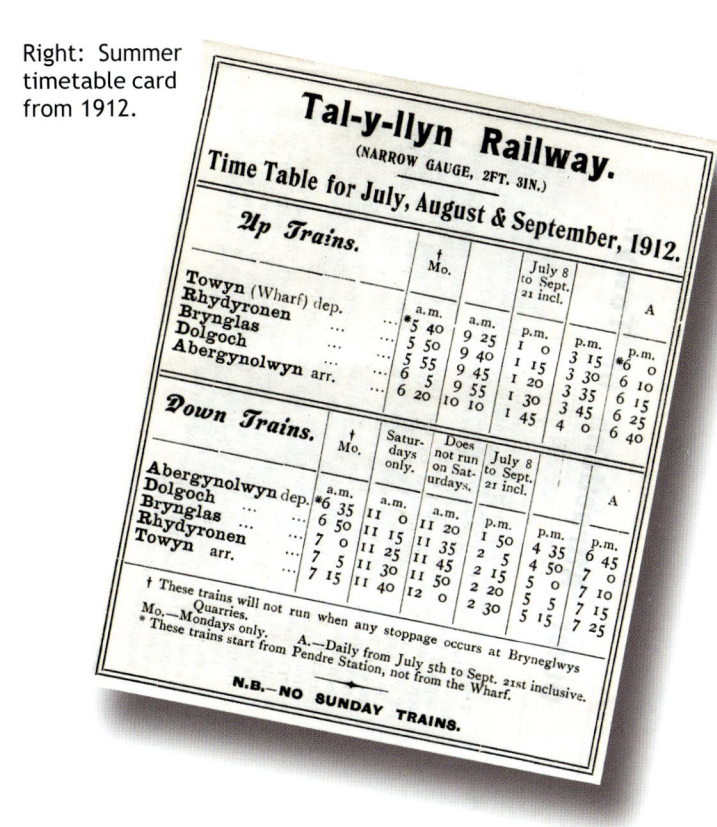

Rails Along The Fathew

151

Passenger Operations

Surprisingly, in 1899 only 2,392 such tickets were issued out of a total number of passenger journeys of 30,743 for the year. Allowing for the option that the tickets issued were returns, thus equating to two passenger journeys, this was still less than 20% of the total and represents an average of around 45 men travelling on each train.

Therefore, who else used the trains, aside from the quarrymen? Well, in the nineteenth century there were a significant number of farmers and local residents who used them, particularly to go to Tywyn for shopping, and other essential business. There were also schoolchildren who boarded in Tywyn during the week, and used the return quarryman's working from Abergynolwyn to get to Tywyn in time for lessons on a Monday morning. It is known that commercial travellers used the trains as well.

Another type of passenger for the early Monday morning return trip was suggested by the *Cambrian News* of 7 April 1876 which stated that:

The return train will also enable ministers visiting the place (Abergynolwyn) *for a Sunday to* (catch) *early trains on the Cambrian Railway, and reach journey's end in more seasonable time.*

Officially there were no Sunday trains on the railway before 1959.

Among other passengers who used the trains on a regular basis was the village policeman from Abergynolwyn in the 1870s and 1880s. He used the service to get to meetings with his superiors. Doubtless there were others too who relied on the railway to conduct their everyday business, certainly before the advent of an alternative bus service and increasing car ownership. Indeed local traffic still continues into the preservation era.

Of course during the summer there were the tourists who had come to see the line and marvel at its delights. Posters and timetable leaflets extolled the virtues of the scenery and the pleasures awaiting the sightseer spending a day on the railway. These summer visitors became increasingly significant as seen by the figures for 1921:

Four-week Period Ending	1st class	3rd class
29 January	0	955
26 February	0	1385
26 March	0	1113
23 April	10	1343
21 May	7	1501
18 June	11	1914
16 July	3	2269
13 August	58	5538
10 September	82	7332
8 October	20	2305
5 November	2	1115
3 December	0	848
31 December	0	948
TOTAL	193	28566

By 1933 passenger numbers had drastically declined as seen in the table below (by this time 1st class had also been abolished):

Four-week Period Ending	3rd class
11 February	80
11 March	213
8 April	166
6 May	219
3 June	397
1 July	311
29 July	692
26 August	661
23 September	2276
21 October	1016
18 November	259
16 December	199
6 January 1934	92
TOTAL	6746

In both cases the peaks in the numbers travelling during the summer tourist season can be clearly seen. However, the loss of quarry traffic, plus the introduction of a competing bus service has had its effect on the overall numbers. Even the numbers of tourists travelling has declined, possibly due to the economic conditions at the time. The graph opposite shows the decline in passenger journeys between 1920 and 1939.

Above: An advertisement for the railway from the 1890s encouraging tourists.

Passenger Operations

The Decline in the Number of Passenger Journeys 1920 - 1939

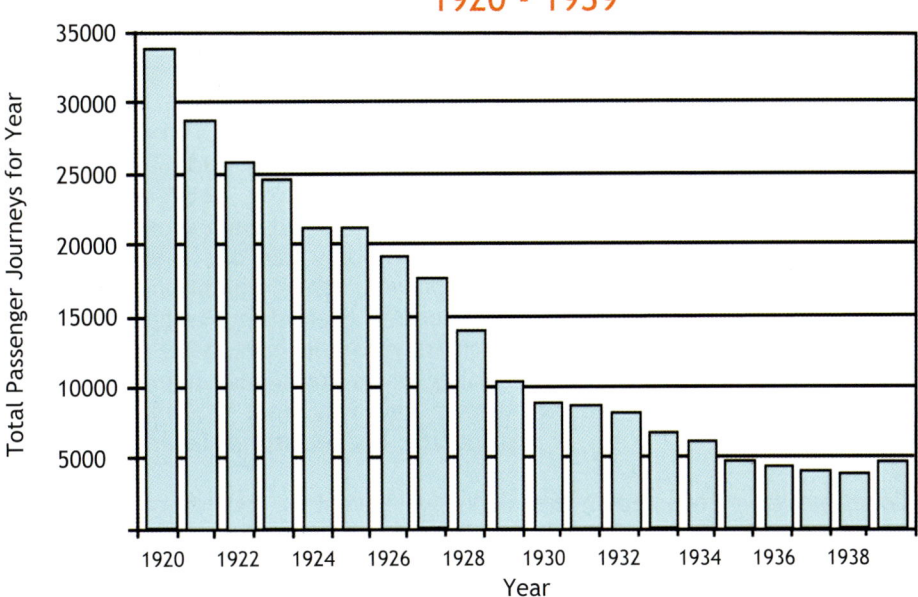

Pre-preservation Special Trains and Events

From the earliest days of the railway there were also events at both Tywyn and Abergynolwyn which attracted passengers, often with special trains being laid on. In Tywyn on Good Fridays there were a number of activities taking place, some of which reflected the solemnity of the day, others seemingly less so. In 1868 it was recorded that both sacred and secular events brought people to Tywyn on the Talyllyn, whose carriages were said to be 'well-filled'.

By contrast the Easter Monday Fair was a uniformly joyous occasion with the town bursting with visitors. That same year the *North Wales Chronicle* reported that the Talyllyn's trains were 'crowded to suffocation'. In 1885 and 1887 newspaper reports stated that hundreds were brought by the railway to the fair. The *Cambrian News* stated in 1887 that:

There were special trains running on the Talyllyn Railway, attached to one of which were seventeen slate-wagons loaded with people for the fair.

There were other events that attracted travellers on the railway too. On Tuesday 2 November 1869 an Eisteddfod was held at Abergynolwyn. Many of the participants and audience travelled up from Tywyn and a procession was made from Abergynolwyn station to the meeting place. This was in time for a 1.30 pm start, which implies that they had travelled on a special train for the occasion.

Certainly special trains were laid on for similar events later, as stated in the *Cambrian News* of 24 August 1877:

As most of the audience came from Towyn and its neighbourhood, there was a greater demand made for railway carriages than the Talyllyn Railway Company could supply. The passengers had accordingly to avail themselves of engine, van, and a large number of railway trucks which were attached to the carriages.

One late night special operated on 13 April 1886 when William Abraham, M.P. for Rhondda, came on a speaking tour of the area. It is recorded that he travelled from Corris to Abergynolwyn to speak at a meeting there at 10 pm, before travelling by special train to Tywyn. Here he mounted the platform at 11.30 pm and the meeting continued until 1.30 am!

Other trips were organised for other reasons. In June 1871 an outing for the pupils of the Towyn Academy necessitated an early start so that they could reach Castell-y-Bere by 10.30 am after walking from Abergynolwyn. Similarly a late return train was organised from Abergynolwyn at 7 pm. In December 1895 a special train was arranged in connection with a presentation to Mr Meyrick Roberts, the Quarry Manager. There were also other trips arranged for various groups and organisations throughout the 19th Century.

While these were joyous occasions, there were other more solemn events. There was a special train arranged in December 1898 for mourners attending the funeral of W.J. Griffith, a young man of 27 who had died. Sometimes it was more than the mourners the train carried.

The *Cambrian News* of 7 February 1902 records the funeral of David Davies who had been killed in an accident at Bryneglwys, it relates:

The body was conveyed from Abergynolwyn to Towyn by a large special train and was met at the Pentref Station on the Talyllyn Railway by a large concourse of people.

Another special train was arranged for the funeral of Hugh Thomas, the father of Edward Thomas in 1903. He was a long time employee of the railway and it is said that on the day:

The quarrymen of their own accord suspended work during the day, and came down in a body by special train

Rails Along The Fathew — 153

Passenger Operations

placed at their service by Mr Yates. It ought to be noted here that the funeral was one of the largest that has taken place in Towyn for many years.

(*Cambrian News* 6 February 1903)

Dolgoch

One of the busiest days in the railway's pre-preservation history came when the Dolgoch Ravine was effectively gifted to the people of Tywyn. The Whit Monday following the donation was particularly busy, as the *County Times* of 22 May 1902 reported:

The officials of the miniature railway had a busy time of it on Monday, no less than six trains being run up and down. It was well patronised, a good number visiting Dolgoch for the falls and pleasure ground.

The following month the *Cambrian News* reported on the annual picnic of the English Presbyterian Sunday School, this stated that:

On account of the small number of ordinary trains on the Talyllyn Railway, arrangements had been made for special trains, and this was fully justified by the large number who joined the picnic party.

Later that year the *Cambrian News* reported that the railway carried a record number of people on one day, when the Agricultural Show was held on 12 September in Tywyn. It said that:

So great was the incursion into the town that day, that the countryside was practically denuded of its population.

All this poses a question, did the railway always keep to the rule of 'one engine in steam'? Certainly all the public timetables were compliant with that rule, but what about these special occasions? It is possible that six return trips were made by one locomotive and train on Whit Monday in 1902, but it would have been a long day. When such large numbers travelled might a second locomotive and train have been involved?

There are some anecdotes from the Haydn Jones era of two trains being operated. The carriages and wagons were reportedly split between the two locomotives, which then followed each other up the line, although of course they only had one brake van between them. In addition as the condition of both locomotives deteriorated their ability to handle heavy trains on such 'high' days would have been impaired. Therefore, two smaller trains could have been an option, after all they were a long way from Whitehall and the offices of the Inspector, but the stories could be apocryphal.

Sadly we have few records of special trains operating during Haydn Jones' time, but doubtless such trips and outings continued. However, like the ordinary passenger traffic, they increasingly had to deal with competition from charabanc trips and similar.

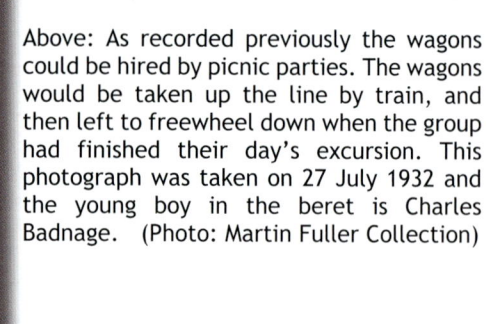

Above: As recorded previously the wagons could be hired by picnic parties. The wagons would be taken up the line by train, and then left to freewheel down when the group had finished their day's excursion. This photograph was taken on 27 July 1932 and the young boy in the beret is Charles Badnage. (Photo: Martin Fuller Collection)

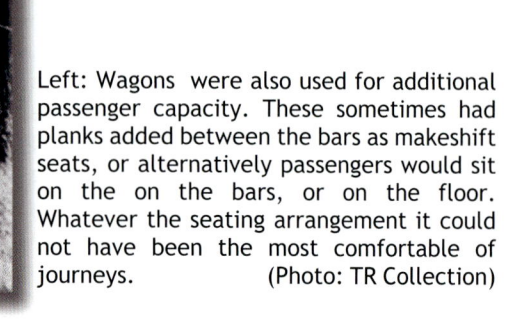

Left: Wagons were also used for additional passenger capacity. These sometimes had planks added between the bars as makeshift seats, or alternatively passengers would sit on the on the bars, or on the floor. Whatever the seating arrangement it could not have been the most comfortable of journeys. (Photo: TR Collection)

154 Rails Along The Fathew

Passenger Operations

Post-Preservation Timetables

Of course, much as with the pre-preservation timetables, it would take a longer book than this to detail every timetable change that has taken place since 1951. Essentially through the 1950s, 1960s and early 1970s there was a significant increase in the number of trains operated.

Following the events of Whit Monday 14 May 1951 when the service had been run to Rhydyronen, it was decided to run two trains a day on Mondays to Fridays from Monday 4 June until 28 September departing from Tywyn Wharf at 10.30 am and 2.45 pm. The journey time was increased to an hour due to the state of the track, which meant the return workings departed Abergynolwyn at 11.45 pm and 4 pm. No trains ran on Saturdays or Sundays.

The service was increased in 1952, as seen in the following table which operated between 2 June and 27 September:

UP	am MF	pm MS	pm WSOa
Tywyn Wharf	10.25	2.50	6.20
Tywyn Pendre	10.30	2.55	6.25
Rhydyronen	10.45	3.10	6.40
Brynglas	10.53	3.18	6.48
Dolgoch	11.10	3.35	7.05
Abergynolwyn	11.25	3.50	7.20

DOWN	am MF	pm MS	pm WSOa
Abergynolwyn	11.45	4.50	7.35
Dolgoch	12.05	5.10	7.55
Brynglas	12.20	5.25	8.10
Rhydyronen	12.28	5.33	8.18
Tywyn Pendre	12.40	5.45	8.30
Tywyn Wharf	12.45	5.50	8.35

MF – Monday to Friday
MS – Monday to Saturday
WSOa – Wednesday and Saturday only between 19 July and 6 September

In 1953 the last public train ran where passengers were allowed to ride in slate wagons. This followed a derailment involving a scout party on 1 August that year which led to claims being made against the company.

For 1954 the evening trains on Wednesdays and Saturdays were eliminated, while the 2.50 pm departure was retimed to 3 pm, made possible by a decrease in the running time to 55 minutes. There was though another innovation, the introduction of a 2.15 pm Dolgoch and Abergynolwyn only service for the peak season, which arrived at Abergynolwyn at 3 pm and returned at 4.30 pm. This led to the sight of two passenger trains at Abergynolwyn in the mid-afternoon. Extra trains could also be run due to the availability of the loop at Brynglas and increasingly ran as required.

However, in 1959, three significant changes took place. The first was the introduction of the first official passenger service on a Sunday departing from Wharf at 2.50 pm from 5 July to 6 September. The second was the speeding up of services, and the last was the introduction of a high peak four departure service for the school holidays on Mondays to Fridays with trains passing at Pendre as follows:

UP	am	pm	pm	pm
Tywyn Wharf	10.25	1.40	3.00	3.15
Tywyn Pendre	10.30			3.25
Rhydyronen	10.42			3.37
Brynglas	10.48			3.43
Dolgoch	11.03	2.10	3.37	4.00
Abergynolwyn	11.15	2.20	3.45	4.10

DOWN	am	pm	pm	pm
Abergynolwyn	11.55	2.25	4.30	5.00
Dolgoch	12.08	2.35	4.45	5.15
Brynglas	12.18			5.25
Rhydyronen	12.24			5.31
Tywyn Pendre	12.36			5.41
Tywyn Wharf	12.40	3.10	5.15	5.45

During 1960 the high peak Monday to Friday service became five departures from Wharf with crossings at Brynglas:

UP	am	pm	pm	pm	pm
Tywyn Wharf	10.25	1.15	2.00	3.00	3.50
Tywyn Pendre	10.30			3.05	cr
Rhydyronen	10.40			3.15	cr
Brynglas	10.46			3.20	cr
Dolgoch	11.00	1.45	2.35	3.35	4.30
Abergynolwyn	11.10	1.55	2.45	3.45	4.40

DOWN	am	pm	pm	pm	pm
Abergynolwyn	11.50	2.00	2.55	4.45	5.00
Dolgoch	12.03	2.08	3.05	5.00	5.15
Brynglas	12.13				5.25
Rhydyronen	12.19				5.31
Tywyn Pendre	12.29				5.41
Tywyn Wharf	12.34	2.45	3.40	5.30	5.45

cr - calls if required

On Saturdays in the high peak only the 2 pm and 3 pm departures ran, and on Sunday there was only one train at 3 pm. With minor changes this service operated in 1961. In 1962 an additional down relief from Abergynolwyn operated at the end of the day. The following year the down relief was replaced by an additional train in the middle of the day. Departures from Wharf were then 10.25 am, 11.55 am, 1.15 pm, 2.10 pm,

Rails Along The Fathew

155

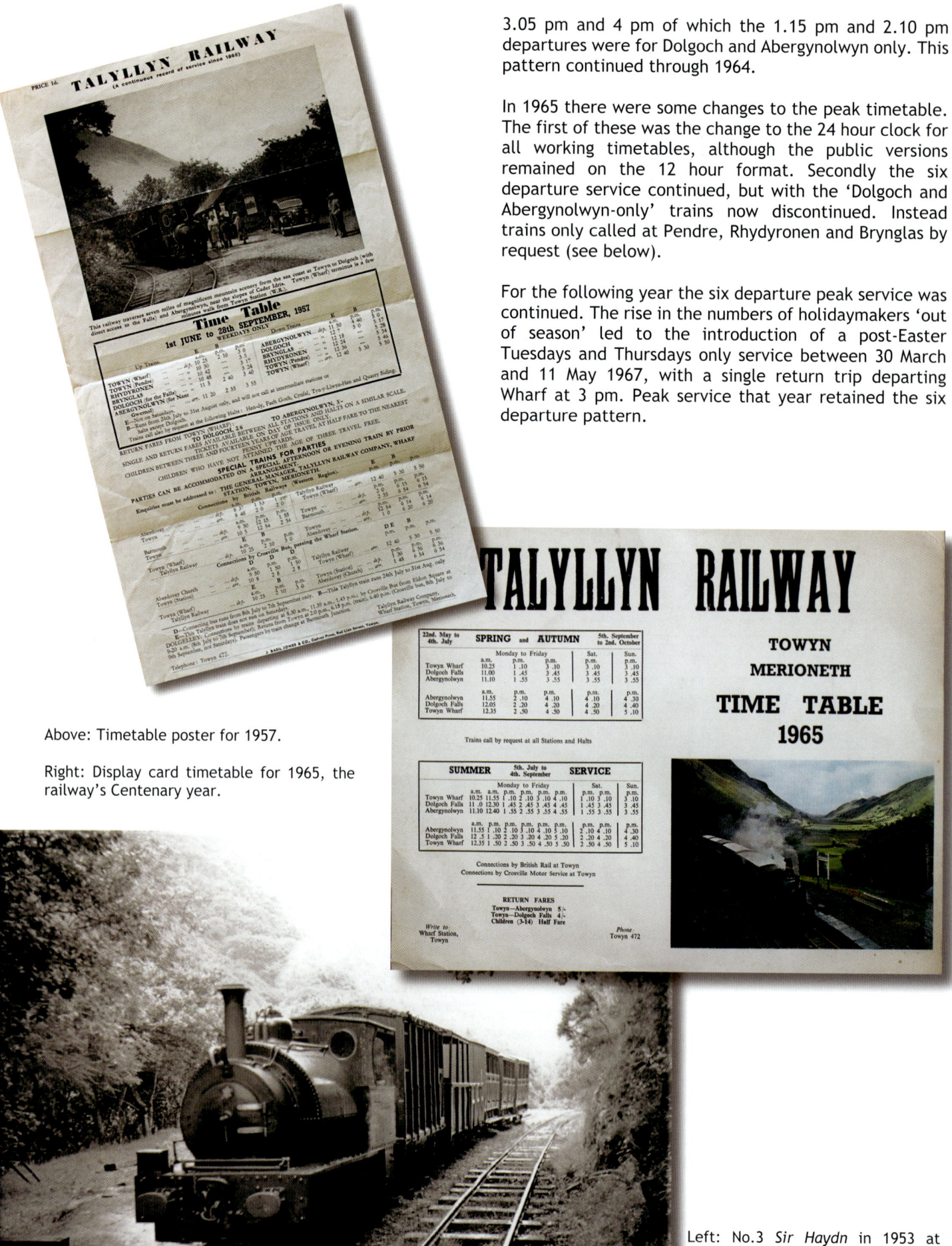

Passenger Operations

3.05 pm and 4 pm of which the 1.15 pm and 2.10 pm departures were for Dolgoch and Abergynolwyn only. This pattern continued through 1964.

In 1965 there were some changes to the peak timetable. The first of these was the change to the 24 hour clock for all working timetables, although the public versions remained on the 12 hour format. Secondly the six departure service continued, but with the 'Dolgoch and Abergynolwyn-only' trains now discontinued. Instead trains only called at Pendre, Rhydyronen and Brynglas by request (see below).

For the following year the six departure peak service was continued. The rise in the numbers of holidaymakers 'out of season' led to the introduction of a post-Easter Tuesdays and Thursdays only service between 30 March and 11 May 1967, with a single return trip departing Wharf at 3 pm. Peak service that year retained the six departure pattern.

Above: Timetable poster for 1957.

Right: Display card timetable for 1965, the railway's Centenary year.

Left: No.3 *Sir Haydn* in 1953 at Abergynolwyn with a train consisting of three original Talyllyn coaches, the original brake van and opens Nos. 7 and 8. (Photo: R. Holcombe)

156 — Rails Along The Fathew

Passenger Operations

During 1968 the post-Easter Tuesdays and Thursdays only service was retained. The peak service was six departures on Mondays and Fridays, seven on Tuesdays and Thursdays, and eight on Wednesdays. This was with the introduction of a 5 pm departure (Tuesdays to Thursdays), and a 7.30 pm Wednesdays only evening train.

The next major shake-up of the service occurred in 1969 with the introduction of the 'three-train' service with three train sets in use during the peak. This led to the introduction of a near 'clock-face' peak service with up to eleven trains departing Wharf Mondays to Thursdays, with an evening train on Wednesdays, as seen below:

Additional services were operated over the Easter school holidays and the spring service was run on Sundays, Tuesdays and Thursdays. Pre-peak services were also increased. At the other end of the season a 2.30 pm departure was run on Sundays, Tuesdays and Thursdays during October. Over the next few years this pattern of service was retained, with minor changes in timings, and also an expansion of out of peak services.

The opening of the Extension to Nant Gwernol in 1976 saw a major revision of passenger operations. As a result of the longer journey times, and also the introduction of an extended refreshment break at Abergynolwyn on the down trip, a fifty-minute interval Monday to Friday peak service was run as set out in the timetable at the foot of the page:

UP		am	am	am	pm	pm	pm	pm	pm	pm	pm	pm	pm
													FX	WO
Tywyn Wharf		10.15	10.45	11.15	12.15	12.45	1.15	2.15	2.45	3.15	4.15	4.45	7.30
Tywyn Pendre	R	10.20	10.50	11.20	12.20	12.50	1.20	2.20	2.50	3.20	4.20	4.50	
Rhydyronen	R	10.29	10.59	11.29	12.29	12.59	1.29	2.29	2.59	3.29	4.29	4.59	
Brynglas	R	10.35	11.05	11.35	12.35	1.05	1.35	2.35	3.05	3.35	4.35	5.05	
Dolgoch		10.45	11.15	11.45	12.50	1.20	1.50	2.50	3.20	3.50	4.50	5.20	8.00
Abergynolwyn		11.00	11.30	12.00	1.00	1.30	2.00	3.00	3.30	4.00	5.00	5.30	8.10

DOWN		am	am	pm	pm	pm	pm	pm	pm	pm	pm	pm	pm
Abergynolwyn		11.15	11.45	12.15	1.15	1.45	2.15	3.15	3.45	4.15	5.15	5.45	8.30
Dolgoch		11.25	11.55	12.25	1.25	1.55	2.25	3.25	3.55	4.25	5.25	5.55	8.45
Brynglas	R	11.35	12.05	12.35	1.35	2.05	2.35	3.35	4.05	4.35	5.35	6.05	
Rhydyronen	R	11.44	12.14	12.44	1.44	2.14	2.44	3.44	4.14	4.44	5.44	6.14	
Tywyn Pendre	R	11.52	12.22	12.52	1.52	2.22	2.52	3.52	4.22	4.52	5.52	6.22	
Tywyn Wharf		11.55	12.25	12.55	1.55	2.25	2.55	3.55	4.25	4.55	5.55	6.25	9.10

R - Calls by Request   FX - Fridays Excepted   SO - Saturdays Only

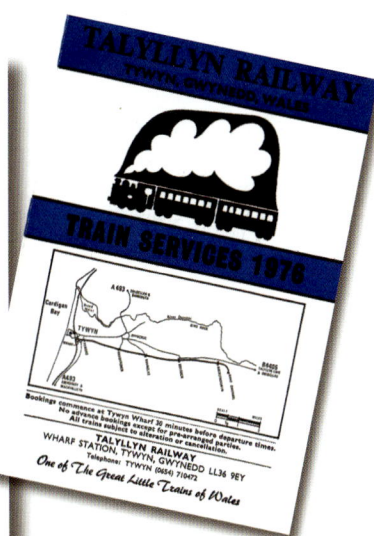

Above and Left: The timetable leaflet from 1976.

Rails Along The Fathew

157

Passenger Operations

Below: Timetable poster for 1988.

Right: The full timetable for 2015, showing the pattern of operation throughout the year.

Peak service was increased to nine departures in 1991 as part of the 40th Anniversary of the Preservation Society, but returned to eight the following year. In 1995 there were significant changes to the timetable including the introduction of a daily named train, 'The Quarryman'.

The peak service was again increased to nine departures for the 50th Anniversary of preservation in 2001, but once more this only survived one season. That year the last regular scheduled evening train was also run.

There was a further reduction in the peak service to seven departures in 2009, and then to six departures in 2013. That year also saw a major revision to much of the timetable, with many off-peak services being reduced as well. This had the benefit of reducing the numbers of staff and volunteers required to operate the services. The year also saw the demise of 'The Quarryman'.

This actually reduced the number of peak train services, but with additional rolling stock in service the overall numbers that could be transported was maintained. At this point serious consideration was being given to the introduction of four-train-set service, but due to falling passenger numbers this was never implemented.

This pattern held until 1982 when the peak Monday to Friday service was reduced to nine departures. The Saturday service was reduced to four departures and there was a Wednesdays only evening train. During 1983 the Saturday service was reduced to two departures, and the evening train had moved from Wednesday to Sunday. In addition, extra trains were run when there was sufficient demand, and by 1989 the Saturday service had been increased to four departures again.

In 1986 the Monday to Friday service was reduced to eight departures, but the full peak service was run during the Spring Bank Holiday week. The increasing importance of the off-peak or 'shoulder' season led to daily running through October being introduced.

The Vintage Train

It had been realised that the fact the Talyllyn possessed both of its original locomotives and all its original carriages could be used as a marketing tool. Therefore, starting in the mid-1960s, there were various attempts to introduce a 'Vintage Train' making use of them.

These included running them in the evenings and on Sundays. More recently there has been a largely successful use of the train on Thursdays during the off-peak in June, July and September. These services have included opportunities for photographic run-pasts, and also either a tour of the workshops at Pendre or a cream tea at Tywyn Wharf.

Passenger Operations

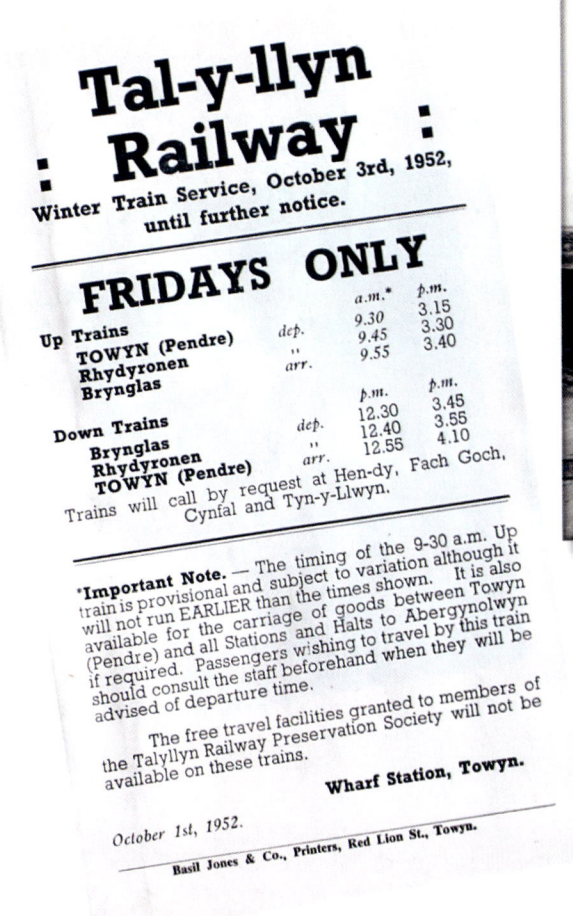

Above: No.3 *Sir Haydn* with a winter service train consisting of carriage No.1 and van No.5 at Tywyn Wharf during the winter of 1953/54. (Photo: R.K. Walton)

The Winter Service

During the post-preservation period there were also several attempts to run a winter Fridays-only train service. This was for those living close to the line to get into Tywyn to do their shopping. The first of these was run for a brief period between 1952 and 1954, but the need for track renewals brought the service to an end.

In 1963 the idea of a Fridays only winter service was revived, due to local demand, and trains ran from 4 October with the following timetable:

UP	am	pm
Tywyn Pendre	11.35	3.05
Rhydyronen	11.50	3.20
Brynglas	12.00	3.30
DOWN	pm	pm
Brynglas	12.15	3.35
Rhydyronen	12.25	3.45
Tywyn Pendre	12.40	4.00

The standard train formation was diesel loco No.5 *Midlander* with Corris coach No.17 and van No.6.

Passenger figures were sufficiently encouraging for the service to be repeated the following winter but then it was discontinued.

It was revived for the winter of 1970/71 and for subsequent winters through to the spring of 1973, but again was abandoned. In 1977 a regular service began for the week between Christmas and New Year, which has continued ever since.

Tickets and Fares

Like much of the early history of the Talyllyn the subject of tickets is shrouded in some mystery. It is presumed that Edmondson card tickets were used from the outset, but no tickets are known dated earlier than 1902. Interestingly, however, there are some tickets that survive which are both undated and also do not have fares printed on them, see below:

Images Courtesy The National Archives

One theory is that the tickets without fares were printed before The Regulation of Railways Act of 1889, which stated they should have the fares printed on them. It is then known that when R.B. Yates became manager he acquired at least two date stamps, one of which was mounted in the brake van when it was fitted as a mobile booking office. These were to prevent the tickets from being used in a fraudulent manner, and from then on tickets were usually date stamped. The tickets were then reprinted with fares.

Rails Along The Fathew

Passenger Operations

Images Courtesy The National Archives

Edmondson tickets continued to be used on the railway, with various colours and markings to denote the types of tickets being issued, long into the preservation era. The advent of Gift Aid necessitated the introduction of computer printed tickets at Tywyn Wharf in 2013, but Edmondson tickets are still in use at other stations and from the brake van booking offices.

The Talyllyn Railway Act set down the maximum level of fares as 1½d per mile Third Class, 2d per mile Second and 3d per mile First. Surprisingly in 1879 a Third Class fare between Tywyn and Abergynolwyn was only 6d and the Second Class fare was 1s. This meant the Third Class fare was less than 1d per mile, and only just achieved that rate when the fares were later increased to 6½d for Third Class and 1s 2d for Second by 1892.

Use of this fare would explain the fact that the Talyllyn never seems to have designated any trains as being 'Parliamentary'. The fact that they ran all trains with closed Third Class carriages at a rate of a penny a mile or less would have satisfied the terms of the Railway Regulation Act of 1844.

When the Cheap Trains Act of 1883 was introduced, which removed passenger duty on fares of 1d per mile or less, William McConnel wrote to the Board of Trade to confirm that their workman's tickets of ½d per mile were also exempt. These workmen's fares survived until 1898 at least, probably much longer, although interestingly no 'workman's ticket' has so far ever come to light.

First Class fares were available between the railway's opening and 1873, when these became Second Class in the returns to the Board of Trade (although McConnel still refers to these as First Class fares in 1883). In 1914 the Second Class fare seems to have been at a rate of 1½d per mile.

In 1917 the government ordered an increase in fares for the railways under its war-time jurisdiction, and the Talyllyn seems to have followed suit. Third Class fares were doubled to 2d per mile.

Second Class was abolished in July 1920 and became First Class with fares 50% higher than Third Class. Around this time return fares seem to have been introduced with fares 50% higher than for singles. First Class was abolished in 1932, and from then on all fares were Third Class.

The next major change in fares came in March 1948 when they were increased by at least 50%, making a Tywyn to Abergynolwyn Third Class return rise from 1s 8d to 2s 6d. These fares remained in force into the preservation-era. It was also at this time that 'Pendre' instead of 'Towyn' appeared on tickets, 'Wharf' having appeared on the tickets since the early twentieth century.

Above: Pre- and Post- 1948 tickets illustrating the use of Pendre instead of Towyn from 1948, as well as the substantial fare increase.

Post-Preservation Fares

In 1955 the first fare increase took place since 1948, despite the huge popularity of the railway. This took a Tywyn Wharf to Abergynolwyn return (the most expensive fare then available) to 3s, a 20% increase. In 1961 the same return fare was increased by a third to 4s.

By the time of decimalisation in 1971 the fare had risen to 35p or 7s. Through the early 1970s, the era of inflation brought about by the Middle East Oil Crisis, and the same fare had doubled to 70p by 1975. At this point the Extension to Nant Gwernol opened, and with the Increased length of run the full-length return became £1. From 1976 fares were no longer printed on the tickets, instead the generic term 'Fare As Advertised' was used.

Above: Post-1976 tickets with 'Fare As Advertised', the right hand ticket shows the use of the Welsh 'Rheilffordd Talyllyn'.

With continuing inflation more increases were to follow. In 1981 the Tywyn Wharf to Nant Gwernol return had become £2, and by 1985 it was £2.80. In 1995 a new 'Day Rover' fare was introduced, for a pound more than a Tywyn Wharf to Nant Gwernol return passengers could have unlimited travel on the line for £8.50.

From 2000 all Tywyn Wharf to Nant Gwernol returns became day rovers. These were priced at £9.50 in 2003 and by 2015 the standard day rover was £16.30. This sounds an horrendous increase since 1951, but in fact when compared with the rise in income levels, and also the increased length of the journey, they are surprisingly in keeping with the increase in people's personal income.

Goods Operations

Slate

For much of its life goods traffic on the line was dominated by slate. In a letter from the A&WCR to Thomas McConnel in March 1864, it is clear that one of the earliest ideas discussed was that of 'piggy-backing' slate wagons on top of standard gauge flat wagons between Tywyn Wharf and Aberdyfi.

This would have saved a considerable amount of handling, and it is unclear why it did not go ahead. A possible explanation was the lack of storage space at Aberdyfi. Later in 1886 the subject was raised again during the dispute with the Cambrian over goods rates between Tywyn and Aberdyfi. At this time the Talyllyn refused to consider it on the grounds that it did not have sufficient wagons available for a rake to be away from the railway. (It is believed that at that time a rake consisted of ten wagons.)

In his initial discussions with the A&WCR McConnel suggested that he anticipated an annual total of 20,000 tons of slate passing between Tywyn and Aberdyfi. In the end the amount of traffic proved to be much less and the interchange at Wharf was able to handle the traffic easily.

Sadly the actual tonnage of slate carried by the railway was not recorded separately, but analysis of the minerals carried on the railway compared to the slate produced at Bryneglwys shows that they follow a similar pattern. There is some variation and the railway appears to have conveyed around 1,000 tons of other minerals per annum. The chart below shows the tonnage of minerals carried on the railway during the McConnel era.

The levels of slate production, although more modest than hoped, were reasonably consistent until around 1903 when they began to decline rapidly. At its peak the slate quarried at Bryneglwys reached nearly 8,000 tons, which would have equated to approximately 200 wagon loads a week. This would have been easily handled with the slate wagon stock available. In fact, so limited was the traffic that there was hardly any need to run separate slate trains, and by the 1890s McConnel told the Board of Trade that nearly every train was 'mixed'.

Slate was also quarried at various times in the Dolgoch ravine and also in the valley above Rhydyronen, but how this was transported and in what quantities is not known. For the Haydn Jones era up until the Second World War the amount of minerals carried is shown on the graph overleaf.

Tonnage of Minerals Carried Per Annum 1867 - 1910

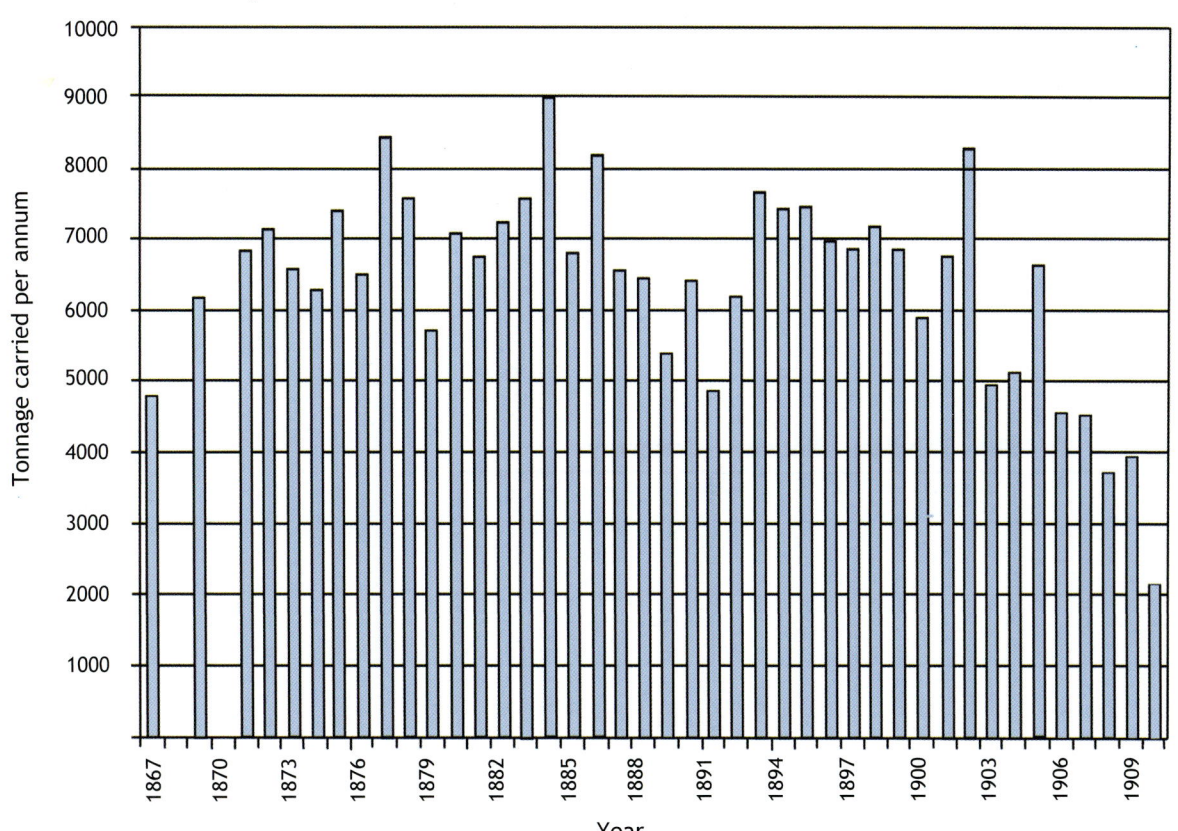

Source: Annual Returns to the Board of Trade

Goods Operations

Tonnage of Minerals Carried Per Annum 1919 and 1938

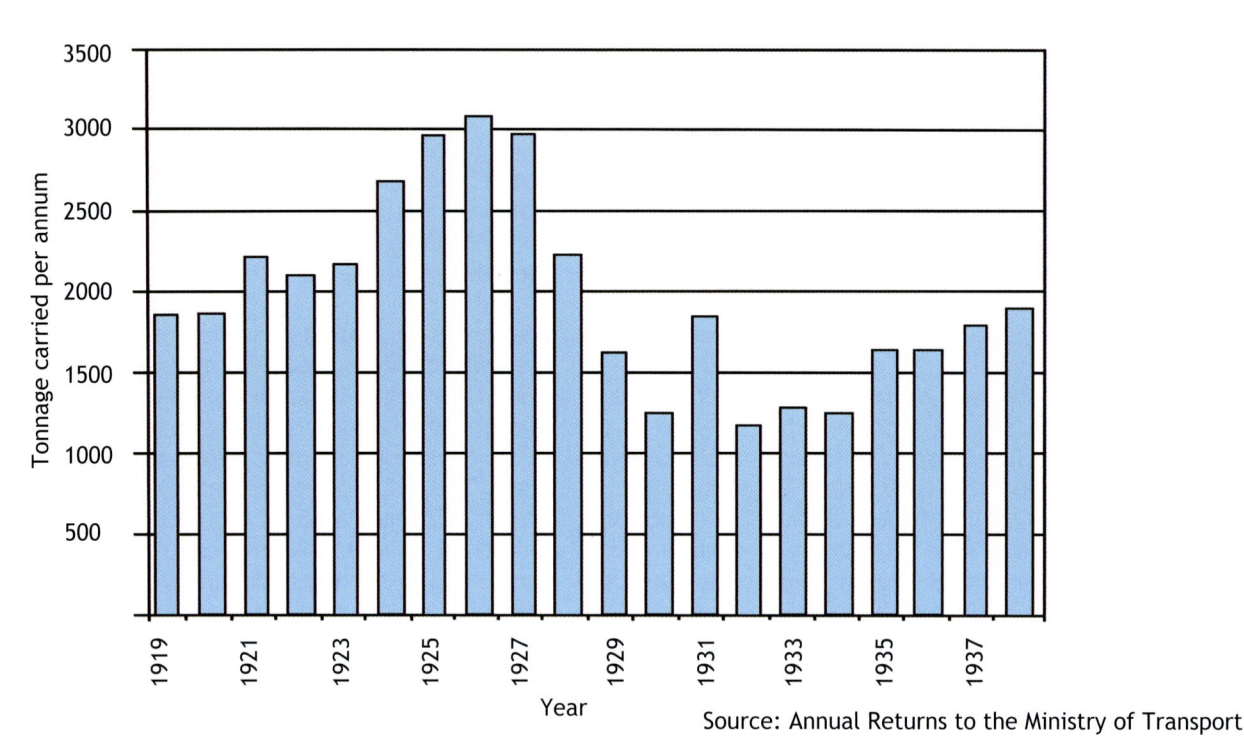

Source: Annual Returns to the Ministry of Transport

This shows how the post-First World War 'boom' turned into a decline during the late 1920s and into the early 1930s. There was, however, a small recovery towards the end of the 1930s. Sadly we do not have the figures for the period of the Second World War, but anecdotal evidence tells us that there was a mini-boom in the slate traffic due to the damage during the Blitz. This meant that slate trains were sometimes run on the days that passenger trains were not operating. With the end of the war and the closure of the quarry the slate traffic rapidly declined with the last of the slate stocks being cleared.

Other Traffic

Slate was not the only traffic carried on the railway, coal was also significant. When the quarry was shut down during the change in ownership during 1910/11, the returns showed that just over 300 tons of coal and other minerals were carried on the railway. It is not unreasonable to suppose that the bulk of this was coal. This coal traffic would have continued until competition from road deliveries made an impact.

There were other sources of goods traffic as well. At Brynglas the woollen and flour mills generated some traffic. Abergynolwyn also needed to be supplied with provisions, much of it transported down the incline, for example, there were regular deliveries of fish from Grimsby.

In addition, the quarry needed to be supplied with equipment and spares as well as provisions for the men living up there during the week. An indication of the variety of commodities carried comes from the goods receipt books, and some of the pages from these are reproduced opposite.

Farmers and Livestock

One of the other major sources of traffic was the farms along the line. In later days these required deliveries of fertiliser and poultry food, and also agricultural implements and even cart wheels.

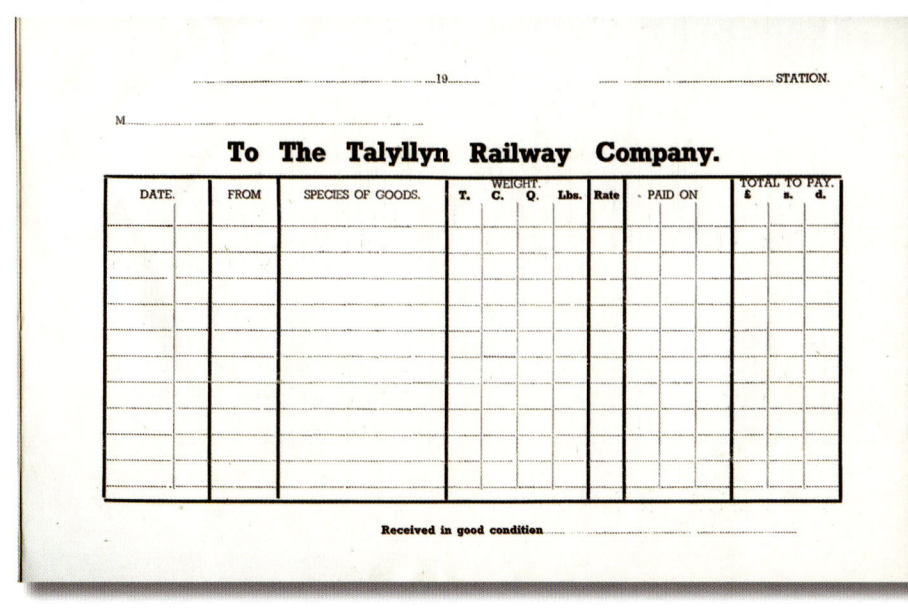

Left: A blank goods receipt form.

Goods Operations

Three pages from the goods receipt books showing the range of goods carried as well as their destinations.

Left: The first page comes from April 1918, when the First World War was still in progress. One point of note is that where a specific address in Abergynolwyn is recorded, e.g. Lan St., short for Llanegryn Street, or Tan St., short for Tan-y-Bryn Street, it indicates that these goods were delivered via the village incline and rail system.

Right: The second page is from February 1926. Being winter the number of coal deliveries is probably not surprising. As already noted the delivery of fish from Grimsby was a regular weekly occurrence.

Left: This page from July 1946 seems to show the last recorded delivery to be made via the village rail system. Together these pages show the contribution the railway made to the local community in providing a delivery service for their supplies.

Goods Operations

Left: Hay made from the grass cut from the lineside was stored at each station and also in the coal yard at Tywyn Wharf. The supply at Wharf was used to pack between the slates, while the stacks at the other stations were sold. Haydn Jones had a barn erected at Pendre, which was used to store hay largely for use at his own home at Pantyneuadd.

Bracken could also be cut for animal bedding, with customers loading a borrowed wagon and then having it transported to where it was required. This can be seen in this photograph where a wooden frame, or hurdle, has been placed on top of a slate wagon and then loaded with bracken as far as the loading gauge would allow.

The people in the photograph have possibly been identified as, left to right: Revd. Daniel Lincoln Jones, one of Sir Haydn's brothers, and his son, Idris, while David Jones is loading the bracken on top of the wagon.
(Photo: TR Collection)

Right: Odd loads could be carried up the line as seen here in August 1923 with a hurdle being carried on the last wagon of the train. Maybe the wagon was destined for the loading of bracken as seen above. Whatever it was for, the position of the man on it seems somewhat precarious as he appears to be sitting on the object outside the edge of the wagon. Presumably the weight of the hurdle was sufficient to counterbalance his mass, but one wonders how finely balanced it all was.
(Photo: J. Edgington/TR Collection)

Left: At Tywyn Wharf a rather more conventional load is being put into the van in 1949. It appears to be a sack, possibly of flour.
(Photo: The Elliot/Dan Quine Collection)

Rails Along The Fathew

Goods Operations

The railway also provided the means of transporting livestock, which could be carried in one of the vans. After the withdrawal of these vehicles in the 1920s, animals were transported in open wagons covered with netting.

Some of the tourists did not appreciate the ways of the local farmers, or the railway, particularly when it came to the treatment of animals. In 1876 one wrote to their local paper complaining that they had witnessed some lambs, whose feet had been bound, being roughly treated while being transported along the line.

Goods Rates

The maximum tolls for goods were set down in the original Act of Parliament. These were for:

Coal, building stone, manure, lime, chalk etc. 2d per ton per mile
Coke, bricks, tiles, slates, charcoal etc. 2½d per ton per mile
Fish, sugar, grain, flour, timber etc. 3d per ton per mile
Cotton, wools, manufactured goods 4d per ton per mile
Horses, mules etc. 4d per head per mile
Ox, cows, bulls etc. 2d per head per mile
Calves, pigs, sheep, lambs etc. ½d per mile

Parcels were to be charged at:
Under 7 lbs   4d
Under 14 lbs   6d
Under 28 lbs   1s
Under 56 lbs   1s 6d
Over this at the company's discretion.

How long these rates were enforced is unknown. In 1878 the railway was reported to charge 1½d per ton per mile for slate. This was even charged to the Abergynolwyn Slate Company.

When the railway increased the rates in 1889 it incensed the shopkeepers of Abergynolwyn, a representative of whom wrote to the *Cambrian News*. In his letter he revealed that the previous rate for the conveyance of coal to Abergynolwyn was 4s per ton, for flour 5s and for shop goods 10s per ton. Meanwhile parcels to Bryneglwys were charged at 2d. These far exceeded the rates laid down in the original Act.

The new rates were to be 6s a ton for flour, mill goods etc. In addition there would be a charge of 1s for parcels to Bryneglwys, but only for those shopkeepers who had opposed the rate increase. Rates were increased again in 1893 (see page 24), causing further complaints, this time with the Tywyn Board of Health becoming involved.

In 1917 the rate for coal between Tywyn and Abergynolwyn appears to have been 4s 4d per ton, and by 1947 it seems to have increased to 5s

6d per ton. The accounts for 1924 also show that slates and slabs were charged at 4s 6d per ton for transport from the quarry.

Preservation Era

Perhaps surprisingly after preservation the railway still carried a significant amount of goods. In 1952 and 1953 consignments of coal, cement, poultry meal, paint and cases of beer were conveyed to various destinations along the line, thus demonstrating that the railway was still meeting the needs of the local community.

Over time the amount of goods carried did diminish, the railway's seasonal nature and also the rise of the motor car and delivery van counting against it. The last recorded item was a tin of sheep mark sent from Tywyn Wharf to Cynfal Halt on 25 June 1975.

This would still though not be the end of goods trains on the railway, for aside from engineering trains others have been run. For example regular coal trains were run from Abergynolwyn to Tywyn between 2004 and 2005 during the rebuilding of Wharf station. Coal having to be delivered to Abergynolwyn and transported down the line, because of the lack of suitable road access elsewhere.

Miscellaneous Loads

In addition the railway has from time to time been called upon to transport interesting and unusual items. There was one very interesting item that was transported on a pair of the railway's bolster trucks, but not along its tracks. The story appeared in the *Merioneth County Times* for 23 January 1902:

A DIFFICULT FEAT.-Last Wednesday a very difficult task in the building trade was safely accomplished by Messrs. Jones, Hughes, and Edwards, when a section of the studio of Mr C. H. Young, which is built of corrugated iron and timber, was safely removed from its position to the new premises recently occupied by Mr Young. The building was first lifted from its foundation, placed on rollers, and moved without mishap to the side of the street

Right: A modern coal train at Tywyn Pendre during the rebuilding of Tywyn Wharf station in 2004.
(Photo: David J. Mitchell)

Goods Operations

where it was left overnight. In the morning it was placed on railway trucks, borrowed from the Talyllyn Railway Co, and much speculation went on as to whether it would reach its destination safely. The builders, however, had no doubt of its success, and their judgment proved correct. A team of horses was hitched on, and the structure was conveyed to its new position two hundred yards away. The total weight was from six to seven tons and one side was composed of 250 square feet of glass, but not a single pane was broken.

More recently other unusual loads have been transported on the railway itself. These include a shed moved from Pendre to Brynglas in 1968 for installation as a ground-frame hut. More recently a Wurlitzer console was transported between Wharf and Pendre for installation in the Neuadd Pendre hall in April 1996.

Mail

In April 1869 it was announced in the *Cambrian News* that arrangements had been made for the conveyance of mails to Abergynolwyn via the Talyllyn Railway. However, there seems to have been a delay in the commencement of this agreement as it was not until 13 August 1870 that the same newspaper reported that:

The Postmaster-General has made arrangements for the conveyance of the letters for Talyllyn, Abergynolwyn, Brynreglwys (sic) Quarries, &c., via Towyn, and thence per Talyllyn Railway, instead of foot post from Machynlleth, as heretofore. Mr Ebenezer Jones has been appointed postmaster at Abergynolwyn, and a foot postman will carry the letters to and from Talyllyn. The box will close at 3.45 p.m. This alteration will much increase the work of Mr Jones, postmaster at Towyn.

This arrangement certainly carried on into the twentieth century and the train was reported as still carrying the mail in 1904.

The Railway Letter Service

In 1891 the Talyllyn Railway was a signatory to the Railway Letter Agreement. This was an arrangement with the Post Office by which a statutory railway company could charge a fee in addition to the normal postage to carry letters on its trains. Most railway companies at the time offered this service, which could be much faster than the normal post. In the Talyllyn's case while it signed up to the Agreement it never made use of it until preservation days.

Then in 1957 the railway began operating its Railway Letter Service, the first stamps being issued on 27 May that year. These were in the form of two sheetlets each of six different designs with a face value of 11d. Since then there have been regular issues of stamps to mark various events, as well as commemorative covers.

Left: Many people will have imagined that when the Preservation Society took over the railway became purely a passenger carrying entity. In fact this was not so, it continued to fulfil its 'common carrier' role, transporting goods as well as passengers along the valley, as is illustrated by this page from the goods book from August 1952.

Right: One power the railway had which was not used before preservation was the right to operate its own Railway Letter Service. This was started in 1957, and in 1991 there was a commemorative cover to celebrate the Centenary of the Railway Letter Agreement signed in 1891.

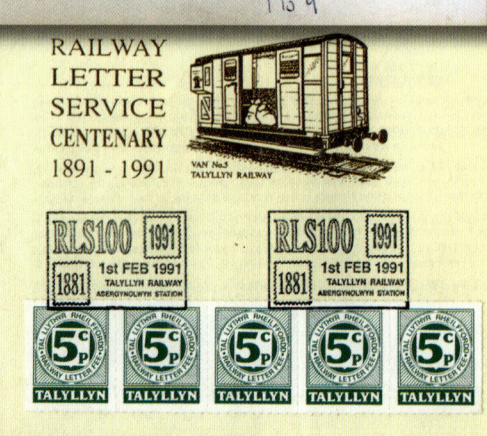

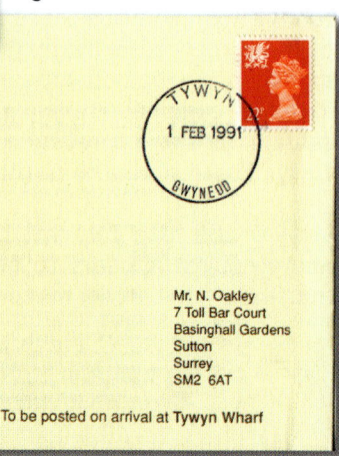

Rails Along The Fathew

Locomotives

Above: A posed photograph of *Talyllyn* and *Dolgoch* (then *Pretoria*) at Pendre apparently 'double-heading' a train c. 1903. The contrast in the quality of the paintwork on the locomotives is striking. *Dolgoch* had recently been repainted and renamed *Pretoria* in June 1900 while *Talyllyn's* paintwork definitely looks tired. However, the locomotive was itself shortly to be overhauled so presumably it received a new coat of paint then. It has been suggested that *Dolgoch* was repainted red at this time, but trying to judge colour with black and white photographs is difficult. John Rowlands is on the footplate of *Talyllyn* and Bob Thomas on *Dolgoch*.
(Photo: TR Collection)

It is to be noted that *Talyllyn* and *Dolgoch* were not officially numbered until Society days.

No.1 *Talyllyn*

Talyllyn was built as works No.42 by Fletcher, Jennings & Co. at its Lowca Engineering Works in Whitehaven, Cumbria. It was a variation to one of their standard tank locomotive designs, and completed on 24 September 1864, but it was not delivered to the railway until the following April.

As stated previously, to overcome its undue vertical oscillation a pair of trailing wheels was fitted in 1867. This gave the locomotive a long fixed wheelbase, which led to the practice of laying the track to a nominal gauge of 2 ft 3 in and a thumb. Later a front sheet and eventually a cab were added.

Around 1899 it received an extensive overhaul back at Lowca Works when work on both the firebox and boiler was carried out. A new saddle tank was also fitted at this time. It was overhauled again at Pendre between 1903 and 1904 when its cylinders were re-bored, and once more in 1916, this time with the assistance of the Festiniog Railway.

More work was done between 1919 and 1920. This was possibly when it was fitted with new frames made from blanks reportedly supplied by Bagnalls. An entry in the 1919 Annual Return shows an expenditure of £408 for materials for locomotive maintenance, which could indicate when these were obtained. In September 1920 it is reported *Talyllyn* was repainted red with white lettering. The last major work to be done on the locomotive pre-preservation was in the early 1930s, when it also received its third saddle tank.

Lack of money for major repairs meant that gradually its condition deteriorated. Eventually it became unfit for use. In 1945 it was steamed for the last recorded time before its rebuilding in 1957/58.

From that time *Talyllyn* was stored in the locomotive shed at Tywyn Pendre. In 1952 it was moved under the barn where it was to remain for several years.

Many thought it would never steam again, but on 23 March 1957 the locomotive was loaded for transportation to the West Midlands. Here it was restored at Gibbons Bros., including a new boiler, and returned to service on 14 June 1958.

There were many problems. One was the long fixed wheelbase, a solution to which was sought in 1963 when the flanges of the centre wheels were removed. The following year it was fitted with a steam brake and stiffer springs.

Locomotives

Left: Probably the second oldest known photograph of *Talyllyn* at what was then King's station, now Tywyn Wharf, in the early 1890s. At this time it still had its original saddle tank. The lining also seems to reflect the original Fletcher, Jennings paint scheme, although it would have been repainted since being delivered. Note also the rear buffers are mounted somewhat differently to normal, with their bases making a diamond shape. Why this was is unknown, and later they were remounted conventionally.
(Photo: E.D.Chambers/ TR Collection)

Right: This photo of *Talyllyn* at Tywyn Wharf is dated 12 June 1920. If correct then the locomotive could just have returned from an overhaul. Later that year it would be repainted in red.
Carriage No.4 behind the locomotive is still in its original form.
(Photo: H.L. Hopwood Copyright Ken Nunn Collection NRM/SSPL)

Left: *Talyllyn* at Tywyn Wharf c. 1938. At this point the locomotive has been fitted with its third saddle tank. This is easily distinguishable because it had an all-welded construction with no external riveting.
(Photo: H.B. Tours/Cozens Collection)

Rails Along The Fathew

Locomotives

Left: Between 1952 and 1957 No.1 resided in the barn at Pendre, where it was often photographed. This example comes from August 1955. Although by this time it had been cosmetically repainted, probably few believed it would ever steam again.

(Photo: J.T. Fraser)

Right: No.1 at Tywyn Pendre in May 1958 after rebuilding by Gibbons Bros. (Photo: J.H.L. Adams)

Left: No.1 at Tywyn Wharf on 24 September 2014 on its 150th Anniversary. The locomotive had just returned from major repairs at Porthmadog after a failure in service had damaged the motion.

Finally in September 1968 it was taken into the works at Pendre for a major overhaul with numerous adjustments being made. It was returned to service nearly four years later in May 1972.

The opening of the Extension again caused problems with the long wheelbase on the sharp curves. This was not solved until the locomotive was overhauled in 1982 when it was fitted with a radial axle for the trailing wheels. It re-entered service on 16 May 1987.

In 1994 extensive boiler repairs were carried out. For the Golden Jubilee of the Preservation Society it went on tour including a visit to the National Railway Museum.

Withdrawn for overhaul in 2004 it returned in March 2007 for some photo charters without a cab, re-entering full service in the August. Over the winter of 2007/08 it was repainted black, which it retained until the end of 2014.

With preparations for its 150th Anniversary already in hand No.1 suffered a major failure on 6 April 2014, which led to severe damage to the motion on the driver's side of the locomotive. Lacking the capacity at Pendre to deal with the damage in the time available, the decision was taken to move *Talyllyn* to Porthmadog for repairs to be undertaken at Boston Lodge works.

On 22 April *Talyllyn* was moved to Porthmadog by road and transferred onto one of the Ffestiniog Railway's flat wagons. It was then hauled across the famous Cob (see page 61) in the fading light before entering the works. It returned to Tywyn on 19 August and re-entered service on 18 September in time for its anniversary celebrations. These took place on 24 September 2014 when a special train was arranged for invited guests.

Locomotives

Left: *Dolgoch* at Wharf c.1930.
(Photo: Real Photographs Copyright NRM/SSPL)

Right: *Dolgoch* on the resumption of passenger services on 19 April 1946 after its heavy overhaul at the Atlas Foundry in Shrewsbury.
(Photo: The Dan Quine Collection)

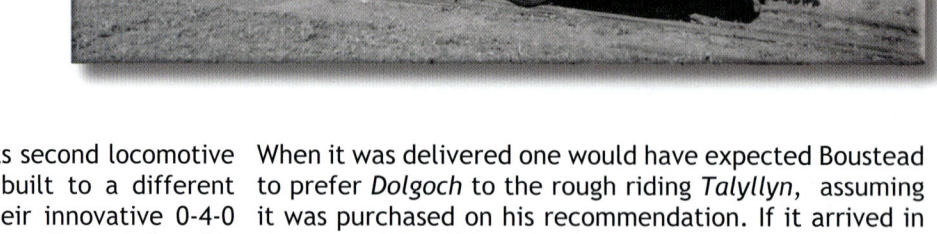

No. 2 *Dolgoch*

In spring 1866 the railway ordered its second locomotive from Fletcher, Jennings. This was built to a different design to *Talyllyn*, being one of their innovative 0-4-0 *Fletcher's Patent* tank locomotives. Essentially this design allowed the rear driving wheels to be placed behind the firebox, which reduced the tendency to vertical oscillation which had afflicted *Talyllyn*.

Instead of the saddle tank fitted to *Talyllyn*, *Dolgoch* was equipped with a small well tank below the footplate and another larger tank at the rear of it. The design produced a powerful locomotive well able to cope with the loads on the Talyllyn. It did however, involve a complicated layout for the motion within the narrow confines of the frames, a fact that Tom Rolt commented on in the early years of preservation.

Like *Talyllyn Dolgoch* was probably originally supplied without a cab or weatherboard. When it did acquire a cab it was a fairly flimsy affair, prone to being dented and bent in various places. Built as works No. 63 it arrived at Tywyn in the summer of 1866 shortly before Tyler's first inspection in the September. Unlike *Talyllyn* it was its horizontal oscillation that he commented on, a fact that led to its crank pins being shortened, probably carried out after *Talyllyn* had returned from having its trailing wheels fitted at Whitehaven.

When it was delivered one would have expected Boustead to prefer *Dolgoch* to the rough riding *Talyllyn*, assuming it was purchased on his recommendation. If it arrived in time it could well have hauled the Archaeological Society excursion in August 1866. It seems more than likely that it pulled the first public service trains in December 1866.

For many years it was widely believed that *Dolgoch* retained its original boiler into preservation, but recent research has shown this is not the case. Paperwork has been discovered indicating that a new boiler, firebox and tyres were manufactured by Brush at Loughborough for the Talyllyn suitable for *Dolgoch* in 1891. It is probable that it had work done in 1900, which was why it was being repainted in the June when it was renamed *Pretoria*.

In 1906 it is recorded that its motion was overhauled with new parts supplied from Lowca at Whitehaven. Then in 1913 it was returned to Whitehaven for heavy repairs, probably including a new firebox. This was probably when the name reverted to *Dolgoch*.

Further repairs were carried out in the mid-1920s, and then in 1935 it was dispatched to the Britannia Foundry in Porthmadog, for repairs, possibly to the boiler and/or firebox. A few years later in 1938 it was at the Atlas Foundry in Shrewsbury for more boiler work.

Locomotives

Left: *Dolgoch* at Pendre on 30 June 1950, during the last months of the Haydn Jones era. The boiler barrel and dome had now been painted black, presumably because that was the only paint they had available at the time. However, the rods have painted red. The door was removable and used to keep the worst of the weather out. It continued to be used into preservation days.
(Photo: S.Bragg/TR Collection)

Right: In July 1975 Graham White guides No.2 *Dolgoch* onto the coaching stock in the North Carriage Shed at Tywyn Pendre at the beginning of the day's work. By then it had a much improved appearance; it has remained a reliable performer ever since and in 2016 will celebrate its 150th anniversary.

Then in 1945 *Dolgoch* was dispatched to the Atlas Foundry for a heavy overhaul at a cost of some £650, during which time the railway was effectively shut for passenger operations. In August 1949 its frame cracked, which had to be welded while all train services were suspended. The cost of the repair seems to have been about £121.

After the Preservation Society took over, as is now well-known, *Dolgoch* was to prove the mainstay during the first year of operation. But it was apparent that it was in need of major repairs. Therefore, on 19 July 1954 it was despatched to Hunt Bros. for major work to be carried out. A new boiler was supplied by Hunslet, and when Hunt Bros. were unable to to do the other work, it was carried out by Gibbons Bros.

Finally it returned to service on 1 July 1963. This time the rebuild was more successful than that of *Talyllyn* and, despite some problems with the valve gear and leading axle, the latter being replaced between 1966/67, it was to remain in service until 1977. During this time it also hauled the opening train to Nant Gwernol on 22 May 1976.

Dolgoch returned to service after heavy overhaul in 1980, being retubed in 1984. Around the same time it was equipped with Belville disc springs for the trailing axle, to improve the ride, and also had stronger buffer springs fitted.

Since 1952 it had been painted in what was known as 'Talyllyn Standard' green. In 1990 there was a change of livery when it was repainted in an approximation of the light green livery applied at Atlas Foundry in 1945. This was the livery it carried during 1951, the first year of preservation. No.2 ran in this livery from 1990 until 2008.

Between 1995 and 1999 it received another overhaul, and later featured in 50th Anniversary of the railway's preservation in 2001. It also appeared on a Post Office stamp issued on 13 January 2004. In 2007 work was done on its firebox and the following year it was repainted maroon, and for a brief period in the summer was renamed *Pretoria*.

Withdrawn from service in 2009 and requiring a new boiler, there was considerable doubt if it would be in service for the 60th Anniversary in May 2011 of the first train to Rhydyronen under preservation. Fortunately, an appeal aided by the magazine *Steam Railway* saw the money come in, and *Dolgoch* was able to play a starring role on the day. Now plans are beginning to be formed for the celebration of its 150th Anniversary in the summer of 2016.

Locomotives

Left: No.3 at Aberllefenni on 7 February 1941. The restricted height of the cab can be seen in this photograph. In 1942 it went to Swindon for retubing. (Photo: W.A. Camwell/TR Collection)

Below: When originally delivered to the Talyllyn No.3 was placed on the line with the chimney pointing up the line as with *Talyllyn* and *Dolgoch*. However, when the vacuum brake was fitted on the Corris the left hand side of the cab was sheeted off, this meant the only exit on the Talyllyn was on the non-platform side. Therefore, when No.4 (on the standard gauge wagon) returned from overhaul in May 1952 the opportunity was taken to turn No.3 by crane with the chimney towards the sea. This was how it was to run until returning from overhaul in 1968. (Photo: TR Collection)

No.3 *Sir Haydn*

The Corris Railway opened on 1 April 1859 as the Corris, Machynlleth and River Dovey Tramroad (CM&RDT) using gravity working to bring slates down from the quarries around Corris to Machynlleth. The gauge was 2 ft 3 in, the same as the Talyllyn would adopt later, but locomotives were not initially considered to be practicable on so narrow a gauge.

Steam locomotives were authorised to be used in 1864, the year after they were first used on the Festiniog, but were not introduced until much later. The same act also renamed the tramway as The Corris Railway.

In July 1878 the company became part of Imperial Tramways Co. Ltd. By this time plans were already in hand for the introduction of steam locomotives. Three identical 0-4-0 saddle tank locomotives were ordered from the Hughes Locomotive and Tramway Engineering Works Ltd., based at Falcon works, Loughborough. The locomotives were delivered during December 1878, they were works numbers 322, 323 and 324. No.322 became Corris No.2, No.323 became Corris No.3 and No. 324 became Corris No.1.

A passenger service was finally started in 1883, but still there was little use for three locomotives and No.3 became the spare locomotive. In December 1885 William McConnel wrote to the Corris asking if he could purchase it, but the price quoted was £700, the amount it cost when new. Eventually, however, No.3 would find its place on the Talyllyn.

Like *Talyllyn* the 0-4-0s were converted to 0-4-2 saddle tanks with the addition of trailing wheels, No.3 being so treated in 1893, when it was also fitted with vacuum brakes along with a new cab and coal bunkers. In 1900 it was fitted with a new boiler.

The Corris purchased a new locomotive, No.4, in 1921, about which more later. Locomotive No.1 was officially withdrawn in 1923. There was then an amalgamation of parts between locomotives No.1 and No.3. This included the transfer of the boiler from No.1, while one frame plate was apparently used from each locomotive.

It is therefore debatable whether the locomotive that returned to service in 1927 was either No.3 or No.1. It has been surmised that it was known as No.3 because it carried No.3's bunkers and maker's plate.

Corris No.2 lasted until 1930 when the Great Western Railway took over the line. No.3 took a trip to Swindon that year for heavy boiler work to be carried out as well as other tasks. This was its final major repair before the closure of the Corris, although it did return to Swindon for retubing in 1942.

Locomotives

The last services ran on the Corris in August 1948, by which time both locomotives Nos. 3 & 4 were based at Machynlleth where they were first examined for potential purchase by the Talyllyn. It was not to be until 1 March 1951 that they were bought for the newly preserved railway.

Some of the events of No.3's early years on the Talyllyn have already been recorded. Although initially in better condition than No.4 its narrow tyres made it sensitive to the vagaries of the track gauge. It would not be until 1953 that it would run regularly in service, having been named *Sir Haydn* in 1951.

Over the winter of 1953/54 the pony truck and wheels were repaired, and in 1956 work was carried out on the firebox keeping it out of service for the summer. It returned to action for the 1957 season, but by this point it was clear that major work would be required. It was last steamed on 16 October 1957 and then laid up.

For various reasons work did not begin on the overhaul in earnest until 1964. During the work its appearance was altered substantially with a new cab and other changes. It was first run, still in grey undercoat, on 23 September 1968. From then on it proved very reliable.

Left: Sometimes the dates on photographs are unreliable. The date on this photograph is August 1957, but as No.3 still has its original Corris coupler and no buffers it is liable to be August 1953. Anyway *Sir Haydn* is seen near Abergynolwyn with a down train. (Photographer Unknown)

Right: The date on this photo is a more believable, 24 August 1955. No.3 had been fitted with buffers in July 1954. These were delivered on the lorry bringing in No.6 *Douglas* on 19 July 1954 and No.3 was photographed with them fitted on 31 July 1954. It is seen here in Tywyn Pendre yard. (Photo: J.T. Fraser)

Left: On 26 September 1957 No. 3 was steamed for one of the last times before it was withdrawn for overhaul the following month. It is seen passing Quarry Siding with a down train.
(Photo: George S. Hearse/Martin Fuller Collection)

Right: When No.3 emerged from its overhaul ten years later its appearance had changed substantially as it had been fitted with a new cab, more suited to build of the Talyllyn crews. It is seen here still in undercoat.
(Photo: David J. Mitchell)

Rails Along The Fathew

Locomotives

The next major interruption came in July 1977 when *Sir Haydn* suffered a fractured main steam pipe which was repaired in six days. In 1978 it was transported to the Brush Works at Loughborough as part of its Centenary celebrations. Between 1982 and 1983 it experienced an identity change when it was repainted red and fitted with a face as *Sir Handel* of the Rev. W. Awdry's Skarloey Railway.

Over the following years some minor work was carried out. In 1986 the cylinders were re-bored and a new saddle tank provided. However, in 1990 it was found to be in need of a new firebox and was withdrawn at the end of the season returning to service in 1993.

Early in 1999 it was repainted red for a series of photographic specials, the livery being maintained for successive years. In June 2003 it visited the Corris Railway for which it was painted a closer approximation to its old Corris livery.

During 2006 it was fitted with a new pony truck and trailing wheels while the following year it was retubed. Over the winter of 2008/09 work was done on its motion with it returning to service for the Spring Bank Holiday week 2009.

In the summer of 2012, with the expiry of its boiler certificate looming, it made another visit to the Corris Railway. The intention was that it would be stored there until being returned to Pendre for overhaul. Later a decision was taken to send it on a publicity tour during 2013.

This included a visit to the Great Central Railway near Loughborough as well as trips on a flat wagon along both the Severn Valley and West Somerset Railways. It was then put on display in the Engine House at Highley on the Severn Valley Railway. Finally in February 2015 it returned to Tywyn, after making an appearance at the Caravaning, Camping and Motorhome Show at the National Exhibition Centre, Birmingham en-route. It then made a special guest appearance at the 150th Anniversary in July 2015 taking part in a locomotive cavalcade, although not in steam.

Left: No.3 in 'standard' green livery at Tywyn Wharf in August 1993. No.4 in its guise as *Peter Sam* is at the rear of the train.

Right: In 2003 No.3 was repainted into Corris livery, which it has remained in ever since. It is seen here at Tywyn Wharf on 11 July 2005.

Rails Along The Fathew

Locomotives

Left: No.4 shortly after being delivered to Tywyn Wharf.   (Photo: TR Collection)

Below: No.4, now named Edward Thomas, at Tywyn Wharf on 24 August 1955. It had been fitted with a new saddle tank by Hunslet, and had had some modifications, including new trailing wheels in 1952, but still had its original cab. It also retained its marine coupling rods.

(Photo: J.T. Fraser)

No.4 *Edward Thomas*

With its original locomotives in poor condition, the Corris Railway ordered a new locomotive from Kerr, Stuart and Co. of Stoke-on-Trent in 1920. This was an 0-4-2 saddle tank of their *Tattoo* class, a design which had been considered by Haydn Jones for the Talyllyn a few years previously.

Works No.4047 was delivered in June 1921. Known on the Corris as simply *The Tattoo* it was soon dealing with the bulk of the line's traffic. Very quickly the boiler wore out and a new one was fitted with a different tube pattern, along with a new smokebox, in 1929

It too paid a visit to Swindon in 1940 for an overhaul including retubing, and evidently continued to be the main locomotive in use. By 1948, although not in a bad state of repair, it did require some substantive work.

When acquired by the Talyllyn it was numbered 4, the same number it had on the Corris, and given the name *Edward Thomas* after the line's former Manager. The Society committee chose the name by a narrow majority over Tom Rolt's choice of *James Swinton Spooner*. The locomotive required retubing, and also repairs to its firebox crown stays. This was work beyond the capacity of Pendre works at that time. Fortunately the railway received a generous offer from the Managing Director of the Hunslet Engine Company, Mr. J. F. Alcock. He was a life member of the Preservation Society and offered to repair the locomotive at Hunslet's works in Leeds.

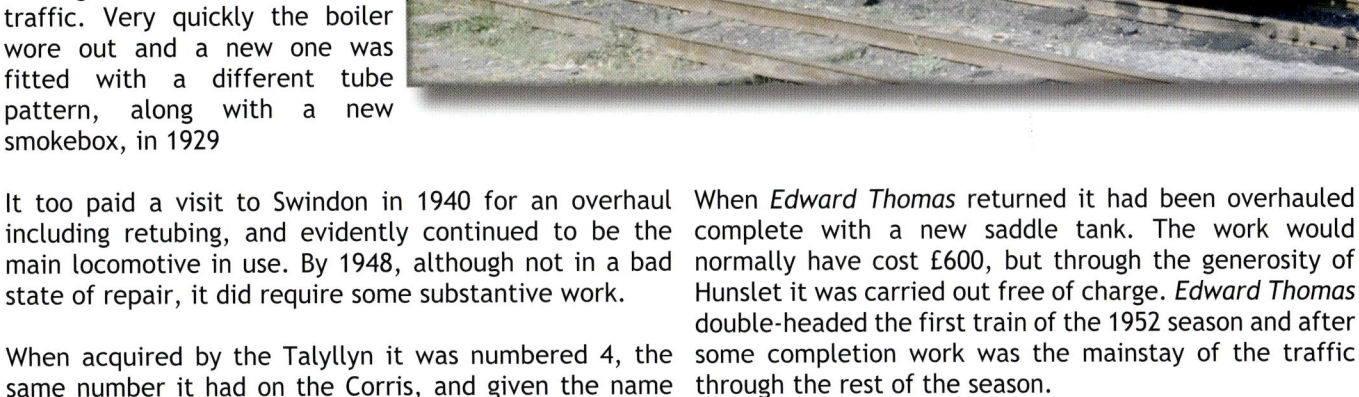

When *Edward Thomas* returned it had been overhauled complete with a new saddle tank. The work would normally have cost £600, but through the generosity of Hunslet it was carried out free of charge. *Edward Thomas* double-headed the first train of the 1952 season and after some completion work was the mainstay of the traffic through the rest of the season.

In 1953 the locomotive was out of action for six weeks when the motion was damaged, returning to service on 7 August. It gained national fame in September 1958 when it was fitted with a *Giesl* Ejector. In this device, instead of the usual single blastpipe, the exhaust fans out into a series of nozzles which eject the steam into a venturi-shaped chimney. This it was claimed would mean the locomotive would use less coal. However, externally the 'fish-tail' chimney changed the locomotive's appearance significantly.

Rails Along The Fathew

Locomotives

The boiler was condemned in October 1963. A replacement arrived on 8 July 1964 and the locomotive returned to service in the August. When the *Giesl* Ejector became life-expired in 1968 it was removed and replaced by the original chimney and blastpipe. This was found to make an improvement to the locomotive's performance.

At the end of the 1975 season it was withdrawn for overhaul including an extension of the cab, returning to service in the autumn of 1977. For the celebration of the 150th Anniversary of the GWR in 1985 it was repainted GWR green, a livery it never actually carried on the Corris Railway.

It remained in this livery until it was painted again in 1988 this time taking on the persona of *Peter Sam* from the Skarloey Railway remaining as such until October 1991. That month it was rapidly repainted into Corris Indian Red for its 70th birthday. This was its livery throughout the 1992 season before returning as *Peter Sam* the following year, a guise it ran in until 2001. There was though, a brief interlude when it returned to the revived Corris Railway in October 1996 for a period back in its old haunts.

Its next major overhaul came in 2001, which included a replacement boiler, and it did not return to service until 2004. This time painted in green as *Edward Thomas*. However, in 2012 it was discovered that it needed a new firebox, which kept it out of service for the season, but it made its return in 2013.

Above: No.4 after being fitted with the *Giesl* Ejector in September 1958. By this time it had had solid disc trailing wheels substituted for the spoked ones. (Photo: J.H.L. Adams)

Right: No.4 at Tywyn Wharf c.1970 after the Ejector had been removed. (Photographer Unknown)

Left: At Quarry Siding with *The Quarryman* on 11 July 2005. Bill Heynes is the driver.

176   Rails Along The Fathew

Locomotives

Left: Andrew Barclay works No.1432 languishes at Abelson and Co. (Engineers) Ltd, Birmingham on 18 June 1949 with No.1431 behind. No.1431 was to remain there for another four years until it was donated to the Talyllyn Railway Preservation Society and became locomotive No.6 *Douglas*. (Photographer Unknown)

Below: No.6 *Douglas* in service at Tywyn Pendre on 24 August 1955. As well as regauging from 2 ft to 2 ft 3 in various modifications were made to the locomotive before it entered service on the Talyllyn including the fitting of a running plate and buffers. (Photo: J.T. Fraser)

No.6 *Douglas*

The locomotive that eventually became Talyllyn Railway No.6 *Douglas* was originally built in 1918 as one of six by Andrew Barclay of Kilmarnock for service with the Airservice Construction Corps. It was works No.1431, built as one of Barclay's *Light* class locomotives which bore a close resemblance to an Orenstein and Koppel design.

Initially it was sent to RAF Manston in Kent, but in October 1921 it was transferred to RAF Calshot on the Solent. This was one of the bases used by the RAF's seaplane service for coastal reconnaissance. A 2 ft gauge line had been laid there linking the camp on the mainland with the hangers and jetties at the end of the spit. With its fellow class member, works No.1453, it ran the service along the line carrying supplies and personnel as required.

By this time the Airservice Construction Corps had become the Air Ministry Works and Buildings Department (AMW&B), and the initials were painted on the locomotives. The locos were worked hard and No.1431 required a new firebox and overhaul in 1928, the work being completed by 1931 at Thorneycrofts based at Woolston in Southampton.

It was overhauled again in 1942, this time at the Southern Railway's Eastleigh works, when more firebox work was carried out and a new smokebox fitted. Services on the line ended on 15 August 1945 when it was discovered that the underframes of the carriages were badly corroded.

The locomotives were auctioned in 1949 and purchased by Abelson & Co of Sheldon in Birmingham. Their intention was to export them to India, but the boilers of the locomotives did not meet Indian standards. The locomotives therefore remained in the West Midlands.

It was spotted by a Society member in the yard and a letter was sent to the owners requesting a possible donation. This resulted in No.1431 being given to the railway in April 1953, and then transported to Hunt Bros. in Oldbury for conversion to 2 ft 3 in gauge.

It arrived in Tywyn on 19 July 1954 bearing the name *Douglas* after the Managing Director of the firm, Douglas Abelson. However, the height of its chimney meant that the track had to be lowered under Hendy bridge and elsewhere in order to allow it to pass underneath. Almost immediately No.6 was put into service and, although it derailed on one of its early trips, it quickly proved to be a useful addition to the locomotive fleet.

In August 1960 it derailed while shunting in Pendre yard and cracked an axlebox. During the following winter it was discovered it also needed extensive work to the firebox and returned to service on 31 July 1961.

Douglas experienced a failure in service on 4 August 1973 when the piston and rod went through the right hand front cylinder cover when a piston-rod cotter came loose. Fortunately the damage was slight and the locomotive

Rails Along The Fathew

Locomotives

returned to service on 6 August. At the end of the season it was withdrawn for a major overhaul during which its frames were straightened and it was fitted with a new smokebox. It returned to duty in time for the peak season in 1975.

In 1984 work was done on the cylinders and pistons, and later it was retubed. It was around this time that the suggestion was made that it should be withdrawn in favour of No.7 when its boiler needed replacing. This did not go down well with sections of the Society membership, with the result that when it was taken out of service in 1992 it was only three years before it was back in service again. The new boiler was partly funded by the Hugh Jones Memorial Fund, No.6 having been Hugh's favourite locomotive. In 1996 it was repainted in AMW&B livery and spent some time at the RAF Museum at Hendon. Then in 1998 it spent a time facing the 'wrong way' for some photo charters. During one of these it suffered some motion damage.

A new role for the locomotive was found in 2001 when it assumed the guise of the Skarloey Railway locomotive *Duncan*. On 30 September 2007 it was withdrawn for another major overhaul, but this was interrupted by the work required to get *Dolgoch* back into service for 2011. This meant that No.6 did not return to service until early 2013, still in a red livery so that it could resume its *Duncan* guise. In 2014 it was briefly repainted to a representation of its original delivery livery for a series of photo charters, but was returned to red afterwards.

Left: No.6 *Douglas* stands at Brynglas waiting for a down train c.1970. Note that the siding has not been installed yet.

(Photographer Unknown)

Right: No.6 in its guise as the Skarloey Railway's *Duncan* on 10 July 2005 at Tywyn Pendre. The air pump has had to be replaced with a spare from *Dolgoch*, which is still in green.

Left: In March 2014 No.6 *Douglas* was temporarily painted in its delivery colours for the Airservice Construction Corps for a series of photo charters, for which it also had its air pump removed. It is seen here at Cynfal on 12 March 2014.

(Photo: David J. Mitchell)

Rails Along The Fathew

Locomotives

Left: Bord Na Móna locomotive No.1 at Tywyn Wharf in September 1969. It is being stripped for parts which would be used in the construction of No.7 *Tom Rolt*. Soon after its arrival in March 1969 someone had scribbled *Irish Pete* on it as it had come from the Irish Peat Board, which can just be made out in the photograph. This became its official name for many years until the decision was changed to *Tom Rolt* in 1989. (Photo: J.T. Fraser)

Right: No.7's boiler is mounted temporarily on the chassis that had been fabricated in June 1975. It was to be another 16 years before the locomotive was completed. (Photo: David J. Mitchell)

No.7 (2) *Tom Rolt*

During the mid to late 1960s when traffic was increasing substantially, consideration was given to a new locomotive for the line. As noted previously several designs were considered but in the end a secondhand 3 ft gauge Andrew Barclay locomotive was purchased in 1969 from the Bord Na Móna (Irish Turf Board).

This was works No.2263, built in 1948 and delivered to a new peat-burning power station at Portarlington, County Laois, along with two similar locomotives. They were a variation of the Andrew Barclay *Light* design. All three were built as peat burners, but their service in Ireland was short-lived and by the end of 1954 all were in store.

Finally in 1969 the three locomotives were sold, No.2263 coming to the Talyllyn for £300. On 26 March it arrived at Tywyn and was placed on a temporary section of track in front of the gunpowder store.

The plan was to convert it into an 0-4-2 side tank locomotive making use of the boiler, firebox, smokebox, cylinders, wheels and motion. Soon after arrival the name *Irish Pete* had been chalked on the side, and at the 1970 AGM this was adopted as its official name.

Initially work steadily progressed on the locomotive, and by 1975 a rolling chassis had been fabricated on which the boiler was temporarily mounted. However, with the decline in passenger numbers the project was largely suspended, and it would not be until autumn 1988 that work would begin again in earnest.

The name *Irish Pete* had not been universally popular and so the 1989 Society AGM revisited the decision, opting this time for the name *Tom Rolt*. On 6 May 1991 it was steamed up to Abergynolwyn to be officially named by Tom's widow, Sonia. In truth No.7 was far from finished and it did not haul its first revenue-earning train until 27 July that year.

Since then the locomotive has continued in service. With its limited use in Ireland it is perhaps unsurprising that little major work has been required on the locomotive save for retubing. This was until 2008 when some work was required to the boiler and firebox. Over the winter of 2014/15 it had some further work done, but was in service for the 2015 season.

Rails Along The Fathew

Locomotives

Left: No.7 *Tom Rolt* running round its train at Nant Gwernol on 16 June 1994.
(Photo: J.T. Fraser)

Right: No.7 *Tom Rolt* on an engineering train at Tywyn Wharf on 10 July 2009. (Photo: David J. Mitchell)

Left: On 15 October 2011 new Corris Railway No.7 (on the right) visited the Talyllyn, and was lined up at Tywyn Wharf with Talyllyn Nos. 4 *Edward Thomas* and 7 *Tom Rolt* for a night photoshoot.

Right: The Old and the New: Nos. 1 *Talyllyn* and 7 *Tom Rolt* together on 24 September 2014 when No.1 was celebrating its 150th anniversary.

180 Rails Along The Fathew

Locomotives

No. 5 (1)

The first No.5 was designed and built by David Curwen, at a cost of £77 9s. It was delivered to Tywyn on 17 October 1952. One of its primary duties was to operate the Fridays only passenger service between Pendre and Brynglas.

It was powered by the engine out of Tom Rolt's boat *Cressy*, a 20 b.h.p. Ford motor driving through an epicyclic gearbox. The drive was on to the rear axle, which was coupled to the front axle by a chain.

At first it gave trouble-free service but was too light and prone to slipping. It was overstrained when asked to haul *Edward Thomas* back from Dolgoch where it had derailed. Although it was repaired and returned to service, it broke down in April 1953 and never ran again.

Eventually its chassis was used for a ballast wagon. However, more recently work has started on rebuilding the locomotive on the original chassis by a Society member.

Above: The first No.5 at Tywyn Pendre on 9 June 1953, already out of service. (Photo: J.H.L. Adams)

Below: The second No.5 *Midlander* also at Tywyn Pendre in June 1957. (Photo: J.H.L. Adams)

No. 5 (2) *Midlander*

The second No.5 has been altogether more successful. It was purchased from Jee's Quarry, Nuneaton where it was known as *Matron*. It had been found by a team from the Midlands Area Group, who were lifting rail from the 2 ft 6½ in gauge line there. Negotiations with the quarry owners followed and it was purchased for £150.

No.5 is a Ruston-Hornsby, works No.200792, 4-wheel type 48DL shunter delivered to the quarry new in February 1941. Formerly it was equipped with a 48 bhp 4VRO engine. After purchase it was converted to 2 ft 3 in gauge at the quarry and then delivered to Tywyn on 23 March 1957, the same lorry taking *Talyllyn* back to the West Midlands. It was given the number 5 in the locomotive roster and named *Midlander*.

Very quickly it proved to be a valuable asset and was used for shunting and engineering work. The locomotive also played a vital role both on the work on the Dolgoch slip in the late 1950s and on the Extension to Nant Gwernol in the 1970s. It was also used on the winter train service between 1963 and 1965.

It received a substantial rebuild in 1963, including parts from an identical locomotive (No.5A) purchased as a source of spares. In 1977 the original engine reached the end of its life and although repairs were attempted it was realised that a new power unit was required. This was obtained by the purchase of another donor locomotive, works no. 200800, with a VRH engine, which was transferred into No.5. In addition, the rebuilt locomotive made use of the donor locomotive's cab and bonnet. No.5 re-entered service in 1980.

In 2000 it suffered a gearbox failure and, following a lengthy rebuild and restoration, was test run again in 2007. It has since re-entered service.

Left: *Midlander* looks well-used in this photo taken at Tywyn Pendre on 16 March 1963 with carriage No.10. (Photo: David J. Mitchell)

Rails Along The Fathew

Locomotives

Left: In the early 21st Century No.5 underwent an extensive overhaul. It is seen here under test at Tywyn Pendre with Rob Frost at the controls on 12 June 2007.

Below: Sometimes No.5 does haul passenger specials such as here on 4 June 2012.

No.7 (1)

The first No.7, which arrived in July 1954, was another short-lived attempt at a home-built internal combustion locomotive. It was based on a Mercury tractor converted for rail operation. Only the back wheel was driven and therefore it was only suitable for light loads. Another feature was that it was fitted with a turntable to allow it to be turned round.

Shortly after its arrival a canopy was added and the engine adapted to run on paraffin by Charlie Uren, becoming unofficially known as *Charlie's Ant* as a result. Sadly, it continued to prove unreliable and was last used in 1958. The bogie wheels are still in use on a works trolley.

Above: No.7 in action at Tŷ Mawr with carriage No.7 and wagons on 1 August 1954. (Photo: J.N. Slater)

No.8 *Merseysider*

In order to provide extra motive power to help with the Extension in 1969, two 3 ft gauge Ruston type LFT four-wheel diesels of 1964 vintage were obtained from the Parkgate Steel Works, Rotherham. They were equipped with YDA 50 b.h.p. engines with three-cylinder air-cooled engines and Dowty hydrostatic transmission systems.

They arrived in Tywyn on 12 June 1969 having been purchased along with a Hunslet diesel, and works No.476108 was chosen to be converted to 2 ft 3 in gauge. A generous donation had been made towards the purchase, the only condition of which was that the resulting locomotive should be called *Merseysider*.

Above: No.7 at Tywyn Pendre after it was fitted with a canopy. (Photo: J.H.L. Adams)

Following regauging and rebuilding No.8 *Merseysider* entered service in late 1970. Later it was repainted and received nameplates. It soon proved itself in service and provided useful extra motive power on the Extension. At the start of the 1984 coal strike it even hauled regular passenger trains.

At the end of the 1994 season the engine was in a poor state and it was intended to replace it with the one from the spare locomotive obtained in 1969. However, the project grew somewhat, and it was not until 2003 that the locomotive re-entered service with a completely redesigned cab and bodywork.

182   Rails Along The Fathew

Locomotives

In 2008 one of its axles sheared which led to it being abandoned in the siding at Brynglas for some time only re-entering service the following year. Then in 2012 it suffered a broken valve along with a smashed piston crown and damaged cylinder head, which was repaired. However, more recently it has suffered a further failure.

Above Right: One of the Parkgate diesels being unloaded on 12 June 1969. (Photo: David J. Mitchell)

Above: No.8 *Merseysider* with its original bodywork (but with an extended cab) at Tywyn Pendre in July 1975.

Right: With its rebuilt bodywork on the curve to the wharf edge at Tywyn Wharf on 9 July 2005.

No.9 *Alf*

In November 1970 two ex-National Coal Board Hunslet four-wheel diesels were purchased from a Manchester scrapyard for £500. They had previously worked at Huncoat Colliery near Burnley and were delivered to Tywyn on 2 December that year.

They were built in 1950 to 2 ft 3 in gauge with 75 bhp Gardner 4LW engines. Designed for underground work they had no cabs and were driven by a jackshaft. The intention was to make one serviceable and use the other for spares.

In September 1971 works No.4136 entered traffic as No.9. It proved an efficient and powerful machine capable of hauling a full passenger train, albeit at a reduced speed of 9 mph. Subsequently it was named *Alf*, after the then Chairman of the Coal Board Lord Alfred Robens, with the name initially painted on the side of the locomotive.

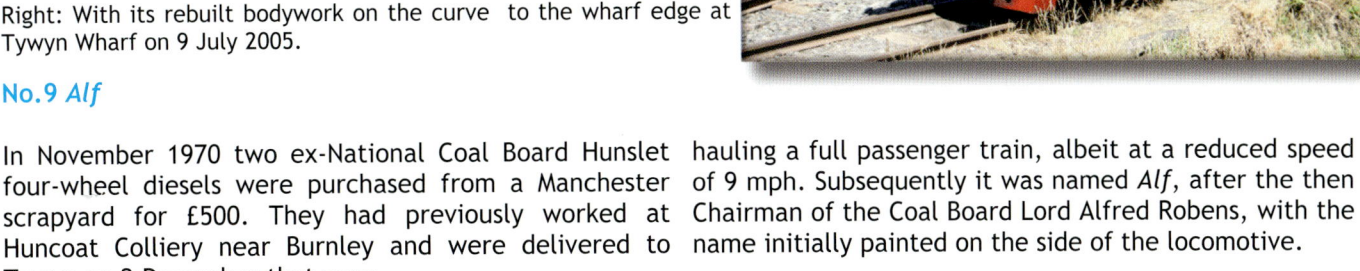

Between 1984 and 1985 it underwent a heavy overhaul. It was provided with brass nameplates in 1986 when it was repainted. In 2007 it was repainted again by the Young Members' Group into a version of standard Talyllyn Green livery, although it ran briefly over the summer in black undercoat.

Left: No.9 *Alf* at Tywyn Pendre in July 1975.

Above: In black undercoat at Tywyn Wharf on 23 August 2007. (Photo: David J. Mitchell)

Locomotives

No. 10 *Bryn Eglwys*

The need for a more powerful, faster locomotive that could also operate air-braked stock led to the purchase in 1997 of another former National Coal Board (NCB) locomotive. It had previously worked at Hemheath colliery near Stoke-on-Trent and was a Simplex Series 'T' four-wheel diesel. Built in 1985 for the 2 ft 6 in gauge line at Hemstock, it was fitted with a Dorman 100 bhp six cylinder air-cooled engine and a twin-disc two-speed torque converter drive.

It arrived in Tywyn September 1997, becoming No.10, but retaining its NCB yellow livery. Its time on the Talyllyn could be described as chequered. When in service it was capable of performing as well as was hoped when it was purchased, but it was also prone to breakdowns and underwent several heavy repairs. In 1998 the locomotive was named *Bryn Eglwys*. It was repainted into green in 2005. When the first of the Baguley diesels entered service No.10 was sold to the North Gloucestershire Railway and left in August 2014.

Nos 11 and 12

When Society members were tracklifting at the 2 ft 6 in gauge line at the Royal Naval Armaments Depot at Trecwn, South Wales, in 2008, they found a number of Baguley-Drewery four-wheel diesels there. These were a class of seven built in 1983 especially for the depot with 99 bhp Perkins engines, an air-operated transmission, and chain-drive to the axles.

It was felt that these would be ideal for use on the Talyllyn, but unfortunately the financial situation at the time meant that the railway was not in a position to purchase any of them. Nevertheless a consortium of members decided to buy three, two of which would be converted for use on the railway with the third used for spares. They arrived in Tywyn in September 2008 and were stored at Wharf station.

Top: No.10 *Bryn Eglwys* is seen passing Rhydyronen station, having rescued a train involved in a breakdown further up the line, in July 2001. (Photo: D.K. Drummond)

Above: No.10 at Tywyn Pendre on 29 May 2009 having been repainted into green.

In July 2014 they were purchased by the railway and the first of them, works No.3779, was sent to Alan Keef Ltd to be re-gauged, returning on 4 September. The second locomotive, works No.3764, was then taken for re-gauging.

After its return in 2014 No.3779 was put into service, with No.3764 returning in August 2015. When both locomotives are in service they will be numbered 11 and 12 on the Talyllyn, and will be named *Trecwn* and *St Cadfan*.

Left: No.11 in the headshunt at Tywyn Pendre on 31 May 2014.

184 — Rails Along The Fathew

Locomotives

Additional Vehicles

In addition to the above locomotives the railway also possesses other vehicles.

Motor Trolley

This was built by John Bate in 1954 originally using the engine from an Austin 7. It proved very successful, and in 1960 it was fitted with a canopy. Later it was given the unofficial name of *Toby*. During drought periods it was used as a fire tender, following service trains up the line. Unfortunately it was severely damaged in a shunting accident in 2008 and remains out of use.

Above Left: The motor trolley seen at Tywyn Pendre.
(Photo: Keith Stretch)

Left: During droughts the motor trolley, now fitted with a roof and canvas sides, acted as a fire patrol. It had an attached wagon equipped with a water tank and fire-fighting equipment and would follow trains between Tywyn Pendre and Brynglas if required. It is seen here, now with the unofficial name of *Toby*, on 1 September 1984. (Photo: David J. Mitchell)

Matisa Track Tamper

Put together from the parts from two ex-MOD variable gauge tampers, purchased in 1989, it was commissioned on 26 June 1990 and remains in use.

Above: The Matisa track tamper in use at Tywyn Wharf on 22 July 2001. (Photo: David J. Mitchell)

Flail Mower

Another vehicle which was designed by John Bate was the flail mower to clear lineside vegetation. It was built using parts of the chassis of spare diesel locomotives 5A and 8A. Other components came from a Smalley 5 excavator with a new Perkins 4-236 diesel engine, fitted with a new McConnel flail assembly, along with a cab that had been fabricated at Pendre. It entered service in 1999.

Left: John Bate is seen here at the controls when it was under test and without a cab at Quarry Siding on 25 June 1999. (Photo: R. Plummer)

Rails Along The Fathew — 185

Passenger Stock

Above: There are few, if any, other railways that are able to run a train of all their original carriages pulled by one of their original locomotives, particularly in their 150th anniversary year. No.1 *Talyllyn* is seen here with such a train at Bryn Erwest on 17 March 2015. (Photo: G. Jones)

Nos. 1 to 5 The 'Original' Carriages

Unsurprisingly the early history of the carriages is unclear. What is known is that the first carriage arrived in January 1866. We also know that there was only one carriage, and presumably the brake van, in service when Tyler made his inspections in September and November 1866, but a second carriage was on the way. Tyler subsequently encouraged the company to order more carriages, both in a letter at the end of September and in his report in the November. In the latter he stated that these needed to be in service by the following spring. Certainly by September 1867 the railway possessed four carriages and one brake van.

It was believed for some time that what is now carriage No.4 (the current numbers were given in 1954), constructed by the Lancaster Wagon Co., was the first to arrive. This was because it is the 'odd one out' and has a more primitive design. However, a few years ago work on what is now carriage No.3 revealed the date of 1865 stamped on the wheel hubs, suggesting that this was the original carriage delivered.

A drawing of van No.5 in the Brown, Marshall archive is dated July 1866, which has been taken to be the construction date for that vehicle. More recently John Bate has stated that he believed the van could have been delivered earlier, and in fact could have been the first to arrive. Certainly it is dimensionally closer to No.3 than it is to the other Brown, Marshall carriages.

A possible scenario is that, if the date found on carriage No.3 reflects the date of construction, then it and van No.5 were the first vehicles to arrive, although in what order is not clear, but there would have been a need for a brake van to be in operation from an early date. Then the second passenger carriage was No.4, of a more basic construction, purchased when money was tight. This would fit with what McConnel wrote to the Board of Trade following Tyler's first inspection. Here he stated that one new carriage had been ordered and 'indeed it is now finished'. He also said that the directors felt the two carriages would be sufficient for the 'next two years'.

As already mentioned, during his November inspection Tyler again urged the directors to purchase more carriages Indeed forewarned by Tyler's letter, and, perhaps with improved finances, McConnel could well have already made enquiries, so that any order could be placed quickly. This could have led to what are now No.1 and No.2 being ordered from Brown, Marshall very rapidly. These have virtually identical bodyshells to one another, with No.1 being originally an all First and No.2 an all Third. They are one foot longer than carriage No.3 and slightly taller.

Passenger Stock

Above: *Talyllyn* and carriage No.1 at Tywyn King's (Wharf) station in the early 1890s. This photo demonstrates that passenger trains could be seen at King's before 1900. (Photo: E.D. Chambers/TR Collection)

Another Talyllyn myth is that the carriages were not numbered before preservation days; as the above photo shows, what is now carriage No.1 is labelled as No.1. However, it is unlikely the numbering bore any relationship to the order in which the carriages arrived. Any numbers seem to have disappeared during the 1900 repaint. The numbers in this section are those applied by the Society in 1954.

While the earliest livery is not known it seems likely that the carriages have been painted brown or red throughout their time on the railway. It is known they were repainted in April/May 1900. They were repainted again in 1920 in a scarlet colour with yellow lining, brown ends and footboards. They also seem to have been repainted during the 1940s.

Carriage No.1

Supplied by Brown, Marshall of Birmingham this was originally an all-First. It was downgraded to Second in 1873 when First Class was discontinued, but upgraded again when First Class was reintroduced in 1920. It was distinguished from Third Class by the use of seat cushions. After First Class was abandoned again in 1931 it still retained the cushions and was therefore popular with passengers.

It has continued in service after preservation with various repairs and repaints. The bodywork was damaged in an accident at Wharf in 1968. Air braking was finally fitted in 1998 over a century after the original exemption was granted.

Above: The First Class carriage at Abergynolwyn c.1940. (Photo: TR Collection)

Left: Carriage No.1 not long after receiving its number during a repaint in spring 1954. Note the large class numbers and the crest that were also applied at the same time. The numbers were similar to those supplied to South African Railways. The carriage was repainted as Third Class in 1962. (Photo: J.H.L. Adams)

Rails Along The Fathew

Passenger Stock

Carriage No.2

No.2 was also supplied by Brown, Marshall as an all-Third, which it has remained ever since. In 1968 the carriage doors were altered so that the handles were on the right hand side. Air brakes were fitted in 1998. All the Brown, Marshall coaches have retained their original axleboxes, now modified for oil lubrication.

Right: What would later be numbered carriage No.2 at Tywyn Wharf station on 6 June 1953.
(Photo: J.H.L. Adams)

Carriage No.3

This is reputed to have been the first carriage delivered on the line. At a later date it was altered with the separate First/Second Class compartment being installed in order to make it a composite. It was in this form that it was to run until preservation. The carriage doors were altered so that the handles were on the right hand side in 1967. More recently it was the first of the original carriages to be fitted with air-brakes in 1997.

Right: Carriage No.3 after repainting at Tywyn Wharf in August 1962, it was now an all-Third. (Photo: Keith Stretch)

Carriage No.4

When first delivered this carriage only had single-skinned wooden sides with external framing. It also had reduced height doors, although these seem to have been soon altered. In 1912 it appears that it was at least re-tyred as the wheel tyres are marked with that date, and was probably fitted with modern oil lubricated axleboxes at the same time, although the fillers for these are very inaccessible, as any Talyllyn guard will tell you. An external wooden skin was added between 1923 and 1925.

In 1951 No.4 had an ungainly gait and was nicknamed 'Limping Lulu', but repairs to one of the springs in 1953 went some way to curing this. At some point pre-1951 it had suffered severe damage to the drawgear at the east end which had been crudely repaired. It was speculated that this was as a result of the accident in 1882, but the truth of this cannot be ascertained. It was fitted with a new steel inner underframe in 1959, which finally cured the 'limp', and received air brakes in 1999.

Above: Carriage No.4 in its original form at Tywyn Wharf in the early 20th Century. (Photo: TR Collection)

Right: Carriage No.4 as rebuilt at Tywyn Wharf station in 1951. (Photo: The Elliot Collection)

188 Rails Along The Fathew

Passenger Stock

Van No.5

When originally delivered by Brown, Marshall van No.5 had an open verandah at one end, as seen in the photograph on page 21. This was enclosed and look-out duckets were added on each side before the end of the 19th Century.

After R.B. Yates took over he converted this end of the van into a mobile ticket office. A small cut-out was added to the ducket on the platform side of the van for the issuing of tickets. Later (c.1920) the doors on the van's south side were removed and the opening panelled over. The south side footboard was removed subsequently.

In the early 1940s the south side ducket was knocked off, reputedly by the wicket on the carriage shed. Certainly the van was reported as out of use around this time. The tyres on the van were also life-expired, and following a derailment the van was taken out of service around 1946. It remained out of use until the wheels were sent to Britannia Foundry in April 1949 for new tyres to be fitted, they were soon returned and the van was returned to service.

In April 1954 a set of windows were cut in the west end of the van, which have remained ever since. More recently it was equipped for air brake working in 1995. Then in November 2014 it was taken to the National Exhibition Centre at Birmingham for display with locomotive No.1. This was the first time it is known to have been away from the railway.

Above: The photograph on page 21 shows the brake van in its earliest form with an open verandah. By the beginning of the 20th Century this had been closed in and look-out duckets added, as seen in the photo above. In the early 1900s the booking office opening was added to the look-out on the platform side.
(Commercial Postcard)

Above: The brake van at Tywyn Wharf in June 1950. Originally there was a set of doors on the south side of the van, as seen on page 127, but this seems to have been removed in the 1920s.
(Photo: The Elliot/Dan Quine Collection)

Above: The brake van at Tywyn Wharf on 6 June 1953. This was before the windows were cut into the west end.
(Photo: J.H.L. Adams)

Right: As seen in 1994 with the windows that were added in 1954 in the western end of the sides, and in the west end, still in place.
(Photo: J.H.L. Adams)

Rails Along The Fathew — 189

Passenger Stock

Corris Van No.6

This had originally been built for the Corris Railway in 1885 at Falcon works. After the closure of that line it was sold to Mr E.B. Cope for private preservation, but he donated it to the embryonic Talyllyn preservation scheme. It served for a number of years, both in an engineering capacity and on passenger trains, often being used to supplement the restricted luggage space.

Eventually the body was replaced in its entirety in 1958. The old body was deposited at Quarry Siding where it served as a shelter for those working there for some years. It ran in Talyllyn red for a time but was repainted brown in 1961. In 1984 it was repainted again this time GWR grey and had its GWR number, 8754, added, but was repainted brown again soon after. Air brake piping and a setter valve were added in 2001.

Above right: Ex-Corris Van No.6 in Talyllyn colours in 24 September 1954, but still retaining its Corris buffers.
(Photo: J.H.L. Adams)

Right: As repainted in GWR colours in 1984.
(Photo: David J. Mitchell)

The 'Penrhyn' coaches

In 1953 the railway was given the first of a series of former 2 ft gauge Penrhyn open workmen's coaches. These were converted into 'new' carriages for the Talyllyn. They were initially fitted with wheelsets from old Talyllyn wagons but these were so worn they had to be replaced before the carriages entered service. The first one to run on the railway was actually No.8 in July 1953, but they are listed here in numerical order.

Carriage No.7

Penrhyn carriage H was converted for the Talyllyn making use of the wheelsets from an ex-Corris wagon (GWR No.31992), as well as strengthening the chassis and fitting a roof. It entered service on 4 August 1953 but derailed and had to be abandoned at Rhydyronen. The carriage suffered a major derailment on an engineering train, resulting in a broken arm for one of the passengers in the September. Eventually it was dumped at the lineside at Fach Goch as a Permanent Way shelter.

In 1955 the running gear was modified and the roof removed and it continued in service until 1960. It was then converted into a tea van in 1963 for use at Abergynolwyn with a new body, lasting in use until the end of 1968. With work on the Extension under way No.7 was modified yet again to be a tool and mess van for use by the 'Gwerns'.

Finally in 1980 it was withdrawn once more to have a new body and underframe built for use as a wheelchair-accessible carriage cum brake van. After much delay, the re-bodied carriage was ready for use in 1992 with a formal launch taking place on 28 June. It was fitted with roller bearings and was equipped for air brakes in 1994.

Left: Carriage No.7 c.1953 when it was fitted with a roof. (Photo: J.H.L. Adams)

Rails Along The Fathew

Passenger Stock

Above: Carriage No.7 being rebuilt into the tea van outside the North Carriage Shed on 29 July 1963. (Photo: Keith Stretch)

Above: Carriage No.7 in use as the Abergynolwyn tea van in September 1968. By this time a special siding had been laid for it at the east end of the station. (Photo: J.H.L. Adams)

Left: Carriage No.7 as currently in service at Tywyn Wharf in August 2015.

Carriage No.8

Carriage No.8 was constructed from former Penrhyn P, with the wheels from another former Corris wagon, and first ran in service at the end of July 1953. Unfortunately it was also prone to derailing and was fitted with softer springs in 1955, with buffers being added the following year.

When it was condemned in 1965, due to the state of the bodywork, it was determined to replace it with a new-build with a steel framework for the body. It was also to be fitted with a roof. Work started on the new carriage in May 1966 and it entered service on 26 July that year, albeit with the running gear from the old No.8. Doors, chest-height guard rails and footboards were fitted in 1970. It has run in this form ever since, except for being fitted with air brakes in 1998.

Above: Carriage No.8 in service on 3 August 1953. An interesting question is what would happen if a coupling broke as the carriage is on the downhill side of the brake van. Still the passengers had a hand brake. (Photo: J.N. Slater)

Right: Carriage No.8 in its rebuilt state in June 2015.

Passenger Stock

Carriage No.9

With increasing demand for passenger accommodation in 1954 two 23 ft 6 in bogie carriage chassis were constructed by W.G. Allen for £380 each. Initially the bodies from Penrhyn carriages C and D were simply bolted one of the frames and carriage No.9 entered service in May 1954, the first bogie vehicle on the railway.

It was decided to build a new enclosed body for the chassis using timber framing and plywood. This was completed in time for the start of passenger services in 1955.

However, the softwood construction soon deteriorated, and so the body was replaced with a new one, constructed by Raymond Tisdale and Co. of Kenilworth. The rebuilt carriage returned to service on 2 June 1968, with modified bogies similar to those fitted to carriage No.10.

Shortly after re-entering service it had two accidents. The first was when the bodywork was damaged in the accident at Wharf on 6 July 1968. Later, in September, it suffered a broken axle.

Save for repairs and repaints it has run in this re-built form ever since. In 1990 it was fitted with Mark 3 bogies, but these were changed for air braking rigged ones in 1994.

Above Right: The first rebuild in service at Tywyn Wharf.
(Photo: TR Collection)
Right: The second rebuild in service in August 2015.

Above: Carriage No.9 in its first form at Tywyn Wharf on 19 July 1954. (Photo: J.H.L. Adams)

Above: Carriage No.10 in its original form at Tywyn Wharf on 19 July 1954. (Photo: J.H.L. Adams)

Carriage No.10

The second Allen-built chassis had a brake fitted to one of the bogies, but it was found that the remaining Penrhyn bodies were too rotten to be used. Therefore, a plywood body was hastily assembled with a small guard's compartment. It entered service on Whit Monday 7 June 1954. However, it is reported that the underframe was still being painted as its first passengers were boarding!

In 1966 it was decided to replace the body with one manufactured by Tisdales to a similar style to the new 'standard' bogie carriage No.18. At the same time new bogies were constructed for the vehicle with the underframe strengthened and modified to allow greater distance between them. The rebuilt carriage entered service on 3 July 1967.

Above: The first rebuild of carriage No.10 at Tywyn Wharf.
(Photo: TR Collection)

Above: No.10 at Tywyn Wharf on 2 July 2015.

It was fitted with new Mark 3 bogies in 1988, and was also equipped with an air-brake cylinder. However, it was not until 1992 that it was equipped for air braking. Between 2005 and 2008 it underwent a major rebuild, which including redesigning the guard's compartment.

Passenger Stock

Carriage No. 11

When Penrhyn bodies C and D were removed from carriage No.9 in 1955 they were reused. Carriage No.11 was completely assembled in two days at the start of August 1955. Work started on the Sunday morning and the carriage made its first run on the Monday evening.

It was constructed with type 3 axleboxes, hornblocks and springs from an old Festiniog quarrymen's carriage with a new steel chassis. Again a set of Corris wagon wheels was pressed into service. Penrhyn body D was then bolted on the top.

In 1958 it was rebuilt along with No.12 to the same design as No.13, the rebuilt carriage entering service in 1959. Platform-side doors were added in 1965, and the following year it was fitted with a roof and ends. New wheels were fitted in 1967, while a south-side guard rail and a platform-side footboard were added in 1970. The bodywork was renewed in 1973 and air brakes fitted in 2000.

Carriage No. 12

Originally rebuilt with a similar set of components to No.11, No.12 was fitted with Penrhyn body C, entering service in 1956. Like No.11 it was rebuilt for the 1959 season, and again a roof and ends were fitted in 1966. In 1970 doors and a footboard were added along with a guard rail on the south side. The bodywork was renewed in 1982, and it was equipped with air brakes in 2000.

Above: Open No.11 at Tywyn Pendre in June 1957.
(Photo: J.H.L. Adams)

Above: Rebuilt No.11 at Tywyn Wharf on 7 April 2015.

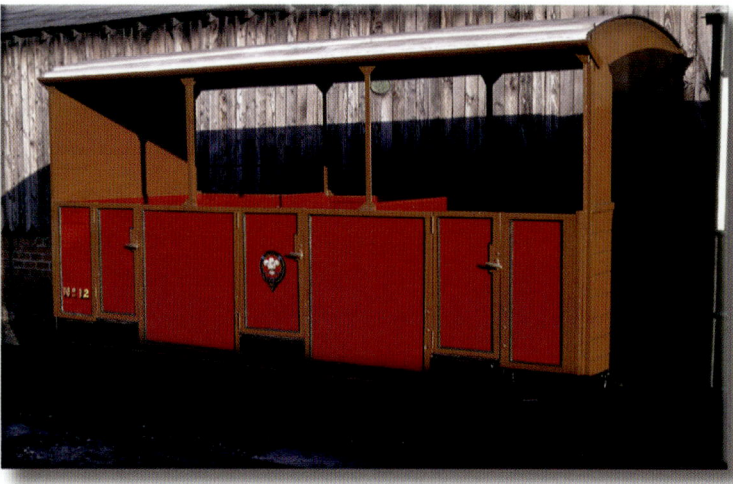

Above: Rebuilt carriage No.12 at Tywyn Pendre.
(Photo: David J. Mitchell)

Below: Carriage No.13 at Tywyn Pendre.
(Photo: J.H.L. Adams)

Above: Carriage No.13 as originally built at Tywyn Pendre.
(Photo: J.N. Slater)

Carriage No.13

Additional numbers led to the need for new rolling stock, and so another open carriage, No.13, entered service in mid-August 1957. This time a 14 ft long body had been constructed at Pendre rather than utilising one of the old Penrhyn ones, and was larger to offer more passenger comfort. It was also equipped with a roof and new wheels over the winter of 1966/67. Again doors, a footboard and guard rail were added in 1970. The bodywork was renewed in 1977 and it received air brakes in 2000.

Passenger Stock

Carriage No.14

In 1956 the railway obtained the first of two coach bodies from the defunct Glyn Valley Tramway (GVT) which had run between Chirk and Glyn Ceiriog and had closed in 1935. The first, having rested in a vicarage garden in Chirk, was purchased by a member in 1956 and donated to the Society. This was the former First Class carriage, No.14, built in 1892 by the Midland Railway Carriage and Wagon Co.

The body was taken to Tywyn for restoration and the provision of new running gear with roller bearings constructed by Allens. It had its first trial on the line in October 1958, tight clearances led to the replacement of the Pendre cottage wall with a fence. After further work it entered full service on Whit Sunday 1959 painted in a representation of its former GVT livery of green and cream.

In 1999 it was taken out of service due to woodworm in the bodywork, and underwent a major rebuild to the body and running gear. It was also fitted with air brakes, the last vehicle to be so equipped, and returned to service in 2004.

Above right: The unrestored body of carriage No.14 at Tywyn Wharf in 1957.   (Photo: TR Collection)

Right: Carriage No.14 with full GVT lining in June 1959.
(Photo: J.T. Fraser)

Carriage No.15

No. 15 was a former GVT Third Class carriage of 1901, the body of which was purchased in 1958 from a farm near Glyn Ceiriog. Unlike No.14 this was taken to the Midlands to be professionally restored at Hunt Bros. It was provided with an upgraded interior to match No.14 and entered service on 23 July 1958. In contrast to No.14 it was originally provided with plain brass bearings, roller bearings not being fitted until 2000 when it was also fitted with air brakes. In July 1985 it was taken back to Glyn Ceiriog, and put on display for a day as part of a commemoration of the 50th Anniversary of the closure of the GVT.

Above: Carriage No.15 being loaded to be transported for restoration.
(Photo: TR Collection)

Left: Both GVT carriages at Tywyn Pendre c.1959.
(Photo: J.N. Slater)

Rails Along The Fathew

Passenger Stock

Carriage No.16

On 5 February 1958 a near-derelict 3 ft gauge coach body, which had been obtained for £25 from the Stanton quarry in Derbyshire, arrived at Wharf by rail. This was eventually converted into carriage No.16 using parts of the original frame, which came into service in 1961. It transpired that it was the last surviving carriage built by Kerr, Stuart, so its destruction could be said to be unfortunate, but the question has to be asked as to what was the alternative at the time?

No. 16 was originally rebuilt as a five-compartment semi-open carriage, entering traffic in 1961. The following year it had a guard's compartment complete with a brake working on all wheels added. The guard's compartment was extended between 1968 and 1969.

In 1979 the old body was removed and a new one was constructed by joiner Fred Hamlin at Pendre. Sadly the rebuilt coach's first duty, although incomplete, was as part of the train carrying mourners to the interment of Fred's body after his funeral.

It formally re-entered service subsequently in May 1981. In 1989 it was fitted with Mark 3 bogies and rigging for air brakes. Full air-braking equipment was installed in 1992. A ducket was added in 1998 to the guard's compartment on the platform side, but this was subsequently 'removed' during a shunting accident and not replaced.

Top: The original Kerr, Stuart body as delivered to Tywyn Wharf. (Photo: Keith Stretch)

Above Right: The first manifestation of carriage No. 16 at Tywyn Wharf station on 29 July 1961. (Photo: Keith Stretch)

Right: No.16 as later rebuilt, photographed in July 1975.

Below Right: The carriage in its current form at Tywyn Wharf station on 28 August 2015.

Carriage No.17

This was the last 'restoration' project before the advent of what became known as the 'standard bogies'. The carriage was found in a garden at Gobowen near Oswestry and purchased for the railway in 1958, finally arriving in Tywyn on 5 May 1959. Originally built by the Metropolitan Carriage and Wagon Co. for the Corris Railway in 1898, it had last run in 1930.

The carriage emerged to enter traffic on Whit Monday 1961, perversely just before No.16. It was fully lined out in near Corris

Above: Some of these responsible for the restoration of carriage No.17. Don Gardiner is on the left, and then Brian Green with his father John. (Photo: TR Collection)

Rails Along The Fathew

Passenger Stock

livery and was a credit to those who had worked to get it back into service. As previously stated when it was first in service a supplement was charged for riding in it, despite it being marked as Third Class, but this did not last long.

Perhaps its most famous passenger was Diana, Princess of Wales, who rode in it between Pendre and Rhydyronen during the visit by her and Prince Charles in November 1982. Since then it has been fitted with Mark 3 bogies and air braking equipment in 1994. In 2006 it was repainted into a closer representation of its Corris livery.

Carriage No.18

Above: Carriage No.17 at Abergynolwyn In September 1963. (Photo: J.T. Fraser)

During the late 1950s and into the early 1960s it was clear that the railway needed more passenger stock. Therefore consideration turned to the idea of building new enclosed bogie coaches. In 1958 design work began on the first of these.

Serious construction work began in 1961, but it was not until 1 June 1965 that it entered service as part of the official Centenary celebrations. Designed as a 30 ft long six-compartment all-Third it was built to high standards and is a credit to those involved in its design and construction. The bodywork reflected the design of the Glyn Valley coaches in style, and it was going to be fitted with a parking brake, but this did not happen.

The only major problem was that the initial design of the bogies was not a success, allowing the carriage to roll. Eventually the bogies were modified to be interchangeable with Mark 2 versions in 1977. In 1994 it had the appropriate rigging fitted for air braking.

Above: Carriage No.18 at Tywyn Pendre in July 1969. Note that it was fitted with doors and window bars on the south-side just like the original coaches. (Photo: J.H.L. Adams)

Subsequent to No.18 the first carriages to be rebuilt in the standard style were Nos 10 and 9. These had bodies constructed professionally by Tisdales in Kenilworth, and were to a simplified design. This was the method adopted for the rest of the new-build carriages.

Carriage No.19

On 19 April 1968 the body for No.19 was delivered to be mounted on a frame fabricated at Pendre, and entered service on 21 June 1969 fitted with Mark 2 bogies. It is a First/Third composite.

During the subsequent years there were the usual minor repairs and repaints, but in 1992 it was noted as having a sagging roof line. This led to the fitting of some additional steel framing to support the roof.

In 1996 it was equipped so that electric storage heaters could be fitted for the winter services, these being removed for the summer months. Air braking equipment was fitted in 1993.

Above: The body for carriage No.19 as delivered in 1968. (Photo: David J. Mitchell)

Passenger Stock

Carriage No. 20

By now there was beginning to be a regular production line of new carriages. Carriage No.20 has a 28 ft long all-Third body, which was delivered on 16 April 1969. It entered service on 19 July 1970. However, due to shortages it had to be fitted with plain bearing axleboxes instead of roller bearings. The latter were fitted in July 1972.

In 1993 it was equipped for air brake working. Then in 1996 the eastern end of the carriage was converted into a saloon to provide wheelchair accommodation. It is seen on the right in its original form.

Carriage No.21

The delivery of new coach bodies continued, the one for carriage No.21, another all-Third, arriving on 30 May 1970 and the coach entering service on 3 August 1971. In 1981 it required major body repairs which resulted in it not running in service until January 1984.

Air braking was installed in 1993, and in 1995 it was the first of two bogie carriages to have its eastern end converted into a saloon to convey wheelchairs. The following year it was equipped to have removable storage heaters fitted for winter operation.

It also acted as a Royal Saloon in July 2005 carrying the Duchess of Cornwall between Brynglas and Tywyn Wharf for the official opening of the new station building.

In 2011 it was found that the body needed major repairs, and it was decided to have the carriage professionally rebuilt at Boston Lodge works. The restored coach re-entered service in 2013, as seen above right.

Carriage No.22

Carriage No.22 is a Brake Third the body for which arrived on 8 July 1971, and it entered service a year later. The following year it had to be fitted with extra shock absorbers to improve the ride.

In 1995 it was fitted for air-braking and in 1996 it was another carriage selected to have fitments for storage heaters added. It was taken out of service in 2008 when it was found the body needed a major rebuild which has taken some time to complete, but it is hoped that it will re-enter service in 2016.

Carriage No.23

No. 23 is another all-Third. The body arrived on 17 July 1973 and it entered service on 29 March 1975, running on plain bearings. Roller bearings were not fitted until 1977. It was fitted for air-braking in 1994, and between 2004 and 2005 the body was extensively rebuilt.

It is currently the last standard bogie to enter service. There were scheduled to be at least two more. No.24 was to be a First/Third composite and No.25 another Brake Third, but these were cancelled with the decline in traffic and the tight financial situation following the opening to Nant Gwernol.

All photos on this page by David J. Mitchell except carriage No.21 (below) by the author.

Rails Along The Fathew — 197

Goods Stock

Once more it is difficult to be precise on the early history of the railway's goods stock. In 1870 the railway declared that it had 114 goods and mineral wagons, which by 1890 had become 70. In the 1912 return Haydn Jones declared there were 100, but this seems to be more an estimate than anything else.

The railway's wagons broke down into several different types:

1. Open wagons
2. Slate wagons with timber bar sides
3. Incline wagons, especially shaped for use on the inclines
4. Pig wagons
5. Bolster wagons for the transport of large loads
6. Covered vans
7. Sheep wagon (a modified van)
8. Gunpowder van

The breakdown of wagons in 1921, according to the official classification, was: 10 opens, 3 covered, 70 mineral, 2 locomotive coal wagons and 3 miscellaneous. The difficulty is to ascertain in some cases (e.g. incline, pig, and gunpowder) into which of the official categories individual wagons fell.

Slate wagons were of two distinct types namely two and three-bars. For both types the overall dimensions of the body were 6 ft long by 3 ft 6 in wide by 1 ft 4 in high and, according to the Annual Returns in Haydn Jones' time, both could take a load of 0.75 ton. There were also more of the two-bar type.

The open wagons were solid-sided and made of timber or iron. In the case of the former they appear to be modified slate wagons. There were two types of iron-sided wagons one straight-sided and the other tapered outwards. The pig wagons were given especially extended sides.

Above: This photograph of King's/Tywyn Wharf station from c.1903 features much that is of interest. On the station building there are noticeboards advertising both the Cambrian and Corris Railways, the latter featuring the tours of Talyllyn Lake and Cader Idris. On the standard gauge a Cambrian Railways covered van and a private owner wagon can be seen. In the coal yard there is a large covered haystack. In the foreground most of the railway's wagon types are on display. There is a rake of ten loaded slate wagons, presumably just arrived from the quarry, a mixture of both the two-bar and three-bar types. At this end there are an incline wagon, a flair-sided open wagon and a straight-sided open wagon. Behind them four vans can be made out to the side of the coal yard. Other points of note include the wooden parapet on the Neptune Road bridge in the background, as well as the numbering of the wagons (Nos. 77 and 62 can be made out, seen more clearly on the left).

(Photo: F. Moore Copyright NRM/SSPL)

Goods Stock

The covered vans were wooden-sided with five planks and had curved roofs. Their dimensions were 7 ft 3 in long by 4 ft 8 in wide, they were 4 ft high at the sides, with a maximum height at the top of the roof arc of 5 ft 2 in. They were all out of service by 1934. The remains of one of these vans survived on the east side of Rhydyronen bridge for many years, until it was retrieved for restoration in 1997. The sheep wagon was a conversion of a covered van with a barred opening in the upper sides.

Finally the gunpowder wagon, as the name suggests, was for the safe transport of explosives to the quarry. Its body was therefore constructed of sheet metal with a gabled-ended design. It was some 6 ft long.

Precisely how many there were of each design of wagon is uncertain, and not all of them were in service at any one time. With the decline in the goods traffic on the line the number of wagons declined as well, as the samples on the right from the Annual Returns illustrate. In addition, a number of wagons ended up at the bottom of the Gwernol ravine as a result of breakaways on the inclines.

Wagons were still repaired and renewed. In the return for 1921 it was said that 16 wagons had undergone heavy repair and 5 light repairs all at a cost of £201. For 1924 it was stated that £70 had been spent on wagon repairs including 4 renewals and 8 light repairs.

Numbers of Wagons for each Classification 1921 - 1950

Year	Open Wagons	Mineral Wagons	Covered Wagons	Misc/Bolster Wagons	Loco Coal Wagons
1921	10	70	3	3	2
1933	10	80	2	4	2
1935	10	82	0	4	2
1938	10	65	0	4	2
1945	6	50	0	4	2
1947	6	42	0	4	2
1950	6	35	0	4	2

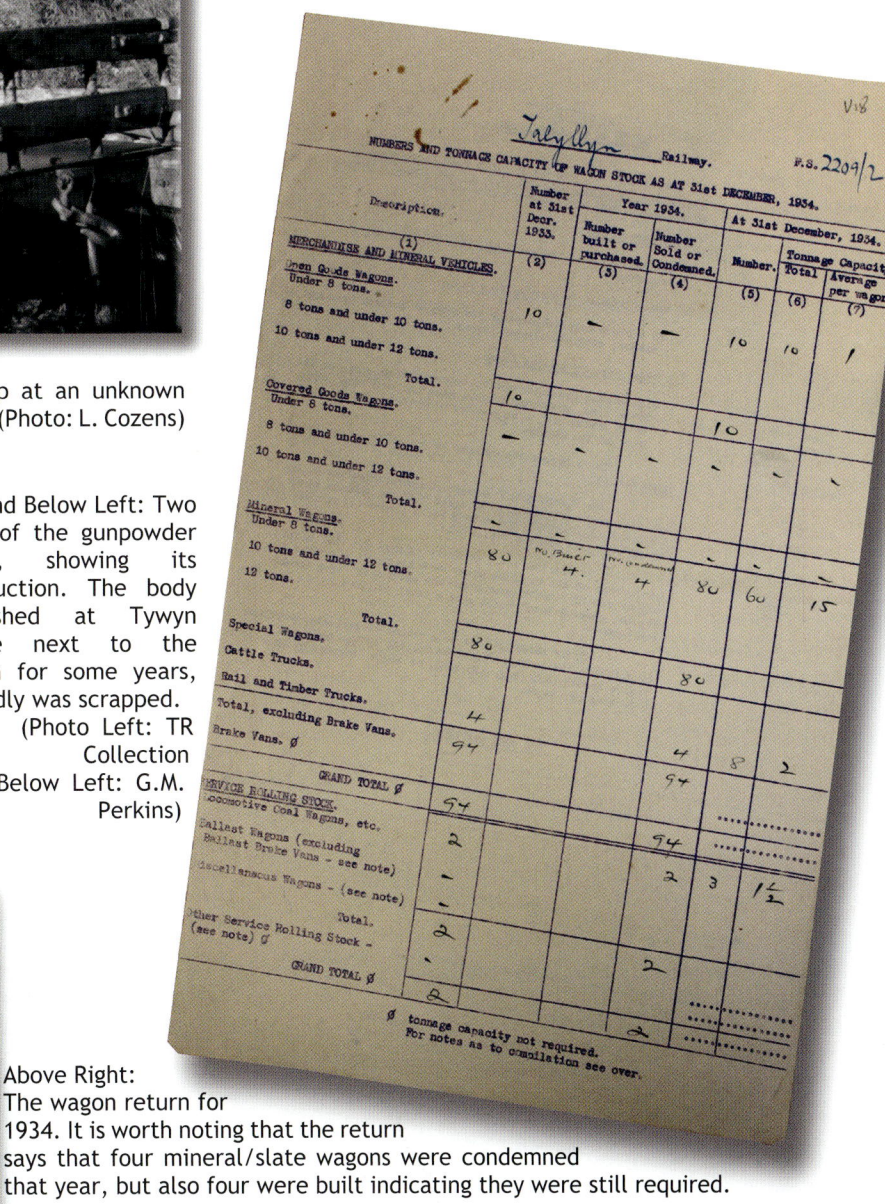

Above: Two two-bar slate wagons in close-up at an unknown location. (Photo: L. Cozens)

Left and Below Left: Two views of the gunpowder wagon, showing its construction. The body languished at Tywyn Pendre next to the station for some years, but sadly was scrapped.
(Photo Left: TR Collection
Below Left: G.M. Perkins)

Above Right: The wagon return for 1934. It is worth noting that the return says that four mineral/slate wagons were condemned that year, but also four were built indicating they were still required.

Rails Along The Fathew

199

Goods Stock

Above: Several wagons were lost down the Gwernol ravine due to breakaways on the inclines and other accidents. Some of these were subsequently retrieved for parts.
(Photo: David J. Mitchell)

Above Left: For many years one of the original covered van bodies was to be seen in the lee of the bridge at Rhydyronen. On 9 April 1955 Hugh Jones was using it as a wood store.
(Photo: J.N. Slater)

Left: In 1997 it was rescued and brought down to Tywyn for restoration. The result of this can be seen on page 202.
(Photo: David J. Mitchell)

After Preservation

The surviving original wagons did not fare well initially under preservation. All were in very poor condition and were cannibalised for other items of rolling stock. In more recent years, however, a number of pre-1950 wagons have been restored or replicas made to complement the original carriages. These are held by the Narrow Gauge Railway Museum Trust.

Space does not permit the detailed examination of the railway's stock of wagons since preservation. Instead a photographic overview is offered. This covers some of the original wagons still preserved on the railway, as well as those that have been acquired since 1951.

Right: The Wagon Stock List from September 1954. A new numbering scheme had been introduced in 1952 and ran as follows:

Steel Body Wagons   Nos. 1 - 19
Wooden Body Wagons   Nos. 20 - 29
Slate Wagons   No. 30 and upwards

Wagon Stock September 1954

No.	Body	Door	Details
1	Steel	End	Ex-Corris Rly. GWR No.31999
2	Steel	End	Ex-Corris Rly. GWR No.31998
3	Steel	End	Ex-Corris Rly. GWR No.31995
4	Steel	Side	Ex-Corris Rly. GWR No.31994
5	Steel	End	Ex-Corris Rly. GWR Chassis No. 31987 Body No.32000
6	Steel	End	Ex-Corris Rly. GWR No.31993
7	Steel	End	Talyllyn Wagon Withdrawn
8	Steel	End	Talyllyn Wagon
9	Steel	End	Talyllyn Wagon (Rebuilt)
10	Steel	End	Ex-Corris Rly. GWR Chassis No.31992 Body No.31987
11	Steel	End	Talyllyn Wagon (Rebuilt)
20	Wood	End	Ex-Corris Rly. GWR No.31982
21	Flat	-	Engineering Tool Wagon Talyllyn Stock
22	Flat	-	Engineering Mobile Generator
23			Formerly Corris No.31992, See No.10 (Withdrawn)
24	Bolster	-	Ex-Corris Rly. Chassis from GWR No.32000
25	Bolster	-	Talyllyn Wagon (Rebuilt)
26	Wood	End	Ex-Corris Rly. GWR No.31991
27	Wood	End	Ex-Corris Rly. GWR No.31990
28	Bolster	-	Built 1954 Talyllyn Stock
30	Slate Traffic Wagon		Talyllyn
32	Slate Traffic Wagon		Talyllyn
34	Flat	-	Altered from slate wagon 1954

Goods Stock

Left: Ex-GWR wagon No.31998, part of the collection of wagons acquired from the then recently closed Corris Railway, at Tywyn Wharf in 1951. This became Talyllyn No.2 in the revised numbering system that was introduced.
(Photo: J.T. Fraser)

Right: A 1950s engineering train could be an eclectic mix as this collection of wagons at Quarry Siding illustrates. Locomotive No.4 *Edward Thomas* is in charge of the ensemble on 29 October 1952, which contains a selection of the ex-Corris wagons the Talyllyn acquired in 1951. The nearest wagon is No.20, an ex-Corris Railway wooden bodied open, GWR No.31982. Further down the line the whole train derailed and had to be abandoned for the night.
(Photo: J.I.C. Boyd)

Left: Another mixed collection of wagons in this 1965 engineering train, hauled by No.5 *Midlander* and driven by Bob Lee, during the relaying at Tywyn Wharf station on 20 February. It includes some tipper wagons, as well as several other types.
(Photo: David J. Mitchell)

Right: Another 1965 view of No.5 *Midlander*, this time it is on the former mineral line, with four flat wagons. Nearest the camera is wagon No.19 constructed out of the chassis of the original No.5. Then come two ex-Festiniog Railway bolster wagons, Nos. 30 and 31, which had been acquired in 1956, and finally an unidentified flat wagon. (Photo: David J. Mitchell)

Rails Along The Fathew

Goods Stock

Above: This two-bar slate wagon was originally rebuilt for the Warley Model Railway Exhibition at the National Exhibition Centre in 2001.

Above: A rebuilt Talyllyn three-bar slate wagon, now part of the Narrow Gauge Railway Museum collection.

Above: A Talyllyn end-door open wagon.

Above: An incline wagon No.117 now held by the Museum Trust.

Left: In 2005 a heritage area was established at Tywyn Wharf and some of the restored wagons were put on display including the restored covered van No.146.

Right: The original wagons are used on special trains, such as photographic charters. One such with a Corris Railway theme is seen at Rhydyronen station in March 2010.

202 Rails Along The Fathew

Goods Stock

Above: Ex-MOD drop-side wagon No.62 at Tywyn Wharf.

Above: Tipper wagons Nos. 53 and 55 on the wharf edge in May 2015. These are of 1½ cu yd capacity and were obtained in 1973 and 1975 respectively.

Above: Ballast Hopper wagon No.23. The body was built at Pendre in 1973, and it is on a later chassis with axleboxes from an old Winchburgh Oil Shale Works wagon.

Above: DN37S is an ex-RNAD bogie wagon from the Trecwn depot, which was regauged for use on the Talyllyn.

Left: A modern engineering train departs from Tywyn Wharf behind diesel No.11 on 8 August 2015. It is composed of a flat wagon, bogie flat No.71, which is an Ex-MOD vehicle. At the rear is Ex-MOD bogie brake van No.70, built in 1987 and used at various Naval Armament Depots until it was acquired by the Talyllyn.
(Photo: B. Fuller)

Rails Along The Fathew 203

Signalling, Blocking and Permanent Way

Signalling

It is unclear whether there was any signalling in place on the railway in its early days. There is only one firm piece of evidence, which is the sale of some signalling equipment to the Mawddwy Railway in July 1867 for £176 16s 4d. Unfortunately the records do not indicate what was sold or why, but the price seems to indicate it was a substantial quantity, particularly as this was a secondhand price.

If signals were ever installed where would they have been put, to what purpose, and why were they sold? Brynglas crossing has been mentioned as one likely place, and indeed it was reported that the hole for a signal post had been found there. But, for reasons already mentioned, it is unlikely that the crossing was in existence prior to Tyler's inspection in September 1866. It would also have had to have been gated and a crossing keeper provided, as it was across a public road. Could signalling equipment have been purchased and then sold after the Broad of Trade's refusal to give permission for the crossing?

Tŷ Mawr and Rhydyronen crossings had been replaced by bridges by the time of Tyler's inspection. Gates had been installed previously, so again had signalling equipment been purchased for these locations before the decision to replace the crossings? If so crossing keepers would have had to be employed to operate them.

Another site for signals would be Pendre, but again if any of the equipment was purchased for this location, it is unlikely to have been installed given the date of sale to the Mawddwy only a few months later. Certainly Tyler doesn't mention any signalling in his report. It therefore seems unlikely that any signalling was actually installed on the Talyllyn.

There is, however, another option and that is the equipment was purchased for Railway No.2 to connect with the A&WCR. It was then sold when construction of this line was finally abandoned, but this is speculation.

Signalling Post Preservation

Soon after preservation there were abortive attempts at signalling. One at Tywyn Wharf station and the other at Brynglas. The first was in place by the time of the visit of Colonel McMullen, the Railway Inspector, in August 1954, but he ordered it be removed and instead a Stop Board provided. Signals had also been installed at Brynglas, but these too were quickly removed as they were not approved.

Point indicators had also been installed at both Wharf and at Pendre the same year. The former seem to have remained in a modified state, but the latter were removed, then re-instated when the ground frame was installed in 1958. These reduced the danger of up trains paying an unscheduled visit to the locomotive shed,

Some unsuccessful attempts at early signalling in 1954.

Top: At Tywyn Wharf. (Photo: J.H.L. Adams)
Middle: At Brynglas. (Photo: J.H.L. Adams)
Bottom: At Tywyn Pendre (Photo: J.N. Slater)

All of which were ordered to be removed by the inspector because they didn't comply with regulations.

Signalling, Blocking and Permanent Way

Above: The replacement Stop Board at Tywyn Wharf station. (Photo: J.H.L. Adams)

Right: Colour light signal at Abergynolwyn.

When Abergynolwyn station was altered in 1976 full colour-light signalling was provided. In 1986 the Inspectorate suggested that similar signalling be installed at Pendre, and a scheme was eventually submitted in 1991. It had also been agreed in principle to install signalling at Brynglas and Quarry Siding in 1990, but in the end none of these schemes was ever carried out.

Blocking

Before preservation the railway was worked, at least ostensibly, on the principle of one engine in steam and there was no need for any track sections to be delineated. However, in 1952 the line was divided into two sections, Wharf to Pendre and Pendre to Abergynolwyn, to allow for additional movements. A train staff was provided for each section, possession of which was essential for a train to enter the designated length of line.

In 1953 the loop was constructed at Brynglas to allow the territorial army possession east of there while passenger trains were still operating. To enable this to happen three new wooden train staffs were made, one for the section Pendre to Brynglas West, one for Brynglas station and the third for Brynglas East to Abergynolwyn.

something that had happened on at least two occasions, due to the driver failing to notice the points were incorrectly set.

The signal at Wharf was replaced in 1955. A green signal lamp, electrically lit, was mounted on a wooden post. About a third of the way up the post, just above the lamp, was a red Stop Board. When the signal was in use trains had to stop at the board unless the green light was showing, the latter being operated from Wharf office.

In 1971, this was replaced by a full colour-light signal. A two-lens subsidiary signal was added in 1974 along with a warning treadle, and the following year two replacement ground disc signals were provided east of Wharf bridge on the south side of the line. These indicate the direction the points are set under the bridge and had been salvaged from the main line station at Tywyn.

Four types of train staff and token:

Top: The original 1951 wooden train staff.

Upper Middle: The 1953 metal Pendre-Brynglas staff.

Lower Middle: The full staff and tickets used on the Brynglas to Quarry Siding section from 1969 to 1972.

Bottom: Electric Key Token for the Wharf to Pendre section.

Rails Along The Fathew — 205

Signalling, Blocking and Permanent Way

Clockwise from top: The new frame being installed in Pendre blockpost, the original frame at Brynglas loop, the frame being installed at Quarry Siding, the frame at Nant Gwernol and the west frame at Pendre.
(Photos: Keith Stretch; TR Collection; David J. Mitchell; I. Drummond and J.J. Davis)

In the summer of that year the sections were modified to Wharf to Pendre, Pendre to Brynglas and Brynglas to Abergynolwyn. A new staff was made from metal plate with welded lettering for the Pendre to Brynglas section and the Pendre to Abergynolwyn staff was re-lettered for the Brynglas to Abergynolwyn section.

These did not last for long as full staff-and-ticket working was introduced the same year along with a new rule book. This allowed two trains to follow each other through a section by one of two methods. The block system allowed a second train (carrying the staff) to enter a section once the first train (carrying the ticket) had cleared part of it. For example a second up train could enter the section at Brynglas once the first train was departing Dolgoch. Only when all the pieces of the staff and ticket(s) were reassembled could a down train enter the section. The other method used was the time interval method under which the second train had to enter the section fifteen minutes after the first.

To provide greater flexibility a Miniature Electric Train Staff (METS) system was commissioned between Tywyn Wharf and Pendre on 1 June 1966. It was intended to extend the system up the line, but it was superseded by the Electric Key Token (EKT) system. This came into operation for the section between Pendre and Brynglas on 19 July 1971 with an intermediate machine at Rhydyronen. The decision to move to a three-train-set peak service also led to the introduction of a new loop and block post at Quarry Siding, the block section between Brynglas and Abergynolwyn being divided appropriately.

EKT operation was extended to Quarry Siding 16 July 1972, and the section between Wharf and Pendre was converted the following year. Finally EKT working was introduced between Quarry Siding and Abergynolwyn in 1976. However, the Extension has been worked by the staff-and-ticket system since opening.

To overcome the need for each block to be manned while the system was in use, a remote operator system was devised. This allowed tokens to be withdrawn and put back into machines even when no blockman was on duty at the other end of the section.

Permanent Way

As already stated, most of the original Permanent Way lasted into the 1950s and 1960s. In fact the first brand-new rail did not arrive on the railway until 1972; until then any replacement rail had been obtained secondhand from elsewhere.

Mention has already been made of the remains of the original construction track found in Wharf cutting. This was of very light construction and probably unsuitable for locomotive use.

For the introduction of locomotive working heavier rail was required. This was flat-bottomed wrought-iron rail with a weight of 40 lb to the yard (although McConnel thought it was 44 lb), heavier than that then used on the Festiniog Railway, in 21 ft lengths. Some 500 tons of it would have been required for the whole line, and it was probably laid in around four to five months between November 1864 and April 1865.

It was laid on wooden sleepers, but was secured by a combination of spikes and chairs. The rails were joined by the two ends of adjoining lengths of rail being butted together in a common chair and secured with a wooden key (see opposite).

Each pair of rails was carried on seven timber sleepers, one under the joint and six others, and secured always in the same sequence. First the chaired joint sleeper, then a spiked sleeper, then a chaired one followed by two spiked, another chaired and finally a spiked sleeper next to the succeeding joint.

Signalling, Blocking and Permanent Way

The method of joining evidently proved unsatisfactory and so it was decided to install fishplates. Tom Rolt records the legend that two men were set to work up the line with a hand-drill to rectify the track joints, but stopping just short of Abergynolwyn. The truth of this is uncertain, there was a break in the fishplated joints just west of Abergynolwyn, but some track on the mineral extension was found to be fishplated. Therefore, the reason for the gap is another Talyllyn mystery.

It would be wrong to think that the track was laid and then not maintained. While the bulk of the rail remained original some rail lengths were replaced and there was a programme of re-sleepering even up until 1950, although eventually this was very limited. As has been mentioned Cynfal bank was also relaid with rails obtained from the closed Glyn Valley Tramway.

During the Haydn Jones era they experimented with using half-round tree trunks obtained from his plantation as sleepers. Generally these proved not very satisfactory, and in some cases they took root and sprouted. In latter days they obtained old sleepers from the GWR which they sawed in half for spot re-sleepering, replacing individual rotten sleepers.

After Preservation

Much of the early effort of the Society went into improving the track. At first this was primarily directed at re-sleepering and re-ballasting. Part of this was to get the track back true to gauge rather than the 2 ft 3 in and a thumb that had been the previous custom. The re-laid track was fully spiked and of course fish-plated.

It also has to be said that the quality of some of the work done in those early days was somewhat dubious. The emphasis sometimes was on the quantity of the work rather than ensuring it was done correctly. This evidently applied to the first visit of the army in 1953, when, according to Patrick Whitehouse, a lot of remedial work was necessary afterwards. Still, without such efforts, it is probable the Talyllyn would not have survived.

Some replacement rail was laid. This had been bought by Haydn Jones from the defunct Corris Railway and was now installed on the up approach to Cynfal bank, for a time known as the Corris Straight. In addition, the section between Wharf and Pendre was relaid, a loop was installed at Wharf and the loop at Pendre renewed.

It would not be until 1955 that the first substantial quantity of 'new' rail arrived from Jee's Quarry at Nuneaton. The line had been fully re-sleepered by 1958, and the following year another substantial source of secondhand rail was found at a quarry at Crich. More was obtained from other sources over time. In addition, the use of secondhand granite ballast obtained from British Railways began, but was later discontinued due to its variable quality.

Secondhand rail, although cheaper, was time consuming as much sorting was needed before it could be laid. Therefore in September 1972 the first batch of new 50 lb rail was purchased with 40 tons being delivered to Tywyn. In addition the ex-BR softwood sleepers being used were proving short-lived, and so in 1971 Jarrah hardwood sleepers began to be laid along with new granite ballast.

On 27 January 1967 the last of the original Talyllyn rail was removed from the main line; now it was some of the replacement rail that needed replacing. Although new rail was being bought the railway was still open to obtaining good-quality secondhand material. Thus it was in 1975 that it obtained a substantial quantity of rail and sleepers from the aborted Channel Tunnel project. More recently substantial quantities of rail and sleepers have been salvaged from the RNAD Depot at Trecwn.

The increasing use of mechanised technology such as the tamper, stone blower, and the like, has transformed the way the line is maintained. Today the Permanent Way is almost unrecognisable from the near grass path the Society inherited in 1951. Not surprisingly along the way some of the character has been lost, but now the track is definitely 'fit for purpose' and well up to modern passenger expectations.

Above: One of the original common chair joints still in-situ at Tywyn Wharf in 1938. (Photo: H.B. Tours)

Right: An early post-preservation point lock in June 1952. (Photo: J.N. Slater)

People

Employers and Employees of the Talyllyn Railway Co. during the McConnel Years
(Based on census returns, newspaper and other reports)

	1860s & 1870s	1880s	1890s	1900s
Managing Director	Thomas H. McConnel William McConnel	William McConnel	William McConnel William H. McConnel	William McConnel William H. McConnel
Office	John A. Roberts Hugh Thomas	John A. Roberts Hugh Thomas J.E. Jones	Hugh Thomas Edward Thomas John Evans Thomas	Hugh Thomas Edward Thomas John Evans Thomas Robert B. Yates
Fitter	William Boustead	William Boustead (to 1884) Hugh Griffiths	Hugh Griffiths	Hugh Griffiths (Contract)
Driver	William Boustead	Robert Pattison Hugh Griffiths	John (Jonathan) Rowlands	John (Jonathan) Rowlands
Fireman	Hugh Griffiths Richard Richards (1865)	Robert Davies (?)	Robert Thomas	Robert Thomas
Guard	Hugh Edwards (1868) Lewis Owen	Lewis Owen (to 1884) Jacob Rowlands	Jacob Rowlands	Jacob Rowlands
Platelayers	David Richards John Williams (1869-?) William Roberts (from 1865)	David Richards John (Jonathan) Rowlands William Roberts Robert Roberts (?)	David Richards David Jones	David (Dafydd) Jones Arthur Pughe
Porters at Wharf	John Roberts	John Roberts David Jones	John Roberts David Jones	John Roberts (d. 1907) David Jones (d.1908) John Lloyd

Note: This table is not exhaustive, but does indicate some of the names that are known.

The Aberdovey Slate and Talyllyn Railway Companies' Backers and Directors

The story of the early days of the Talyllyn Railway has already been recounted. One thing that needs to be emphasised is that while the McConnels were the prime movers behind the scheme to acquire the Bryneglwys quarry and build the railway, they were certainly not the only ones who backed it.

In order of the number of shares held the first shareholders of Aberdovey Slate Co. were (numbers of £100 shares held in brackets):

Thomas Houldsworth McConnel (125), Frederick Swanwick (75), James McConnel (70), John Kennedy (50), James Murray (50), James Worthington (50), William McConnel (50), Thomas Swanwick (50), Edward Hardcastle (50), Samuel Norris (50), Murray Gladstone (35), Thomas Hilton (20), George Wood (15), Wainwright Bellhouse (10), Francis Greg (10) and John Hadfield (10).

(Total shares 720)

As can be seen, although the McConnels held the largest block of shares between them, they were not majority shareholders. Most of the shareholders appear to have been involved in the cotton trade in some way or another. Among the exceptions were Frederick Swanwick of Whittington near Chesterfield and his son Thomas, the former stated to be a Civil Engineer. It has also been reported that they had connections with the Stephensons, the famous railway and locomotive engineers.

It was from this group that the first directors of the Talyllyn Railway were drawn, they were:

Thomas Houldsworth McConnel, James Murray, Thomas Swanwick, Murray Gladstone, James McConnel and Samuel Norris.

The McConnels

As already stated the McConnel family at this time consisted of three brothers: James, William and Thomas. William was in charge of the family business McConnel & Co. Cotton Spinners of Manchester and it seems that he was the one to encourage the diversification of the family's business interests.

It was also William that got the family involved in the quarry at Bryneglwys, but it was Thomas who became the Chairman of both the slate and later the railway company until his death from tuberculosis in 1873. Initially Thomas was the largest shareholder in the slate company, but by 1870 William had taken on this mantle owning shares with a nominal value of £14,400.

On Thomas' death William became the Chairman of both companies, and maintained this role until the liquidation of the slate company in 1882. By then he had purchased the assets of the slate company, and the shares in the railway, for £18,000. James had been a shareholder in the slate company from its formation, and a founder director of the TRCo., until his death in 1879, but seems to have played no active role in either enterprise.

People

The other members of the McConnel family to become involved in the quarry and the railway were William's son, William Houldsworth McConnel. He had trained as a civil engineer and was reportedly in India when his father took over the quarry and railway. William became the Secretary of the railway, and took over both enterprises when his father died. Two of William's other sons were also involved with the railway company. John Wanklyn McConnel, William Houldsworth McConnel's elder brother, is given as a director in 1886, and his younger brother, Henry Wilson McConnel, is a director in 1901.

After the McConnels ended their links with the quarry William Houldsworth McConnel lived with his family near Basingstoke in Hampshire, and was the director of a number of companies, mainly to do with the coal industry. During the First World War he worked at the Admiralty in the Department of the Director of Torpedoes and Mining developing the paravane. Here he was given the honorary rank of Lieutenant-Commander and received an OBE for his work. He died in November 1943.

Planning and Construction

While the question of whether there was a main contractor for the Talyllyn Railway remains unresolved, there are a few names associated with the planning and construction of the line that are known:

James Swinton Spooner was possibly the most well-known name. He was the second son of James Spooner, whose name will always be synonymous with the Festiniog Railway. Trained as a Civil Engineer, he worked as a surveyor in New Zealand and Australia, before returning to Wales. After his work on the Talyllyn he doesn't seem to have been involved with any other railways, instead he concentrated on civil engineering projects. He died in 1884.

William E. Williams was an interesting character, he was an apprentice to James Swinton Spooner, and is recorded as an 'inspector on the Talyllyn Railway' in the report on his marriage to Maggie Jones, a well-known singer, in November 1864. In 1874, he was appointed as Chief Engineer & Supervisor for the Trinidad Government Railway & Sewage Works in the West Indies, and later served in Jamaica. Later he returned to Wales to work for the Ffestiniog Urban District Council. He also became a well-known Welsh bard, under the name Gwilym Alltwen, and won a Bardic Chair at the Llanberis Eisteddfod in 1873 as well as various other prizes.

Evan Humphreys' obituary in 1894 described him as contractor to the Talyllyn Railway for many years, but he was not employed by the company as far as is known. In 1871 he is described as a stone mason, and later as a builder and contractor. Therefore, there is quite a possibility that he assisted in the construction of the railway, probably the buildings. Could the workshops at Pendre be examples of his handiwork?

Another less familiar name from the railway's early days is David Howell, a solicitor from Machynlleth. He was very much involved in the development of railways in this part of Wales. This included being the Company Secretary to the Newtown and Machynlleth Railway. He was also solicitor to the Mawddwy (or Mowddwy) Railway, and was involved in securing its Act of Parliament in the same session as the Talyllyn. As mentioned previously it was also to the Mawddwy that the Talyllyn sold some signal equipment in 1867.

In addition he was a member of the Cambrian Archaeological Society, who were the first known passengers on the Talyllyn Railway in August 1866. Given his previous experience and the connections, one suspects he played a significant role in the early life of the Talyllyn which has previously gone unheralded, making links between the various organisations.

Management and Clerks

One name that remains nearly throughout the McConnel era is that of Hugh Thomas. Born in 1842, Hugh Thomas reputedly served the railway from when it first opened in 1865. His role in the company seems to have varied. At first he was a Clerk, then in the 1880s and 1890s he was described as the Manager. Finally his obituary described him as the Chief Accountant. He was also very involved in the local community and when he died in January 1903 his funeral was described as one of the largest the town had seen. Hugh was also the father to John and Edward who would also serve the company.

Another early employee of the McConnel years was John A. Roberts, who acted as the Slate Agent, but he is listed in *Bradshaw's Guide* as the Traffic Manager between 1875 and 1884. In addition, when the assets of the slate company were first put up for auction in 1879, those with enquiries regarding the railway were instructed to contact Roberts. By 1891 though he is listed as living in Llanfihangel-y-Traethau with his wife and mother, and was engaged as a coal merchant. It is probable that when he left Hugh Thomas succeeded him as Manager.

In turn Hugh Thomas was succeeded as Manager by Robert Burton Yates, who came into William McConnel's employ in November 1899. Quite how his role interacted with Hugh Thomas is uncertain at this point. However, his arrival seems to have coincided with a raft of changes to the railway. These included the repainting of the carriages and renaming *Dolgoch*.

Right: R.B. Yates pictured in 1908. (Photo: G.M. Perkins)

People

Left: Edward Thomas, Hugh Thomas and Jacob Rowlands c.1897. The crest on Jacob's hat appears to be an intertwined T,R and C.

Right: Hugh Griffiths in the early 1890s.
(Photos: TR Collection)

He also seems to be responsible for advertising that passengers could start their journey at King's station. It was Yates who instigated the mobile booking office, and obtained ticket dating machines. He remained with the company until April 1911 when it had been handed over to Haydn Jones, although he remained in the area for a few more years.

As already indicated, two of Hugh Thomas' sons, John Evans and Edward were also based in the Wharf office. Both seemed to have joined the railway from school. John was the elder and is listed as an Office Boy in the 1891 census. He remained with the Talyllyn as its Accountant until the end of the Haydn Jones era.

Edward was also to serve the company until 1950, latterly taking on several roles including Manager and Guard. He became almost synonymous with the Talyllyn Railway during the 1940s and 50s, and is immortalised in the name of locomotive No.4. Both were involved in the local Presbyterian church. A third brother, Hugh worked as an Engine Fitter at a works in Porthmadog.

Another person associated with the line during this time, although seemingly not employed by the railway, was John Edwards. He acted as the shipping agent for the railway in Tywyn until his death in 1903 at the age of 48. Also working in the office in 1889 was J.E. Jones. He is reported as gaining his Pitman's shorthand certificate that year, but otherwise nothing is known about him.

Locomotive Men

The role of the William Boustead has already been mentioned. He came down from Fletcher, Jennings at Whitehaven to repair *Talyllyn*, and was quickly offered the job of Locomotive Fitter. He and his wife Anne moved down, first to Abergynolwyn where their son William was born, and then to the cottage at Pendre.

Here they remained until 1884, when they emigrated to Australia. It is reported that a number of men had also left the area for Australia in 1884, which suggests some kind of advertising/recruitment drive in the area. Clearly the family had become part of the local community as a farewell gathering was arranged at the English Presbyterian church on 1 October 1884 when a presentation was made. The next day a benefit concert was held to say farewell to William Junior. It is also recorded that William Senior built an organ for his son, which was purchased by the Wesleyan Methodist chapel before his departure.

Life in Australia seemed to suit the Bousteads and they settled in Ballarat. Here there was a locomotive works that had already produced locomotives very close to the Fletcher's Patent variety, and so one suspects there were other former Fletcher, Jennings employees there. William Junior became a well-known musician and teacher in the Ballarat area.

Following Boustead as the Fitter was Robert Pattison. He was born in Manchester and came to the area because of his wife's connections. He did not last long on the railway. Tradition had it that he was blamed when the trucks ran over the wharf edge and on to the Cambrian's rails in July 1886. He was dismissed and promptly took a job on the Corris. How true this is is uncertain, but he was in the employ of the Corris very soon after this date.

He was followed by Hugh William Griffiths, who started on the railway as a teenager. By the time of the 1881 census he had become a locomotive driver at the age of 19. After Pattison's departure he became the Fitter as well as a Driver during the late 1880s and 1890s. In the 1900s he continued to work on the locomotives, but now it was on a contract basis. It is said he trained his son, Oswald, to fire and drive locomotives on the railway as well. Hugh's grandson, Steve, also became an employee of the railway company for a few years.

After Hugh Griffiths came Hugh (Gas or Old) Jones. His father, David Jones, was listed in the 1881 census as a labourer and platelayer, but he was not the same David Jones who worked on the slate wharf.

People

The 1901 census describes Hugh as a Gas Stoker, and it is known he worked for the Dysynni Gas Company, hence his nickname Hugh Gas. Quite when he started working for the Talyllyn is unclear. The 1911 census describes him as a bicycle repairer, but the Talyllyn employee record shows that he was also employed as the Fitter on the railway. Possibly there was some hiatus while the railway was run down at the end of the McConnel era, although it was certainly not unusual for railway employees to have other occupations.

Hugh Jones remained in the railway's employ until the mid 1930s, but then apparently left and went to the Towyn & Aberdovey Electric Power Company. He did though return to the railway from time to time to offer advice and assistance. He also continued to sign the Annual Returns to certify the condition of the track and locomotives between 1931 and 1939. When the Preservation Society took over he would appear at Pendre occasionally to offer advice to Tom Rolt.

At some point during the 1880s John Rowlands became a driver. He was the younger brother of Jacob Rowlands and had reputedly started as a platelayer, but by 1891 was listed in the census as an engine driver, and similarly for the 1901 and 1911 censuses. However, he either did not transfer to Haydn Jones' employ, or he left the railway not long after.

Those who fulfilled the role of firemen are less easy to track down, two names only are definitely known for the McConnel era. The first is Richard Richards who was the fireman of the train that was nearly sabotaged in 1865. He does not seem to have remained on the railway for long. Later he is listed as a farm labourer and even at one time a road repairer.

The other name that we have is of Robert Thomas who sadly died in December 1909 at the age of 41. His obituary stated that he had worked as a fireman on the Talyllyn for seventeen years. He also acted as a driver, as he did for the McConnel's trip to Nant Gwernol c.1898.

Above: Bob Thomas c.1903.

Guards

The first guard known about on the railway is Hugh Edwards. He is mentioned as being the guard on the railway in 1868, but he does not seem to have remained on the Talyllyn for long, being listed as a railway porter at Caersws in 1871.

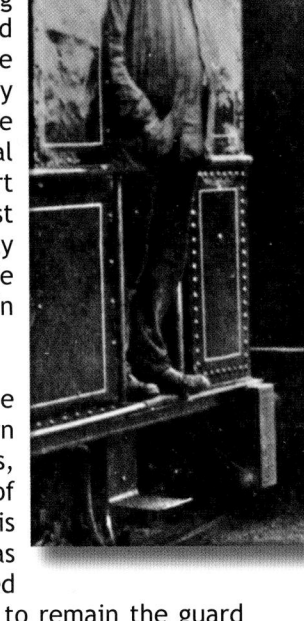

Right: John Rowlands in the early 1900s.

Following him was Lewis Owen. It is not known when he started working for the railway although it was said that he had been employed by the company for many years. In January 1881 his actions in fighting a large fire in Tywyn earned him a special mention in the local paper's report about the conflagration. The last report of him as a Talyllyn Railway employee was in January 1884. He too left for Australia, settling in Williamstown.

He was succeeded by perhaps the most well-known of the Talyllyn Railway's guards, Jacob Rowlands, John's brother. He took on the role of guard in the 1880s and also moved his family into what was later known as 'Railway View', the cottage attached to the sheds at Pendre. Jacob was to remain the guard until his death on 18 December 1928. Many photographs of the period feature him in his distinctive uniforms.

Permanent Way

The first recorded Permanent Way worker was William Roberts, whose name appears in connection with the court case surrounding the potential act of sabotage in August 1865. William was a witness to the event, and was called to give evidence. It seems that he stayed with the railway for some time afterwards, living at Bryncrug, and is listed as a platelayer in the 1881 census. However, how much longer he remained in that role is not certain.

Another member of the track gang at that time also had a court appearance, only this time it was in the dock. John Williams was brought before the court in January 1869 for failure to contribute to the welfare of his mother with whom he lived in Abergynolwyn. At the time he was said to earn 3s 4d per day, and was ordered to pay 2s 6d a week to his mother. This he failed to do and so he was jailed for two months in the March. By 1871 he seems to have resumed work as a platelayer, and in 1881 he was married with a son and was working as a quarryman. They were, though, still living with his mother.

David Richards is the last member of the early track gang we know about. In 1871 he was the occupier of *Plas Coch* at Rhydyronen, and he and his wife Mary remained there until at least 1891. He was probably the occupier before the Jones family. They had two children David and William.

During the 1880s further names were added to those who served on the track gang. John Rowlands has already been mentioned. Another name that is sometimes mentioned

People

Left: Photo reputed to be of David Jones. (Photo: TR Collection)

is Griffith Rowlands, who is listed in the 1881 census as a platelayer, but he does not seem to either be related to John or Jacob Rowlands, or to have worked on the Talyllyn as far as is known. Robert Roberts is listed as a platelayer living in Bryncrug in the 1881 census, and could well have been a Talyllyn employee.

In 1900 another name was to join the list of track workers on the Talyllyn and established a family connection that would last until the present day. David (or Dafydd) Jones moved into *Plas Coch* with his family in 1900, having previously worked as a farm labourer. He was made the Foreman Platelayer in 1902.

David and his wife Anne had seven children, the youngest of whom, Hugh Ellis, born in 1904, eventually followed his father onto the railway. The employment register shows that David left the railway on 17 March 1928, suffering from ill-health. He died in 1935. By this time Hugh was working on the line, and the family's occupancy of *Plas Coch* would continue.

Slate Wharf Workers or Porters

In addition to those employed in operating the trains there were also a number of people who worked at the slate wharf at Tywyn. They would sort and stack the slates, as well as load them onto the standard gauge wagons. One of these was David Jones who, when he died in 1908, was said to have worked for railway for 30 years. He lived at 4, Station Road.

Another was John Roberts, who again when he died in 1907 at the age of 78 was said to have worked for the railway for 40 years. This again probably meant he had worked for the railway since it opened.

As this was unskilled work there would have been many who would have only been transient in this role. One name from the 1901 census is John William Lloyd, who is listed as a slate loader. He also features in a newspaper article from September 1903 when he was injured stopping a horse and cart that had bolted. Later, in the 1911 census he is said to be a bricklaying labourer, probably working with his brother, Thomas.

Employees of the Talyllyn Railway Co. during the Haydn Jones Years
(Based on company records, census returns, newspaper and other reports)

	1910s	1920s	1930s	1940s
General Manager	Richard Barnett Henry Haydn Jones	Henry Haydn Jones	Henry Haydn Jones	Sir Henry Haydn Jones
Office	Edward Thomas John Evans Thomas Griffith L. Evans (Goods Agent)	Edward Thomas John Evans Thomas David Jones (1925 - ?)	Edward Thomas John Evans Thomas	Edward Thomas John Evans Thomas
Fitter	Hugh (Old or Gas) Jones Robert Williams (1916 -1926)	Hugh (Old or Gas) Jones A.M. Howard Jones	Hugh (Old or Gas) Jones	
Driver	John Rowlands Dick Price William Lewis (1916 -?)	William Lewis	William Lewis Hugh Ellis Jones Robin Rowlands Peter Williams	Peter Williams Hugh Ellis Jones Idris Williams Dai Jones
Fireman	John Edwards	David Ellis Davis (1920 -1927) Lewis Davis (1927 - 1930)	William Jones Humphrey Humphreys	Basil Jones Dai Jones
Guard	Jacob Rowlands	Jacob Rowlands		
Platelayers	David (Dafydd) Jones (foreman) Arthur Pughe Richard Thomas Edward Davies	David (Dafydd) Jones (foreman) Arthur Pughe (to 1928) Richard Thomas (to 1926) Edward Davies	Hugh Ellis Jones	Hugh Ellis Jones Morris Lewis Rhys Jones
Porters at Wharf	John Edwards John David Rowlands (from 1915) Evan Harries Evans (from 1916) Samuel Pugh (from 1916) Evan Evans	John Edwards John David Rowlands Evan Harries Evans (to 1925) Samuel Pugh (to 1925) Evan Evans (to 1929)	Hugh Ellis Jones Morris Lewis	

Note: This table is not exhaustive, but does indicate some of the names that are known.

Sir Henry Haydn Jones

Haydn Jones was born the third son of four in 1863 to Joseph David Jones and Catherine Daniel, and was brought up in Tywyn after the death of his father. His brothers Owen Daniel, John Daniel and Daniel Lincoln, all became successful in their own fields. Owen was a Major in the army, General Manager of the North British & Mercantile Insurance Co., and finally Sheriff and Deputy Lieutenant of Merionethshire. Meanwhile both John and Daniel became Congregational Ministers.

People

Haydn Jones himself became involved in several businesses around Tywyn, most notably an ironmonger's shop on the High Street above which he had his office. At the same time he was pursuing his political ambitions. In 1889 he was elected to Merioneth Council. Then in January 1910 he was elected to the House of Commons, and was re-elected unopposed in the second General Election that year which occurred in the December. He was to remain a Member of Parliament until he stepped down in 1945, having been knighted in 1937.

Management and Office

In the Talyllyn Railway Archives there is a list of employees drawn up around 1921 and maintained until around 1930. This has formed the basis of the first two columns of the table opposite. It still leaves some questions outstanding, such as when John Rowlands left the company. He was still listed as an engine driver in the 1911 census, but is not mentioned in the 1921 list.

There is one person who played a role in the early days of the Haydn Jones era that has gone relatively unnoticed, and that is Richard Barnett. He is listed as the Company Secretary of the Abergynolwyn Slate and Slab Company from its inception in 1911 until 1919. He is also listed as the Traffic Manager of the railway in the Board of Trade returns in 1912 and 1913.

He appears to be the same Richard Barnett who, as Clerk to Towyn Urban District Council, was responsible for calling the public meeting to discuss the future of the railway in 1910. He was also the Secretary to the County Education Committee, which Haydn Jones had been on, as well as having other roles in local government.

He continued with his local government role while also working for the railway, which can definitely be said to be multi-tasking. All of which seems to have taken its toll, as he had a long illness early in 1919, which co-incided with his leaving the railway company. It was also around this time that he got married and so doubtless he had to make some time to be at home. After his departure, Edward Thomas became the Company Secretary, while Haydn Jones styled himself as the Manager. John Thomas is listed as the Company Accountant.

Fitters

It is interesting that the 1921 list has two fitters listed, Hugh (Old or Gas) Jones, and also Robert Williams, who is said to be in the role between 1916 and 1926. His part in the Talyllyn story is unclear, and nothing further is known about him. Another mystery name is A.M. Howard Jones who signed the 1929 and 1930 Annual Returns as Chief Engineer. Again nothing further appears to be known about him.

When 'Old' Hugh Jones left the railway is also a mystery, as, according to the company returns, the railway stopped employing a separate Fitter from around 1933. This was possibly when 'Old' Hugh went to work for the Power Company. Except that, as already stated, he signed the Annual Returns as Chief Mechanical Engineer for all the years between 1931 and 1938. This perhaps indicates he was still working for the railway on a contract basis. Hugh Ellis Jones then signed the Returns for the locomotive side from then until the end of the Haydn Jones era.

Drivers

The subject of Drivers is also somewhat confused. It is likely that when John Rowlands left Dick Price was promoted to driver. He apparently had been an agricultural worker, but had joined the track gang before going to work on the locomotives as a fireman.

Above: Dick Price c.1916.

William Robert Lewis followed Dick Price, the 1921 list stating that he joined the railway in 1916, and there is photographic evidence of him still working on the railway in 1931. In 1901 he was an underground worker at Bryneglwys, but the 1911 census has him and his family living in Glamorgan working as a coal miner. The family subsequently returned to Tywyn, and it is said that his wife and daughter ran a sweet shop on the High Street.

Robin Rowlands, the son of John, is said to have driven in the 1930s, although apparently not for very long due to his asthma. It is possible that Hugh Ellis Jones then took up the driving role, before the arrival of Peter Williams.

Peter was at first employed as the foreman of the track gang with Hugh Ellis Jones taking on the locomotive side, but then apparently the two swapped roles. Peter had worked in the Bryneglwys quarry and had also been a coal miner in South Wales. In addition, he had had a brief sojourn in Canada where he had become a platelayer on the Canadian Pacific Railroad before returning to Tywyn.

On his return he went to work at Bryneglwys, before joining the railway around 1935. The family came to occupy the cottage at Pendre, and Peter was to work on the railway until at least 1941, although when he left the railway's employ is unknown. He did though remain at Pendre, and acted as crossing keeper, becoming a firm supporter of the preservation of the railway.

During the mid to late war years Hugh Ellis Jones was the main driver on the line. After the war he was assisted by his son, Dai, until the latter was called up for national service in 1948. This led to Peter Williams' grandson, Idris, being employed as the driver in 1949, so Hugh could concentrate on the track. Idris had a reputation for being somewhat reckless, which seems to have contributed to the cracking of *Dolgoch's* frames in August 1949.

People

Above: Jacob Rowlands on duty with fireman David Ellis Davies in the centre and William Lewis on the right c.1921.
(Photo: TR Collection)

Firemen

The 1921 list does come to our aid in sorting out some of the issues around firemen in the early years of the Haydn Jones era. As stated previously it is likely that Dick Price started out as fireman to John Rowlands before being promoted. The next name is that of John Edwards, seen as the boy with the hoop in the photo on page 25. He left the railway to work with his father who was a local coal merchant.

There are two names that cover the 1920s. David Ellis Davies, who worked for the railway between December 1920 and January 1927. He in turn was followed by Lewis Davies, the cousin of John Edwards, who only remained in the job until September 1930.

In the 1930s it appears that 'Old' Hugh Jones' son William did some firing for a while, and later Peter Williams' son John was to be found on the footplate. William Lewis' son, also William, was reputed to have done some firing as well, although when exactly is not known.

In the late 1930s Humphrey Humphreys was known to act as fireman, before he gained employment on the Corris Railway. There he became the last driver when the line closed in 1948. In the 1940s Hugh Jones' sons Herbert and Dai could be found on the footplate. Then in 1949 a young lad called Basil Jones was employed as a fireman.

Guard

After Jacob Rowlands' death in December 1928, the staff returns indicate that no-one was regularly employed in the position of guard. It seems that a number of people did undertake the role, possibly those whom Haydn Jones could spare from other parts of his business empire. In the latter years of the Haydn Jones era it was Edward Thomas himself who famously fulfilled the job.

Platelayers

The economies of the Haydn Jones era can be seen in the reduction of some of the semi- and un-skilled workers on the railway. In 1911 the railway had four members of the Permanent Way team led by David Jones. However, by the 1930s this had become only two.

Originally David was joined by Arthur Pugh(e)(the name is recorded both with and without the 'e'), known as Blind Pugh. He had been partially blinded by his former employer, a farmer, but had recovered sufficiently to be employed in the quarry, and then on the railway as a platelayer living at Rhydyronen.

Sadly, an accident in 1926 caused him to lose his sight completely, and so he had to leave the company's employ in January 1928. He still continued to live at Rhydyronen for many years, being known to Tom Rolt and the early preservation volunteers. He died in 1956.

Little is known about the next two names we have. The first is Edward Davies. He was in the employ of the company from at least 1911, and remained so until at least the 1930s. The second name is Richard Thomas, who was employed between 1911 and 1926.

David Jones finished working on the railway in 1928 before his death in 1935. By then his youngest son, Hugh Ellis Jones, had started working on the line, following in his father's footsteps.

Born in 1904, Hugh had originally started work at Bryneglwys at the age of 14, but due to issues with the slate dust was transferred to working at Tywyn Wharf loading slate around 1931. He then moved onto the Permanent Way gang, and was also encouraged to work on the locomotives by 'Old' Hugh Jones.

After a time working on the locomotives after 'Old' Hugh Jones left, Hugh Ellis returned to the track, swapping roles with Peter Williams. As the foreman platelayer was paid more than the driver, there was another benefit to this. This was particularly important as his wife Florence died in 1939 and Hugh was left to bring up his three children David Richard (or Dai), Violet May and Herbert, with the help of his now widowed mother.

Interestingly although Hugh Ellis signed the Annual Returns for the condition of the locomotives as Chief Mechanical Engineer for 1939 and for the post-war years until 1950. (No signatures certifying the condition of the locomotives or track were submitted during the war years). This was not the case for the Permanent Way, as will be seen, emphasising the fluidity of the roles at that time.

Hugh Ellis left the railway at the end of the Haydn Jones era, but returned later, and continued to work with his two sons until his retirement in 1973. He died in 1989.

Herbert, his younger son, helped his father out on occasions, recalling that he was on *Dolgoch* when it brought the last load of slate down from the quarry. Herbert (or Herbie as he was commonly known) was not formally employed on the railway until 1955, and continued to serve until he was forced to retire due to

Rails Along The Fathew

ill-health in 1978. Sadly he died in 1983. He and his family were the last occupants of the cottage at Pendre, moving out in 1966.

Meanwhile his elder brother, universally known as Dai, did not start work on the railway immediately after leaving school, but eventually Sir Haydn was persuaded to take him on at a pound more a week than his father, Hugh. Following national service Dai returned to the railway in 1950, and although there was a short hiatus he remained with the railway until he retired in 1986, passing away in 2008.

Both brothers were known for a wicked sense of humour. The author recalls one day working as an Assistant Guard when Dai was driving. Between us we led the Guard, my best man, a merry dance. Happily Dai's son David now works for the railway, and his grandson, Thomas, is volunteering in the locomotive department.

Hugh's brother Rhys also worked on the railway at the very end of the Haydn Jones era. According to the Annual Returns for the period Rhys was responsible for the track between 1949 and 1950, while Hugh looked after the locomotives. He later returned to work for the railway between 1956 and April 1968.

Slate Wharf Workers or Porters

Here again the reduced output from the quarry led to fewer labourers at Tywyn Wharf being required, and so the workforce here was reduced over time, with only one person being employed in the role from 1933.

In the 1910s there were up to five people working on the wharf. The names that we have include John Edwards, who is shown to have served through the 1920s. Another long server was Evan Evans, who was employed there from at least 1911 until 1929.

John David Rowlands started on the wharf in 1915 and seems to have remained there until at least the 1930s. Like the others who worked there little is known about him. However, it doesn't appear he was directly related to the other Rowlands who worked on the railway.

Among the other names Evan Harries Evans worked for the railway for nearly ten years between 1916 and 1925, as did Samuel Pugh. Moving into the 1930s Hugh Ellis Jones had a spell at the wharf before moving to the track gang.

Morris Lewis did various jobs for the railway during the late 1930s, continuing through the Second World War. He signed for the condition of the track on the 1945 Annual Return in March 1946, but probably left the railway soon afterwards.

Other names have been mentioned as being employed on the railway, but those that have been recorded here are the ones where there is some evidence to support their involvement. It was also Sir Haydn's practice to shuffle his labour force between his businesses as needs and demands dictated, so others could well have been at work on the railway at various times.

The Preservation Era

Since 1951 thousands of people have worked on the Talyllyn Railway either in a voluntary or paid capacity. It would therefore be nigh-on impossible to produce even a list of them all without omissions and oversights. Therefore, what I have chosen to do is produce some snapshots of life on the railway through these years by means of a photo-montage. This highlights the work done on various aspects of the railway and some of those involved.

Right: One of the first working parties at the Abergynolwyn village winding house on 27 March 1951. Left to right are Owen Prosser, Eric Lees, Harvey Gray, Bill Oliver, Bill Faulkner and Denis 'Maggi' Maguire, plus Bill Faulkner's dog. (Photo: O. Prosser)

People

Left: With few mechanical aids in the early days of the Preservation Society there was a lot of hard manual labour. This can be seen here with a working party lifting rail from the old mineral line beyond Abergynolwyn for use elsewhere on 21 March 1954.
(Photo: J.N. Slater)

Right: The Area Groups of the Preservation Society have played an important role through the years. Here a London Area Working Party is in action unloading sleepers at Tywyn Pendre on 30 October 1954. In the foreground left to right are Don Coventry, David Thomas, John Hicks and William Jones. Meanwhile in the background with the sleeper are Edgar Sherborne and John Suckling. Also note locomotives No.6 *Douglas* in the background and No.7, the Mercury tractor. On the left the original body from carriage No.9 is lying on its side. (Photo: J.N. Slater)

Left: Here a group is erecting scaffolding in preparation for the installation of the first footbridge over the cutting at Dolgoch in April 1957. This was to allow passengers easier access to the ravine and the falls.
(Photo: Keith Stretch)

Rails Along The Fathew

People

Left: The Braich-y-rhiw bridge just east of Rhydyronen had emergency repairs following the Railway Inspector's visit in 1952, but a more permanent solution was required, and so it was replaced in October 1961. John Halliday, affectionately known as the 'brutal quarry master', is on the right supervising the work.
(Photo: David J. Mitchell)

Right: One extra passenger working in the 1950s was the evening train to take volunteers back to Rhydyronen. The train would then remain there overnight before bringing people back down in the morning. No.4 *Edward Thomas* is seen ready to depart with a single carriage on 14 August 1959. The Jones family were also allowed to run a locomotive to Rhydyronen and stable it under the bridge overnight. (Photo: Keith Stretch)

Left: When No.1 *Talyllyn* returned from rebuilding it was taken for a test run. Here it is at Quarry Siding with a number of notables including George Skelding and Albert Morris from Gibbons Bros. on the left. Then come the Earl of Northesk, Tom Rolt, Bill Faulkner, Eric Gibbons and Ken Cope. (Photo: J.H.L. Adams)

Right: A group of young members have obviously decided to see how many they can squeeze into an open wagon on the old mineral line just east of the Abergynolwyn winding house at Easter 1965. (Photo: David J. Mitchell)

People

Left: More hard labour building a new loading chute at Quarry Siding on 16 April 1960.
(Photo: Keith Stretch)

Right: Work goes on inside the workshop in June 1974 with Don Southgate on the left and Colin Roobottom, for many years the Society Treasurer, on the right. (Photo: TR Collection)

Left: They also serve who sit on committees, the Engineering Committee meets al-fresco in September 1966.
(Photo: J.H.L. Adams)

Right: The Jones family gather at Tywyn Wharf on 30 September 1995 to mark the return to service of No.6 *Douglas*, which had received a new boiler funded by the Hugh Jones appeal. Dai Jones is on the footplate, while his son David, now an employee of the railway, stands just to the left of the cab.
(Photo: David J. Mitchell)

218   Rails Along The Fathew

People

Right: The rail saw is seen in use at Tywyn Wharf in the early 1960s. It was built using the wheels of the Mercury tractor No.7.
(Photo: J.N. Slater)

Left: Building for the future: The Talyllyn's *Tracksiders* group was formed in 1996 to give youngsters an introduction to the joys of working on the railway in all weathers. Here a group is at work under the supervision of Ian Evans (on the right) at Nant Gwernol in May 2007.
(Photo: Bob Morland)

Right: Weedkilling is now specialist work needing the right equipment, as demonstrated here by the track gang at Dolgoch on 4 June 2011.

Left: This photograph went 'viral' on the internet when it was published in March 2013. It shows what the railway claimed was the world's first all-female ballast tamping crew. They were operating the *Matisa* tamper at Tŷ Dŵr on the Extension. In the photo are left to right: Rebecca Sharpe, Pippa McCanna and Debbie Sharpe. The railway's claim has not been challenged. (Photo: Keith Theobald)

Right: Many of our volunteers undertake more than one role. This is illustrated here by Debbie Sharpe, who is the cleaner on No.7 *Tom Rolt* about to exchange tokens with Nigel Adams, the blockman, at Quarry Siding. Also on the footplate are Jonathan Mann and Sarah Freeman, while Liz Garvey, the guard, looks on from the train. The train was *The Rolt Centenarian* run to mark the Centenary of Tom Rolt's birth on 16 April 1910.
(Photo: Bob Morland)

Rails Along The Fathew 219

The Narrow Gauge Railway Museum

Right: Between 1960 and 1976, *Cambrai*, an 0-6-0T metre gauge locomotive built by L. Corpet et Cie. of Paris in 1888, which had worked at the Eastwell and Waltham Ironstone Quarry Railway, stood outside the Museum. It is seen here while the building was being extended in the mid 1960s. *Cambrai* is now based at the Irchester Narrow Gauge Railway Museum.
(Photo: David J. Mitchell)

In 1951 an embryonic scheme was started for a museum of narrow gauge artefacts from the Talyllyn and other lines. Originally based in the old gunpowder store, it opened in 1956. By this time a number of sizeable exhibits had been obtained, including one of the original Guinness Brewery locomotives from Dublin, and the ex-Penrhyn vertical-boilered *George Henry*.

The Museum quickly outgrew the store and so it was moved to the former walled coal yard by the Neptune Road bridge. This was built up and roofed over into a purpose built structure which was officially opened in September 1959. More exhibits were being acquired, among the most well-known was the French metre gauge locomotive *Cambrai* which arrived in 1960.

With more exhibits the building was extended again, the work being completed in 1966. The original Museum Committee had also been reformed into the Narrow Gauge Railway Museum Trust in 1964. By 1970 the main acquisition phase of the Museum had come to an end, with the emphasis now on consolidation and conservation.

Around 2000 plans for the Wharf redevelopment were being considered. It was realised that incorporating the Museum into the proposed new building, could not only open the way for a grant from the Heritage Lottery Fund, but would also encourage more visitors. As a result the Museum came to occupy a two storey space at the western end of the building with a glass wall between the ground floor and the café area. The new Museum opened with the rest of the building in 2005.

Above: Ex-Welsh Highland Railway locomotive *Russell* arrived at Tywyn Wharf in 1955; remaining there until it was removed for restoration in 1965. It is seen here on the left outside the old gunpowder store. On the right is one of the 1 ft 10 in gauge locomotives built for the Guinness St James' Gate Brewery in Dublin by William Spence Ltd in 1895. It was the first locomotive donated to the Museum in 1956.

Right: Inside the original Museum in the old gunpowder store showing some of the artefacts on display.
(Both Photos: R.D. Butterell)

Narrow Gauge Railway Museum

Left: The exterior of the extended Museum building in 1968. (Photo: J.H.L. Adams)

Right: Inside the Museum in 1973 showing the former Dundee Gasworks locomotive No.2. This was built for the 1 ft 11½ in line at Dundee gasworks by Kerr, Stuart in 1907. (Photo: J.H.L. Adams)

Left: For many years the ex-Crewe Works locomotive *Pet* was on display in the Museum. In June 1987 it was temporarily removed, after a fair amount of effort, to appear at an exhibition in Crewe to mark the 150th anniversary of the opening of the Grand Junction Railway. Coincidently the person in charge of the exhibition was the author's wife, who was also the historical consultant for the event.

Subsequently *Pet*, which is part of the National Collection, moved to the National Railway Museum at York. (Photo: David J. Mitchell)

Right: A view of the lower gallery from the stairs in the new Museum in August 2015.

Rails Along The Fathew

The 150th Anniversary

Over the weekend of 3 - 5 July 2015 a unique gathering of locomotives took place at Tywyn Wharf to celebrate the 150th Anniversary of the opening of the Talyllyn Railway. There were two visiting locomotives. First was the Ffestiniog Railway's *Prince*, the oldest working 2 ft gauge locomotive in the world, built in 1863. Also returning to Tywyn was the Welsh Highland Heritage Railway's *Russell* back at Wharf after 50 years, having been there for 10 years awaiting restoration between 1955 and 1965.

Left: On Saturday 4 July 2015 a record was set for the number of narrow-gauge locomotives in steam at Tywyn Wharf, with seven steamable locomotives present. Left to Right they are *Russell, Prince, Talyllyn, Dolgoch, Edward Thomas, Douglas* and *Tom Rolt*. *Prince* and *Russell* are running on especially laid sections of 1 ft 11 ½ in gauge track.

Right: Special guests on Friday 3 July were Timothy West and Prunella Scales seen here with the crew of *The Sesquicentenarian* special train. Left to Right: Andy Vick, Simon Jenkins, Liz Garvey, Marc Smith and Andrew Young.
(Photo: A. Young)

Left: Saturday 4 July ended with a night shoot involving *Russell, Prince, Talyllyn* and *Dolgoch*.

Rails Along The Fathew

Bibliography and Acknowledgements

Above: Shades of Red: The afternoon sun on Saturday 4 July brings out the shades of red on, left to right: *Prince, Russell, Dolgoch, Talyllyn* and *Sir Haydn*, which although its boiler certificate had run out had been brought down to be part of the festivities.

Bibliography

Books and Articles

Cambrian Railways 1859 - 1947, C.C. Green, Ian Allan, 1997.

Railways in Gwynedd 1759-1848 by D. Gwyn, in *Early Railways 5*, Ed. D. Gwyn, Six Martlets Publishing, 2014.

The Cambrian Railways A New History, Peter Johnson, Oxford Publishing Company, 2013.

Bryneglwys Slate Quarry, Alan Holmes with Sara Eade, 2013.

Railway Adventure, R.T.C. Rolt, originally published 1953.

Rails Along The Derwent: The Story of the Derwent Valley Light Railway, J. Stockwell and I. Drummond, Holne Publishing, 2013.

Talyllyn & Corris Steam Locomotives, M. Fuller, Sara Eade Publishing, 2014.

Talyllyn Century, Ed. R.T.C. Rolt, David and Charles, 1965.

Tal-y-llyn Railway, J.I.C. Boyd, Wild Swan Publications, 1988.

Talyllyn Railway Locomotives & Rolling Stock, John Bate, David Mitchell & Nigel Adams, Cheona Publications, 2003.

Talyllyn Revived, A.T. Holmes, Talyllyn Railway, 2009.

The Chronicles of Pendre Sidings, J.L.H. Bate, Rail Romances, 2001.

The Festiniog Railway Volume One: History and Route, J.I.C. Boyd, Oakwood Press, 1975.

The Talyllyn Railwaymen, Sara Eade, Sara Eade Publishing, 2015.

Primary Sources

Extensive use have been made of primary sources, including those in the Talyllyn Railway Archive; The Narrow Gauge Railway Museum Trust; The National Archives at Kew; Search Engine at The National Railway Museum, York; the Gwynedd County Archives; The Welsh National Library, Aberystwyth; Welsh Newspapers Online and the *Talyllyn News*.

Bibliography and Acknowledgements

Acknowledgements

A large number of people have helped in the development of this book, in reality too many to list here. I would, however, particularly like to thank the following people for there assistance in making this book possible:

John Bate, Andy Best, Lawrie Bowles, Eddie Castellan, Anthony Coulls, Alan Doe, Sara Eade, Martin Fuller, Lawrence Garvey, David Mitchell, Don Newing, Dan Quine, John Robinson, Mark Stephenson and Roger Whitehouse.

Especial thanks must as ever go to my wife, Di, for putting up with the disruption to our lives during the past couple of years.

I am also grateful to the staff at The National Archives, Kew; Search Engine at The National Railway Museum, York; The Gwynedd County Archives, Dolgellau and The National Library of Wales for their assistance and patience.

This book would not have been possible without the pioneering research done on the history of the Talyllyn Railway by those who are no longer with us. Therefore, I would like to record my appreciation of the work done by the late:

James Boyd, Tom Rolt, Keith Stretch, Christopher White and Jeremy Wilkinson.

To them and many others we owe a huge debt of appreciation.

Other Books Currently Available From Holne Publishing

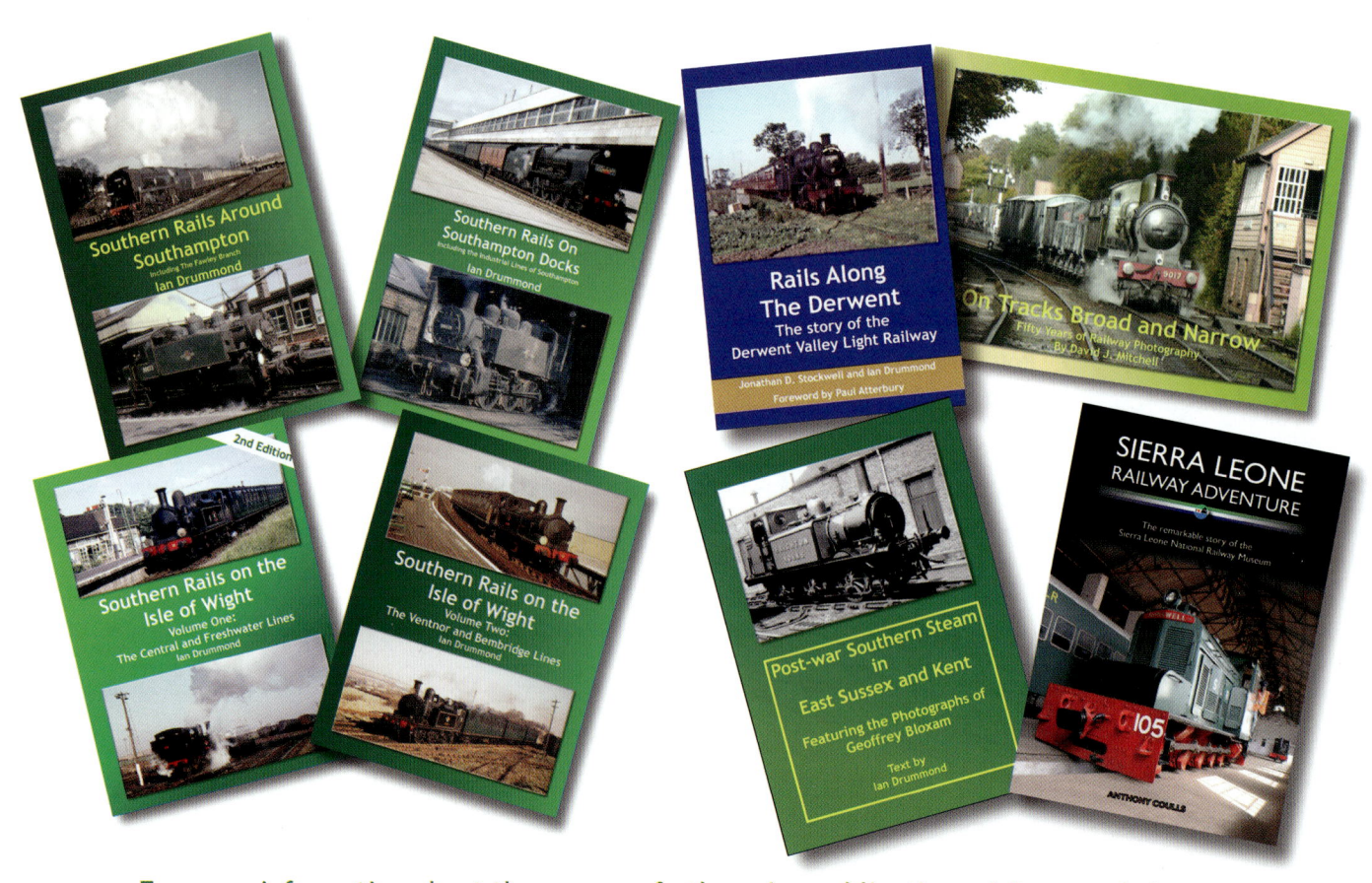

For more information about these or our forthcoming publications visit our website at:
www.holnepublishing.co.uk or e-mail us at: enquiries@holnepublishing.co.uk
or write to:
Holne Publishing, PO Box 343, Leeds, LS19 9FW